Equal Partners?

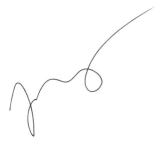

Equal Partners?

How Dual-Professional Couples Make Career,
Relationship, and Family Decisions

Jaclyn S. Wong

UNIVERSITY OF CALIFORNIA PRESS

University of California Press
Oakland, California

Library of Congress Cataloging-in-Publication Data

Names: Wong, Jaclyn S., 1989- author.
Title: Equal partners? : how dual-professional couples make career, relationship, and family decisions / Jaclyn S. Wong.
Description: Oakland, California : University of California Press, [2023] | Includes bibliographical references and index.
Identifiers: LCCN 2022038150 (print) | LCCN 2022038151 (ebook) | ISBN 9780520384569 (cloth) | ISBN 9780520384576 (paperback) | ISBN 9780520384590 (ebook)
Subjects: LCSH: Work-life balance—United States—History—21st century. | Dual-career families—United States—History—21st century.
Classification: LCC HD4904.25 .W6525 2023 (print) | LCC HD4904.25 (ebook) | DDC 306.3/6—dc23/eng/20221230
LC record available at https://lccn.loc.gov/2022038150
LC ebook record available at https://lccn.loc.gov/2022038151

Manufactured in the United States of America

32 31 30 29 28 27 26 25 24 23
10 9 8 7 6 5 4 3 2 1

Contents

Tables

## CHAPTER I

Gender, Work, and Family in the Twenty-First Century

Julie and Max met playing music together in college. "He was a year ahead of me in college, so he was a scary upperclassman at the time," Julie said, chuckling as she recounted their relationship history. After being friends for a few years, Julie and Max started dating. At that point, they both wanted to be doctors and ended up going to separate medical schools in different cities. They kept up their long-distance relationship for several years, taking turns driving over two hours each way to visit each other every few weeks. Max described this long-distance arrangement as "frustrating, especially at first because we didn't really know how much we would be seeing each other." The couple hoped their next step of training—medical residency—would finally put them in the same city. They imagined that once they were in the same location, they could make more serious plans related to their relationship, like living together, getting married, and perhaps having children. Yet when I asked Max how he ended up in a residency program in a small city three and a half hours away by plane from Julie, he said:

> Out of all the places I interviewed, I liked [the Mountain West institution] the best. Knowingly, it wasn't ideal for our relationship because if I was to move to [Julie's city] that would have been simpler. But it would have probably been better to go to places like [the East Coast] where there would be more programs for her to apply to. I knew already that she was applying to [residency] programs this year, like now. My second choice on the list was [an eastern institution], and for example, [that East Coast city] has four or

five [residency] programs [in her specialty] where [this city] has one. So, it was maybe not the best decision at that point, but it was the place I liked the best.

Recall that Julie was a year behind Max in school. When I began interviewing her, she was preparing to submit her residency applications. I wanted to know what she was going do. Did Max and Julie have a plan for her transition between medical school and residency? Maybe she would only apply to Max's hospital and risk getting rejected, without any backup options for her training. Max's hospital was the only institution in a sparsely populated part of the country, so even if Julie considered other "nearby" programs, the next closest option for her was an eight-hour drive or an hour-and-a-half plane trip away. Maybe they would decide that Julie should move to Max's city regardless of whether she could continue her medical career. Perhaps Julie saw other career paths for herself and would consider changing occupations if her residency application did not work out. Maybe she thought taking a break from pursuing a medical career, or giving up having a career altogether, was the right fit for her at this point in her life. That decision would still allow her to accomplish her other goals: she and Max could live in the same place, get married, and start a family. Or Julie could apply broadly to the best residency programs across the country. That plan would maximize Julie's training opportunities but could extend the couple's long-distance relationship—unless Max decided to quit his program to follow Julie or found a way to complete his training wherever Julie ended up. Whatever they chose, what would this decision mean for Max's and Julie's careers and for their relationship for the next year—or for the next five years?

Participation in paid work is increasingly expected of both young men and women in the United States.[1] Americans with postsecondary, graduate, or professional degrees like Max and Julie are particularly likely to express high professional ambitions, with men and women both expecting to pursue careers. At the same time, these highly educated young people want marriages or other long-term, committed relationships, and many expect to have children as well. Given the assumption that men and women in different-gender relationships will both work for pay, many of these young adults hope to share housework with their partners and equally share the responsibilities of raising children while maintaining two careers.[2] Yet we know that working couples' realities often deviate from these egalitarian ideals, usually with women trading off paid work to take on unpaid family care. Will this contemporary cohort of young adults repeat this pattern, or will they come closer to achieving equality in work and family?

This book documents what partnered men and women like Max and Julie do when difficult decisions about careers, relationships, and families have to be made. These couples' expectations for egalitarian partnerships in which both partners are equally responsible for working for pay and providing unpaid caregiving may sound good in the abstract but may not become a reality. Men and women may face material and cultural challenges that can block their attempts to have equal relationships as they launch careers and build their families together. Yet there may be pathways toward gender egalitarianism in work and family, and these contemporary young couples may be blazing those trails toward more equal partnerships.

Using data from 156 interviews collected over the course of six years from the partners of twenty-one different-gender couples, I argue that consistently supportive workplace contexts, partners' steadfast attitudes about gender egalitarianism, and men's and women's jointly coordinated efforts all need to come together for couples to experience gender equality in work and family. I show that weaknesses in any of these areas can divert partners away from equal sharing and toward gendered power imbalances in these domains. If workplaces present material challenges to dual earner-caregiver partnerships, if men's and women's attitudes about gender equality shift over time, or if partners fall out of step in aligning their activities with each other, couples may find themselves in work-family arrangements that deviate from an egalitarian division of labor. Because there is self-reinforcing feedback between workplace conditions, cultural attitudes, and partners' interactions, a couple's particular balance of work and family—and the resulting power dynamics across partners—is likely to persist over time. Yet changes to men's and women's work-related landscapes; their attitudes about gender, work, and family; or the way they take action together can reverberate through a work-family ecosystem and result in a new balance that may be more—or less—gender equal. By illustrating the way couples navigated their job applications, learned to balance two demanding work schedules, helped one another grow in their careers, and coordinated childcare, I shed light on the state of gender inequality in work and family among young professionals in contemporary American society.

THE STALLED GENDER REVOLUTION
IN THE TWENTY-FIRST CENTURY

The stories of couples like Max and Julie are embedded in and influenced by their broader social context. The gender revolution—the movement of women into the paid labor force and men into the household and family—has mostly stalled in the United States in the twenty-first century.[3] Women make up 47 percent of American workers,[4] but they still earn 82 cents for every dollar that men make.[5] Such earning disparities are even starker when broken out by race and ethnicity: Black women make 62 percent and Latina women make just 55 percent of what White men earn annually.[6] Women remain concentrated in feminized, lower-paid occupations like teaching and nursing and are underrepresented in company leadership roles and other workplace positions of power.[7] Even if women equally participated in all occupations, though, most of the gender wage gap comes from within occupations, so disparities across men and women in paid labor would remain.[8] Not only do men and women work in different occupations and receive different levels of pay, men and women experience different employment rhythms. Women are less likely than men to work full-time and are more likely to have gaps in their career histories,[9] a pattern that became especially clear during the COVID-19 pandemic.[10] These résumé characteristics may be interpreted negatively by employers,[11] making it harder for women to reenter full-time positions if they ever deviated from the "standard" pattern of employment. In a stratified society in which incomes and occupations matter to individuals' access to power,[12] men remain more powerful than women in the domain of work.

Men's and women's unequal performance of unpaid labor at home further reflects persistent gendered power imbalances.[13] Women remain responsible for the majority of household chores and childcare despite their participation in paid labor. Prior to the COVID-19 pandemic, women spent an average of eighteen hours a week completing housework and thirty-five hours caring for children while men spent just ten hours on household chores and seventeen hours taking care of children.[14] These figures jumped for both men and women during the pandemic lockdowns, but the gender gap persisted.[15] Even though men's participation in domestic and family-related work varies by race and class and has increased over time,[16] they tend to do different tasks from women. For example, when men spend time on childcare, they are more likely to do the "fun" activities with children like reading to or playing with them, while women are more likely to do the routine physical work associated with childcare like bathing and feeding them.[17] It is unsurprising, then, that married mothers do more housework, sleep less, and have less leisure time than single mothers, despite having a partner who could presumably relieve them from these burdens.[18] If power is also measured by one's freedom from obligations to complete unpaid, devalued, or undesirable labor,[19] men remain more powerful than women in the domestic realm, too.

Cultural norms—attitudes and beliefs surrounding gender, work, and family—and structural factors—material conditions that shape men's and women's paid work in the labor market and unpaid work in families—both contribute to this stalled gender revolution and reinforce power imbalances across men and women. At the cultural level, ideas about gender, work, and family link men and masculinity to paid employment while linking women and femininity to unpaid family care.[20] To successfully perform gender given these cultural logics, men must work for pay,[21] and women must put family first.[22] These messages may resonate particularly loudly for White Americans and upper-middle-class Americans[23]—meaning these specific gender attitudes are bound up with race and class privilege—but also circulate among communities of color and working-class Americans.[24]

These societal beliefs about gender, work, and family are reinforced by structural conditions at work.[25] Greedy white-collar workplaces that demand long hours and expect "face time" pressure workers, often presumed to be men,[26] to devote their energy to their jobs at the expense of other activities.[27] Difficult working conditions are exacerbated in working-class jobs and can push workers, especially women with family care responsibilities, out of the labor force.[28] Paired with a lack of supportive organizational- or state-level policies like guaranteed childcare support, paid time off for personal and family care, and other resources for people to complete activities outside of paid work, men and women must find individualized solutions to balance their responsibilities.[29] Caitlyn Collins, for instance, shows that American mothers who lack access to public policies supporting working parents are more likely to see themselves as personally responsible for achieving work-family balance than their counterparts in other countries with more expansive social safety nets.[30]

When these material conditions intersect with cultural beliefs about whether men or women should work for pay or provide unpaid care to the family, many different-gender couples may be pushed to adopt

a traditional, gender-unequal division of labor.[31] Research by Mary
Blair-Loy and Pamela Stone depicts how masculinized logics at work
and feminized ideals of motherhood push professional women toward
gender-traditional roles.[32] Blair-Loy's and Stone's respective interview
studies show that workplaces structured around an ideal worker with no
other responsibilities—that is, a man with a wife at home who takes care
of the housework and children[33]—hamper professional women's ability
to advance at work. When women enter these masculinized workplaces,
they are assumed to have parenting responsibilities and are mommy
tracked—placed into part-time positions with no upward mobility or
otherwise given no accommodations if they do have other responsibilities. At the same time, cultural norms around intensive motherhood
pressure women,[34] especially White upper-middle-class women, to devote their time and energy to raising children, supporting husbands, and
caring for the home. These workplace pushes and domestic pulls result
in women leaving careers to become full-time mothers. If women return
to work, the persistence of family-unfriendly workplaces and race- and
class-based pressures to mother intensively channel women into freelance jobs or positions in feminized fields—both of which are characterized by lower earnings and few pathways to leadership relative to the
professional career tracks they left behind.[35]

Yet cultural attitudes, workplace conditions, and public policies may
be changing for contemporary young adults. Endorsement of gender-
traditional work-family arrangements is low among Americans aged
eighteen to thirty-four. In the 2021 General Social Survey, only 22 percent of young men and women agreed or strongly agreed that it is better
for men to work outside the home and for women to take care of the
home and children.[36] Instead, young adults are more likely than their
counterparts in the past to support an egalitarian division of labor in
which labor market, household, and family responsibilities are equally
shared. For example, a recent study found that young adults in America
hold strong egalitarian opinions about the ideal way to divide work and
family responsibilities across partners.[37]

In addition to these attitudinal changes, some institutional changes are
taking place across the United States. A few state and local governments
and various private employers have adopted policies to provide workers
with parental leave and job protection for those who take time off for
family reasons.[38] For example, California's paid family leave policy offers 55 percent of weekly wages up to $1,129 and up to six weeks off for
family care leave. Further, workplaces increasingly offer employee-driven

flexible working arrangements such as remote work, a policy that has become even more available in response to the COVID-19 pandemic.[39] These cultural and structural changes may offer contemporary young people more opportunities to build equal partnerships with shared work and family responsibilities than men and women had before.

Still, cultural and structural barriers to gender equality in work and family remain. A detailed probe into young Americans' cultural attitudes suggests that support for gender equality in the public sphere outpaces support for equality at home.[40] Men and women support women's entry into and advancement at work but still hold gender-essentialist beliefs about women's "innate" desires for intimate relationships, "expertise" in all things domestic, and "natural" capacity to do care work. Ellen Lamont finds, for instance, that although young adults want to partner with an equal in terms of education and work accomplishments, they continue following gender-traditional dating scripts because they believe men and women have fundamentally different romantic and family orientations.[41] These gender-unequal patterns continue into young adults' long-term, committed cohabiting and marital relationships. Research by Amanda Miller and her colleagues shows that young adult cohabitors often establish a gender-unequal division of housework without much discussion and assume that men's careers will take primacy over women's careers when they become parents, even if both partners currently have equally strong career orientations.[42]

Neotraditional attitudes that a woman can work as long as it does not interfere with her family responsibilities may become especially pronounced when working conditions do not facilitate equal sharing of all responsibilities. Prior research has found that when workplace and public policies do not exist to support gender equality, people who would have otherwise preferred egalitarianism instead endorsed gendered work-family arrangements.[43] For example, Kathleen Gerson's interview research and David Pedulla and Sarah Thébaud's survey-experimental research show that most young men's and women's "Plan A" for balancing work and family in the future involves sharing these responsibilities equally with their romantic partners.[44] Yet these attitudes are contingent on material supports for dual earner-caregiver households. When asked what they would do if external conditions at work made egalitarianism hard to achieve, the young people in Gerson's study and in Pedulla and Thébaud's research express gendered "Plan B's": men favor a neotraditional arrangement in which their careers are prioritized, but women prefer to forgo partners in favor of working while raising children on their own. Structural lag, the condition in which laws, policies, and workplace arrangements have not changed to keep up with evolving cultural attitudes surrounding gender, work, and family, therefore remains a formidable barrier to young people who might want equal partnerships. Margaret Usdansky points out that this "gender-equality paradox"—the contradiction between spoken egalitarian attitudes and inegalitarian behaviors due to structural constraints—is particularly characteristic of the beliefs and actions of men and women with high socioeconomic status in different-gender couples.[45]

These conditions in the stalled gender revolution frame my research on how coupled young professionals like Max and Julie launch careers, build relationships, and start families. Given this structural and cultural landscape in gender, work, and family in the twenty-first century in the United States, I ask: What work-family trajectories do people in different-gender relationships follow as they launch and build careers, maintain relationships, and start families? How do conditions at work and cultural norms shape these pathways? Further, what do these trajectories tell us about the state of the gender revolution and its likely future? Quantitative scholars who want to study men's and women's work-family trajectories do not yet have the data to describe contemporary young adults' career and family pathways on a national scale. But qualitative research focusing in detail on a smaller sample of couples' intentions, behaviors, and outcomes in work and family during the young adult years can uncover important patterns that hint at how future generations will experience their work and family life course. Ultimately, I address whether these pathways indicate resistance to gender inequality at work and at home, and therefore advancement in the gender revolution, or if these pathways suggest that couples reproduce gender inequality in the division of labor, thus continuing to stall the gender revolution.

THE CURRENT STUDY

To answer these questions, I designed a multiyear study of young dual-career couples as they embarked on their working lives and made decisions about relationships and parenthood together. Specifically, I recruited child-free, different-gender couples from a range of graduate and professional degree programs in a major midwestern city to participate in a six-year study consisting of four interviews per person spaced out over time. I chose this group of couples and designed a study with multiple individual follow-up interviews purposefully to document evolving gender dynamics within couples throughout young adults' career launch and family formation pathways.

My focus on socially advantaged men and women was strategic. I decided to interview aspiring dual-professional couples because these educationally elite men and women with strong career orientations and high earnings potential were well positioned culturally and structurally to contest gender inequality in work and family. Prior research suggests that highly educated, socioeconomically advantaged couples are more likely than less-advantaged people to express attitudinal support for gender equality.[46] With two people pursuing well-paid professional careers—recall, for example, that Max and Julie both wanted to be doctors—these couples were also more likely to have material resources to sustain an egalitarian work-family arrangement.[47] Recruiting educated, dual-career couples therefore made it particularly likely that I would observe gender-egalitarian decision-making, allowing me to more easily assess what conditions could move the gender revolution forward.

Also, child-free men and women transitioning from school to work in early adulthood were especially likely to be making decisions about careers, relationships, and families. Studying young adults in their twenties and early thirties at this life stage made examining gender dynamics in work and family pathways easier for me to observe as a researcher because many life changes were likely to take place within the timeframe of my study. Career decisions were particularly salient because I began interviewing people when they were completing graduate or professional degrees and actively looking nationally and internationally for jobs to launch their careers. Work-related decisions at this stage of early adulthood could be crucial for other decisions about moving in together with romantic partners, getting married, and having children, too.

I recruited research participants using university email lists as well as referrals from my networks and from the interviewees. My final sample included forty people from twenty-one couples: twenty-one graduate and professional school students who were in the final year of their degree programs and nineteen of the students' spouses or romantic partners. Two of the twenty-one partners declined to join the study, and I describe this limitation in more detail in the methodological appendix. Thirty-two of the forty participants were White. Their ages ranged from twenty-two to thirty-five, with twenty-eight being the average age when I began the study. Ten of the twenty-one couples were married when I recruited them. The median relationship time among all couples was five years, and the median marriage duration among the married couples was two years.

Preparing to graduate with elite credentials such as JDs, MDs, and PhDs at the start of the study, the students were actively searching for professional jobs or applying for further training across the nation or the world. Their partners were not always in the same field, but they were all pursuing careers requiring specialized training (like software engineering) or graduate degrees (like medical doctor or data scientist) as well. Many partners were firmly established in their professions by the sixth year of the study. They worked as physicians, senior scientists, professors, and associate directors earning individual salaries well above the US household median for that year, with most earning close to, if not exceeding, six figures.[48] Over the study period, six of eleven unmarried couples got married, and five couples out of the whole sample broke up or got divorced. Eleven couples had children over the six-year window of my study.

Relying on volunteers to participate in my study affected the demographic composition of my final interview sample. Therefore, the work-family pathways I identify may largely reflect White, upper-middle-class, different-gender couples' experiences of gender, careers, and family. Future research should seek to understand how marginalization due to racism, capitalism, cisnormativity, and heteronormativity further shapes work-family pathways among other groups. We might expect, for instance, that racism restricts access to supportive, well-resourced workplaces for people of color, making equal sharing more difficult to achieve.[49] Yet people of color may hold different attitudes about gender, work, and family, enabling coordinated behaviors—like relying on extended and fictive kin for childcare[50]—that result in egalitarian arrangements despite work-related barriers. Although my sample is demographically homogeneous and privileged in multiple ways, the couples I interviewed still provide a useful case for examining gender egalitarianism and inequality. Without having to contend with the additional challenges faced by working-class and poor individuals, gender and sexual minority individuals, and people of color, this group arguably had an especially strong shot at launching and maintaining two equally important careers while establishing equal sharing in their relationships and household responsibilities because of their multiple advantages. Further, key insights from the broader theories I develop about gender, work, and family processes from this case study may be generalizable beyond White, upper-middle-class professionals in different-gender relationships.[51] I speculate on the implications of my study for partners who do not fit this socially advantaged profile in chapter 6 but call on other scholars to conduct empirical research on this topic.

Limitations aside, my study design had several strengths for documenting couples' career launch and family formation pathways. First, in contrast to prior research, I interviewed people multiple times over the course of six years (2013 to 2019) to capture how career and family pathways unfolded organically over time. Specifically, I conducted baseline Time 1 interviews when the men and women were preparing to graduate from school and started searching for jobs. I collected Time 2 interviews several months after baseline when job offers were (or were not) extended and couples had to decide what to do. Then I conducted Time 3 interviews one year after baseline when men and women were settling into their new jobs and adjusting to new responsibilities. Finally, I conducted Time 4 interviews five years after Time 3 to capture how men and women experienced advancing or changing their careers, getting married or breaking up, and transitioning to parenthood or deciding to remain child free indefinitely.

Other studies that interview people at one point in time are limited in their ability to examine these kinds of trajectories. They rely on either retrospective accounts that are prone to people misremembering how things happened or hypothetical accounts in which people imagine the pathways they think they will take in the future without being able to directly capture those events. For example, although Kathleen Gerson's interviews with young Americans reveal that men and women have egalitarian "Plan A's" but gendered "Plan B's" for their future work and family life, these cross-sectional, speculative interviews cannot tell us what men and women actually did in the face of barriers to gender equality in work and family. In particular, Gerson's findings of the gendered "Plan B's" begs the question of what happens when a man and a woman in a couple cannot have an egalitarian arrangement and have to reconcile their situation together. A longitudinal study design may enable us to answer that type of question. By talking to the same people several times over six years, I was able to keep a better record of people's work-family trajectories, directly compare people's ideals or expectations to their behaviors and outcomes, and more carefully document change over time. Although I concluded data collection for this study before the COVID-19 pandemic began in 2020, this longitudinal approach allowed me to make predictions about how couples might have responded to the pandemic based on their previous patterns of action. I lay out my thinking on this topic in more detail in the epilogue.

A second strength of my study is that I interviewed both partners in each couple. Many studies on gender inequality in work and family include women only.[52] A few researchers have spoken to men about these issues.[53] However, very few studies include data from both men and women in the same couples, even though this approach provides many benefits for understanding career and family trajectories.[54] Decisions about work, relationships, and family life are often made by partners, not by individuals. For example, Blair-Loy and Stone hint at how men's devotion to their own careers and inadequate domestic contributions factored into couples' decisions that women should exit their careers. Yet without interviews with men, we cannot understand how conversations and interactions between partners could lead to different work and family outcomes for men and women. Talking to two people in each partnership therefore gave me more information than was available in previous research. This methodological approach allowed me to verify events in a couple's unfolding story. At the same time, discrepancies or disagreements across partners' accounts were valuable points of data allowing me to identify differences in men's and women's experiences of otherwise shared events. For instance, Max really liked the hospital he picked for his residency, but Julie had not even considered it as an option for her own training before she learned that Max matched to this program. The experience of Max starting a residency program, then, was positive for him, but was more mixed for Julie as it became a new factor she had to consider for her own applications.

Once I recruited couples for the study, I met each person individually at a university office, a coffee shop, or the interviewee's workplace or home to have a conversation. Sometimes we spoke on the phone if participants lived outside of driving distance from me. By Times 3 and 4, most people had moved away to take a job, so I relied on phone and online video interviews for this portion of the study. At each interview session, I asked participants about each partner's work or school status; their short-, medium-, and long-term career plans; how they saw their careers fitting in with their personal lives and their relationship or family goals; and whether and how men and women coordinated work and family activities with their partners. Each interview varied in length, with most taking over an hour to complete and some lasting around three hours.

I had an easy time talking to most people because the topic of work and relationships was at the forefront of many men's and women's minds. For example, Julie remarked that figuring out how to find two jobs in the same place and how to line it all up with the couple's plans to get married and have children was all she and Max talked about with friends and loved ones anyway, so talking with me was no extra burden on her. Others mentioned that they appreciated having someone outside their social circle to talk to about these difficult decisions about careers and family. People even candidly shared sensitive details about their lives with me, including marital infidelity, sexual problems, and income information over six years of repeated interviews. Those readers interested in a deeper discussion of research methodology, including further details about the inspiration for this project, may read more in the methodological appendix.

WORK-FAMILY ECOSYSTEMS: A FRAMEWORK FOR
ANALYZING STRUCTURE, CULTURE, AND JOINT
ACTION IN COUPLES' DECISION-MAKING

To provide a sociological analysis of couples' work and family pathways, I developed a *work-family ecosystems* framework for examining structure, culture, and joint action among partners. At the beginning of this chapter I noted that structural conditions—material resources and constraints stemming from workplaces and public policies—and cultural forces—attitudes, beliefs, and norms about gender, work, and family—both contribute to the stalled gender revolution. Sociologists also recognize that individuals' actions play a role in shaping people's experiences and our collective outcomes as a society.[55] Individual agency, though bounded by social structures and cultural norms, matters for the advancement of the gender revolution. Although we have a wealth of scholarship to help us understand how *an individual* interacts with the conditions of their society, we have fewer tools for talking about how two actors navigate their society *together as a unit.*

Shin-Kap Han and Phyllis Moen, building on tenets of life course theory, offer a starting point for considering how structure, culture, and action might look in the context of a marital or romantic partnership.[56] They argue that scholars must analyze "coupled careers" to paint a fuller picture of work and family.[57] The coupled careers model requires us to understand men's and women's professional careers as interlocking within a relationship. Further, men's and women's family careers—their relationship and marital history, the caregiving roles they each play—are interdependent across the partners and intertwined with their professional careers. This web of two careers and a shared relationship and family life evolves over time as couples move across life stages.

I build on the idea of coupled careers to more precisely theorize how partners may navigate work, relationship, and family decisions given their broader structural and cultural landscape. First, I more explicitly incorporate theories of power into our thinking about coupled careers. I draw on Richard Emerson's classic scholarship to deem a person or group as powerful if they have relatively greater access to valued resources in society such as income and status.[58] I expand these criteria following contemporary sociologists Norene Pupo and Ann Duffy's work: a person or group is also powerful if they are relatively free from obligations to perform unpaid or otherwise devalued work; a person is powerful if they benefit from labor that they do not perform themselves.[59] Taking these two ideas together, power relations across partners are revealed when we consider (1) who earns more money or enough money to be independent of their partner; (2) who has the more important career, as gauged by whether the couple makes changes to their lives to support that person's profession; and (3) who does more unpaid or otherwise devalued work. Second, I more specifically detail how coupled careers may crystallize or change over time. Stability in people's structural and/or cultural contexts as well as partners' patterns of interaction may encourage path dependence in partners' coupled careers. Changes to structure, culture, and/or couple-level action, on the other hand, may promote transformations in couples' careers and home life.

Let us consider how to bring power to the forefront of analyzing the way couples may travel along a work-family pathway during the stalled gender revolution. First, two people in a couple might be situated differently in their social structure, affording them different levels of access to resources and therefore power. For example, although Max and Julie both wanted to be doctors, Max was pursuing a men-dominated medical specialty, while Julie was pursuing a women-dominated one.[60] Although it is easy to point to Max's and Julie's individual preferences to explain their particular career pursuits, the gendered nature of medical specialties in the United States made it likely that Max and Julie would end up in gendered subfields with slightly different training requirements. Importantly, Max had more options for advancing his career than Julie did, as Max could be trained in his specialty in more hospitals across the country than Julie could in hers. Further, Max could expect to earn more in his specialty than Julie.[61] In this couple, then, Max would be structurally advantaged in the workplace, whereas Julie would be relatively disadvantaged, making Max the more powerful partner in this relationship.

Second, two partners in a couple might be subject to different cultural norms. As mentioned previously, men and women face different cultural imperatives about work and family. Men face pressure to devote themselves to work above all else, and women face pressure to devote themselves to their families. These norms encourage men to pursue activities that may ultimately afford them more power in our current society while pointing women toward activities that are less likely to give them power. Given these cultural scripts, it might have been expected that Max would choose the hospital he thought was best for his career even though it was not ideal for his relationship. Perhaps Julie would feel more pressure to take her relationship and the couple's plans to have children into account when deciding where to apply for her residency. This particular cultural orientation toward gender, work, and family creates gender complementarity at the couple level for different-gender partnerships, so there might not be tension across Max and Julie if they both agree with these cultural scripts.[62] Yet Julie might recognize the power imbalance associated with gender complementarity and not endorse these broader beliefs about gender, work, and family. This situation could then challenge the ease with which she and Max might make decisions about her residency in the context of their relationship and family plans. If this were the case, Julie and Max would differ in their levels of agreement with these broader cultural norms. Max would be more aligned with, and more likely to benefit from, dominant cultural messages than Julie, and the partners would be misaligned with each other in their attitudes.

In a partnership in which both people want to foster a good relationship with one another and avoid disempowering each other, Max's actions would be influenced by Julie's structural situation and cultural beliefs, not just his own external context. If we were examining individuals only, we might expect that Max would take action to get and maintain a job and act as the main financial provider for the household. After all, he is structurally advantaged by his many work opportunities and may believe, as many Americans do, that men should pursue a professional career to successfully enact upper-middle-class masculinity. However, rather than taking individual action, Max might coordinate his actions with Julie so that the partners could stay on the same page with each other as they consider their structural and cultural resources and constraints as a unit. A partner's work-related opportunities and constraints can become incorporated into one's own set of perceived opportunities and constraints in the context of the couple's shared life. Additionally, if one partner expresses a certain attitude about resolving work and family tensions given their understanding of the couple's external landscape, the other partner may be motivated to align their own attitudes with the first partner to achieve solidarity as a unit.

When partners have taken stock of their workplace resources and limitations and reconciled their beliefs about the situation to form a shared assessment of the couple's circumstances, they can take joint action to move forward in their two professional and family careers. Maybe Julie is committed to continuing her career as a doctor. Maybe Max considers it important for the couple to stay together, though not at the expense of Julie's career. Max might then find a way to use his workplace advantages (perhaps his established connection to his residency program) to facilitate a career opportunity for Julie that could reunite the couple (potentially by exploring his institution's partner-hiring policies). These conditions may reveal how partners come to equally participate in paid labor and share unpaid relationship maintenance responsibilities—and therefore more equally share power.

Let us now consider how partners' coupled careers may crystallize or change over time. The coming together of structural support or constraints, egalitarian or gender-traditional attitudes, and multiple possible forms of joint action creates a self-reinforcing equilibrium for the partners' web of coupled careers. Workplace conditions and cultural beliefs enable certain kinds of joint action. At the same time, partners' coordinated behaviors can set them up to experience specific workplace conditions, which in turn can inform their attitudes about what is possible for future actions. The feedback between structure, culture, and joint action perpetuates this equilibrium, producing path dependence in couples' work-family trajectories. For example, as Max and Julie grow in their careers and in their relationship, they may continue to conscientiously reject the cultural pressure on women to care for the home and family, viewing that set of responsibilities instead as tasks that ought to be shared by partners. If Max ends up outearning Julie due to differences in their medical subfields—as men-dominated areas of medicine tend to pay more than women-dominated ones[63]—maybe the couple could use the extra income to pay for day-care services when they become parents so that both partners can continue full-time careers while sharing the remaining childcare responsibilities.

Yet this equilibrium can be an unstable one. A change in the partners' work-related conditions, cultural attitudes, and/or the way they take action together may ripple out to alter the ecosystem of their coupled careers. Rather than traveling down a straightforward pathway, we may see couples weave their way along more winding work-family trajectories. Indeed, previous research suggests that individuals' attitudes change as they encounter opportunities and constraints related to work and family.[64] Perhaps Max and Julie will experience an increase in the demands of their medical careers, putting too much pressure on the two working parents, even with paid daycare. This work-related challenge, combined with ever-present norms in favor of intensive motherhood, could change how the partners feel about their division of paid work and childcare. If Max outearns Julie and makes enough to support a family mainly on his income, the couple may decide that Julie should scale back her career to take over the couples' domestic and caregiving responsibilities. A new equilibrium might then set in for the couple. Max may work full-time (or more) while Julie may work part-time (or not at all) as the lead parent in the relationship. These joint actions will set each person up to face very different workplace opportunities and constraints and can shape how the partners feel about gender, work, and family later on. In fact, previous scholarship has found that women's gender attitudes become more traditional following the transition to motherhood if childbearing coincides with a withdrawal from the labor force.[65] Women who maintain full-time employment across the transition to parenthood, on the other hand, show no changes in their gender attitudes when they become mothers.

A bird's-eye view of the numerous work-family ecosystems that different couples experience allows us to assess the state of the gender revolution. Examining the way partners work together over time to reconcile their workplace demands and align their cultural understandings of men's and women's participation in paid work and domestic duties can shine a light on how dual-professional couples resist or reproduce gender inequality in work and family. What we learn from Max and Julie and the other couples in this study ultimately provides a window into the state of the gender revolution in the United States in the second decade of the twenty-first century.

The analyses in this book use this framework to make sense of partners' positions in their social structure; the cultural pressures each person might face; and the actions partners take together to accomplish their work, household, and family responsibilities over time. When couples encounter supportive structural conditions (i.e., availability of jobs for both partners, flexible working conditions, and resources to facilitate housework and childcare), culturally support egalitarianism (i.e., value sharing all responsibilities equally), and jointly take action to make the most of these favorable conditions (i.e., both partners use flexible working policies to share childcare, thus equally enacting their egalitarian ideals), we could expect to see egalitarian work-family trajectories. If any of these factors fail to come together—if couples face challenging structural conditions at work, express attitudinal support for gender traditionalism, or do not successfully coordinate their actions to use resources available to them to facilitate equal sharing—we might be more likely to see gender-unequal work-family pathways. Feedback between structure, culture, and joint action encourages path dependence, meaning the balance of work and family in a particular couple is likely to persist over time. However, the equilibrium in a couple's work-family ecosystem can shift in response to changes in workplace conditions, life events prompting changes in attitudes, and changes in the way partners take coordinated action.

CHAPTER PREVIEW

Chapters 2, 3, and 4 each describe one of three work-family pathways—ordered from the most egalitarian to the least—that couples experienced over six years as they launched careers and made decisions about their relationships and having children. In each chapter I identify the structural and cultural conditions that enabled or prohibited couples' ability to both prioritize careers and share family responsibilities. Each chapter also describes how partners coordinated their actions to maintain gender equality or reproduced gender inequality in their behaviors as they navigated the structural and cultural circumstances surrounding their careers, relationships, and families.

Chapter 2 profiles the *consistent compromiser* pathway. These partners maintained two equally important careers over time and shared all family responsibilities when they became parents. In terms of their professional resources, consistent compromisers had relatively high levels of access to job opportunities and workplaces that offered resources to accommodate relationship and family responsibilities. Partners also consistently expressed cultural attitudes in favor of gender egalitarianism and sharing responsibilities as a team. Finally, couples actively and cooperatively leveraged these conditions to ensure that they maintained an equal balance of work and family responsibilities across both part-ners over time. In particular, consistent compromiser men regularly used their workplace advantages like flexibility and autonomy over where and when they worked to benefit women's careers and their families. At Time 1, when students prepared to graduate from school, men and women worked together to formulate a couple-level plan to jointly search for jobs given a relatively favorable job market. Several months later at Time 2, when the realities of the job market challenged some of these couples' ideal plans, men revised their own career plans to sup-port women's careers. This decision enabled couples to maintain equal-ity in their careers as partners transitioned to their first jobs at Time 3, eight months to a year and a half after men and women began their job searches. Despite successfully establishing an equitable balance in their careers early on, men and women faced challenges to maintain-ing equality five years later at Time 4. Women, but not men, experienced poor mentorship, workplace harassment and discrimination, and job in-stability, all of which negatively shaped their career progress relative to their partners. Further, women were less able than men to negotiate child-care accommodations at work without facing professional penal-ties once they became parents. To support women's careers and maintain equality given these gendered external barriers, men took on an equal if not larger share of parenting responsibilities. Despite this equitable, progressive arrangement at home, partners constantly had to work to maintain egalitarianism in the face of careers that demanded workers' total devotion without providing supportive family policies. Men and women were exhausted by constantly negotiating equal working and parenting arrangements and lacked time for their marriages and friend-ships. These stressors point to greedy workplace and family conditions that made having careers and raising children difficult for all people and for women in particular.

Chapter 3 illustrates the *autonomous actor* pathway. Regardless of men's and women's access to job opportunities or workplace supports for work-life balance, autonomous actors stood out for understanding gender egalitarianism to mean two things. First, they expressed attitu-dinal support for men's and women's equal right to pursue their best individual opportunities. Second, they believed men and women were equally responsible for preserving their partner's autonomy by refrain-ing from holding each other back in their pursuits. This gender-neutral logic belied a gendered pattern of actions in which men passively stated their support for whatever women wanted to do, but many women actively compromised their careers for the couple. At Time 1, when partners began looking for jobs, men like Max made individual-focused career plans and invited women to do the same. Women like Julie were left to "make a personal choice" about whether to pursue their own best options or make interdependent plans that accounted for the relationship. When actual job offers came on the table (or not) several months later at Time 2, men deferred to women to make whatever decision would be best for them—effectively leaving the fate of the couple and their careers up to women. Most women opted for long-distance relationships to allow both partners to separately pursue their careers. Other women compromised their own careers to keep the relationship together—some by suspending their career pursuits indefinitely. And some women acted more like men and did what was best for their own careers without considering their partners and relationships. Couples' work-family outcomes at Time 3, about a year after partners began the job search process, varied depending on women's actions at Time 2. What was consistent, though, was that women did more work to manage the ongoing uncertainties in the partners' careers or (long-distance) relationships. If women did not do so, partners broke up. This gender-neutral autonomous logic leading to gender-imbalanced compromising for the relationship changed over the five years leading up to Time 4. At Time 4, both men and women made couple-focused rather than autonomous work and family decisions. Men's increased job security and confidence in their professional skills helped them feel more comfortable in making joint career plans to support women's careers and to make decisions as a couple rather than as an individual. For example, in contrast to Time 1, at Time 4 Max felt confident that he could find a new job in his field if he had to, so he was more willing than before to follow Julie in her career pursuits. This trajectory highlights how gender equality in work-family *outcomes* can often mask gender inequality in work-family *processes*.

Chapter 4 details the *tending traditional* pathway. These couples' pragmatic prioritization of men's careers and openness to women temporarily exiting their careers to care for future children resulted in a much more gender-unequal division of labor than men and women ever expected for themselves. They initially expressed greater acceptance of a neotraditional division of labor because their understanding of egalitarianism was that temporary, circumstantial imbalances across partners would (theoretically) even out over time. When couples encountered external barriers to launching two careers—namely men's unemployment—these cultural attitudes prompted men to assert the importance of their own career pursuits, leading women to suspend theirs. The early decision to prioritize men's careers created lasting constraints on women's professional options. At Time 1, tending traditional men and women formulated shared plans to sequentially look for jobs. After the man landed a job, couples reasoned, the woman could conduct a narrower, more targeted search. However, several months later at Time 2, when men continued to be unemployed, men emphasized their desires for careers at any cost, prompting women to pause their own professional plans to ensure that men could launch their careers first. Couples' revised plans to focus exclusively on men's job searches created an imbalance in men's and women's career trajectories by Time 3, a year after couples began their joint job searches. Whereas men embarked on their careers as planned, women faced unemployment or underemployment. Five years later at Time 4, men and women continued maintaining a neotraditional work-family arrangement despite souring on this division of labor. Women were constrained in relaunching their careers by their family responsibilities and by men's established careers. Men were reluctant to leave their elite jobs and risk losing income and benefits for their families. The couples that destabilized this neotraditional equilibrium only did so by breaking up or divorcing.

Chapter 5 provides more in-depth comparisons of the three work and family pathways presented in chapters 2 through 4 to underscore how workplace structures; cultural attitudes about gender, work, and family; and partners' joint and coordinated actions all needed to come together for couples to experience egalitarian work-family trajectories. For example, structural support for dual-professional couples—such as strong labor markets for two careers in the same city or formal processes to help spouses of employees with job placement—had to exist for partners to maintain egalitarian work arrangements. Otherwise, partners could find themselves taking the tending traditional pathway of work and family. However, workplace or other policy supports were not enough if couples did not jointly take action to leverage that support. If partners used autonomous logics to pursue career opportunities rather than making shared plans for equally and consistently compromising, partners could miss opportunities to take coordinated actions to achieve egalitarian work-family outcomes. This chapter also provides comparisons of the short-term (Time 3) and long-term (Time 4) career and family outcomes of men and women on these three trajectories to highlight how couples' work-family equilibria can persist over time. Consistent compromiser men and women were more likely than the partners on the other two pathways to get the gender-equal work and family outcomes that they imagined for themselves at the start of the study. They had the highest rates of employment over time and the highest individual earnings by Time 4. Although men and women on all three work-family pathways expressed interest in becoming parents, consistent compromiser couples were more likely than the other couples to have children over the six-year study period. Finally, consistent compromisers were less likely than autonomous actors and tending traditional couples to break up or get divorced—in fact, all of the consistent compromiser couples remained intact over time.

Chapter 6, the concluding chapter of the book, discusses the implications of these findings for the gender revolution in the twenty-first century. I suggest that the gender revolution has advanced in certain ways, but that there are persistent as well as new challenges to completing the gender revolution. Men's active support of women's careers through more equal involvement in chores, parenting, and household decision-making indicates that the gender revolution has advanced in terms of men's integration in unpaid household, relationship, and care work. Yet conditions in the workplace continue to slow the full realization of the gender revolution. Gendered harassment and discrimination still hold women back in their careers relative to men. Further, the cultural link between work and masculinity remains tight, as revealed by the way men's professional confidence and stability was key in shaping their support for women's careers. Relationships are not totally equal if sharing all work and family responsibilities hinges on whether men are stably attached to paid work. This point and other patterns I explore in chapters 2 through 5 raise questions for both further research and public policy: What exactly does it mean to have gender egalitarianism? Under what conditions is egalitarianism even desirable? What will it take to achieve gender equality in work and family? I conclude by speculating the answers to these questions and discussing what workplace structures and cultural attitudes toward gender, work, and family need to change to promote equal sharing and equal experiences in careers and family. Although individual- and couple-level solutions may not foster permanent, widespread social change in the gender revolution, as systemic solutions can, I also describe a number of actions people can take to survive in, and hopefully challenge, the structural and cultural contexts surrounding work and family as they exist now. One lesson comes from Max, who learned over six years of making career and family decisions with Julie that "you have to work together to get everything done. . . . I think we've

changed a lot—just communicating constantly about what we're doing."
From his perspective, learning to make decisions interdependently with
Julie, rather than operating autonomously, and coming to equally share
their responsibilities as workers, partners, and parents was ideal: "That's
been the biggest thing that's changed, how we interact. I think it's good.
I've been really happy."

This book ultimately makes three key points: (1) partners can experience gender equality in work and family if they are embedded in supportive structural contexts, culturally endorse egalitarianism, and take
well-coordinated joint actions—any weaknesses can divert couples away
from equal sharing of paid and unpaid responsibilities; (2) adopting a
lens of gender neutrality or degendering the landscape of careers and
family in our current society ignores unique gender-based structural and
cultural challenges women face at work and at home; and (3) men's
structural and cultural power can be leveraged to benefit women's
careers and create gender egalitarianism for couples.

The following chapters lay out the evidence supporting these points.
I first detail the *consistent compromiser* pathway, the most egalitarian
work-family trajectory in this study. These couples' stories reveal how
workplace conditions, cultural attitudes, and partners' coordinated actions all had to come together perfectly to enable men and women to
achieve egalitarianism and maintain it over time.

CHAPTER 2

Consistent Compromisers

The whole plan while we were doing long distance was for me to
go to [medical] residency in [a northeastern city] in order to be in
the same place when she's in business school. So I applied to all the
hospitals in [that city]. I wouldn't apply anywhere else. [My residency
is] three years, so she decided to work another year, go to business
school for two years, then [we] both would be getting a job at the
same time, three years from now. . . . Ideally, we would get engaged
a year after being in the same place, if not sooner, and maybe married
the next year. And then we get a job somewhere and settle down, buy
a house, and have kids a couple of years after that—figure out the
whole work-life balance thing with kids. Like, what kind of conflicts
will we have because our professions will be very demanding. . . .
We've also had a discussion about gender roles and taking time
to have kids: whether I'll stay home, or she'll stay home, or both.
Our viewpoint is that it's going to be about how much we can do
as a couple. It will be a matter of understanding how we can spend
time together as well as going about our business. I'm okay staying
home with the kids. I think what's important to me is that she's
also invested and available in the family. I'm confident she will be.
So I think we're in a pretty good place.

—Jared, Time 1

Jared and his partner Hannah envisioned having two careers and sharing childcare in their life as a couple. Their shared plans for a joint
career launch and their hopes for equal involvement in raising children
capture the collaborative essence of couples' work and family decision-
making on the *consistent compromiser* pathway. Favorable workplace
conditions, the couple's commitment to equally sharing work and family responsibilities, and partners' deliberately coordinated actions to leverage these structural and cultural conditions came together to enable
consistent compromisers to regularly resist gender inequalities at work

24

and at home as partners encountered turning points in their careers and transitioned to parenthood over a six-year period.

Consistent compromisers stood out from the autonomous actors (chapter 3) and tending traditional couples (chapter 4) in the way that men interacted at work and in their relationships. They regularly leveraged or made compromises within the favorable conditions of their own careers and took the initiative to equitably share housework and childcare to enable women's continuous attachment to their careers. Given external workplace barriers and cultural norms that disadvantage women at work and at home, men's actions were key to creating an equal balance of work and family, and therefore an equal balance of power, across partners.

Conscientiously looking for and creating conditions in which partners could always share work, relationship, and family responsibilities resulted in a gender-equal equilibrium in careers and family for these partners in the short term. Over the longer term, however, challenges stemming from the workplace, like gender-based harassment and the greedy, all-consuming nature of professional careers,[1] posed a continuous threat to couples' equal balance of work and family. Still, consistent compromisers worked together within these broader structures to make innovative work and family arrangements that preserved equal sharing of all responsibilities as much as possible.

The experiences of Cristina and Anthony, Vanessa and Alex, and Rick and Nora serve to illustrate this pathway. Details about the other consistent compromisers appear in table 2.1.

THE COUPLES

Cristina and Anthony were both preparing to graduate from the same public policy master's program when they joined the study. They had been a couple for nearly four years and had been married for just under a year. Cristina was passionate about international urban development and was looking for jobs in governmental and nongovernmental agencies, "a place that is fast-paced, more client-oriented, in the sense of the public, the constituents . . . agencies where you are really affecting people's lives directly." Anthony had similarly high career aspirations. He wanted an academic career and was applying to PhD programs. The partners praised each other often in their separate interviews, both as competent professionals and as supportive spouses. For example, Anthony remarked several times as he described his professional accomplishments

TABLE 2.1 CONSISTENT COMPROMISERS

Partners & occupations	Relationship status at Time 1	Time 1 *Partners compromised to target mutually beneficial cities*	Time 2 *Men compromised/ leveraged their careers to support women's careers*	Time 3 *Partners launched careers & established shared household routines*	Time 4 *Partners continued careers & shared parenting, but women faced harassment & slower growth at work*
Cristina, MPP student Anthony, MPP student	Married, living together	Applied together to jobs in select cities	Anthony chose city & helped Cristina find job	Both employed in new city Jointly set up new rhythm for work & life	Anthony advanced in his career Cristina faced harassment but advanced Co-parented 1 child
Vanessa, scientist Alex, STEM postdoc	Married, long distance	Applied together to jobs in 1 city	Alex shifted career plans to account for Vanessa's career	Both employed in new city Jointly set up new rhythm for work & life	Alex advanced in his career Vanessa faced harassment & advanced slowly Got married Expecting 1st child
Nora, STEM PhD student Rick, STEM postdoc	Married, living together	Applied together to jobs in select cities	Rick chose job to facilitate job opportunity for Nora	Both employed in new city Jointly set up new rhythm for work & life	Rick advanced in his career Nora advanced more slowly Co-parented 1 child
Katie, STEM PhD student Will, STEM PhD student	Married, living together	Applied together to jobs in select cities	Will chose city with most job opportunities for Katie	Both employed in new city Jointly set up new rhythm for work & life	Will advanced in his career Katie advanced more slowly Co-parented 2 children

Ashley, STEM PhD student Jake, entrepreneur	Married, living together	Ashley applied to jobs in their current city	Jake shifted career plans to enable Ashley to take job in different city	Jake changed careers & moved to new city for Ashley's job	Ashley advanced her career slowly & moved to new city for Jake's graduate program Remained child free
Joyce, software engineer Jeff, STEM PhD student	Married, living together	Jeff applied to jobs in select cities	Jeff shifted career plans to account for Joyce's career	Both employed in same city to continue their rhythm for work & life	Jeff advanced in his career Joyce's job churning slowed her advancement Co-parented 1 child
Anna, STEM postdoc Peter, STEM PhD student	Engaged, long distance	Both applied separately to jobs broadly	Peter shifted career plans to account for Anna's career	Both employed in Anna's city Jointly set up new rhythm for work & life	Peter advanced in his career Anna advanced more slowly Got married, then started long distance again Trying to have children
Hannah, consultant Jared, MD student	Unmarried, long distance	Jared applied to jobs in Hannah's city	Jared took job in Hannah's city	Both employed in Hannah's city Jointly set up new rhythm for work & life	Both advanced in their careers Got married Trying to have children

MPP = master of public policy

and upcoming plans, "I am here thanks to her." They both considered family to be important to them and wanted to start having children in a few years after they became established in their careers. Cristina and Anthony's process of coordinating two careers and transitioning to parenthood over the six-year study period shows how each person's consistent compromising within their favorable professional contexts allowed them to maintain the broader conditions that supported the partners' equilibrium of work activities, their relationship, and their family unit.

Vanessa and Alex met in graduate school, where Vanessa was completing a master's degree and Alex was completing a PhD in the same natural science field. When they joined the study, they had been in a relationship for two years and had been engaged for a little over a year. Vanessa remembered knowing very quickly that she wanted to marry Alex: "He never got frustrated with me even when I was at my worst, and that's one of the reasons that I know he's right for me. We really complement each other with our mannerisms. When we're together, we're at our best." At the time of their first interviews, they were living in different cities. Vanessa led an active life filled with work, volunteering, and recreational activities. She cared about climate change issues and had recently started a job in a mid-Atlantic city as an environmental scientist. Alex was easygoing, ready to laugh or make a lighthearted joke. He was finishing a postdoctoral research position in environmental science at a southern university and was applying for academic jobs mostly in and around Vanessa's city. They planned to get married when they were both in the same place again. Alex and Vanessa's story highlights how men's attitudes toward egalitarianism on the consistent compromiser pathway prompted them to make compromises in their own careers to benefit women's careers and their families when unfavorable work-related contexts challenged the couples' dual-professional ideals.

Nora, a PhD student, and Rick, a postdoctoral fellow, both did research in the natural sciences and wanted academic careers. They started dating when Nora was halfway through her PhD program and Rick was in the final year of his. They had been married for two years when they joined the study. Each partner held high opinions of the other's academic work and took each person's aspirations as a scientist seriously. Rick repeated in his interviews, "she is a really good scientist," and Nora asserted in hers, "Rick is a very good scientist and very successful so far, and he loves it." Nora was looking for postdoctoral research positions at universities where Rick was interviewing for faculty jobs. They wanted to start a family in the upcoming year and hoped to both have jobs by the time Nora got pregnant. Nora and Rick's experiences provide an example of how men leveraged their workplace resources to facilitate professional opportunities for women and permit equal sharing of childcare across partners.

TIME I: SHARED PLANS FOR
A DUAL-CAREER PARTNERSHIP

Consistent compromisers took stock of their work-related resources and constraints at Time 1 when they began their job searches to identify the conditions that would make it possible for both partners to pursue careers while sustaining their relationship. These partners deliberately made couple-level plans for a joint life together as men and women prepared to graduate from their degree programs. Spouses Cristina and Anthony, both graduating from the same public policy program, coordinated her job search with his applications for further schooling. Cristina discussed collaboratively making plans that accounted for each partner's career goals:

> We are trying to figure out how to match up that situation. He basically targeted cities where I would like to work. He's applying to cities that are also options for me, and I'm also applying to cities where he likes the programs that are being offered. So that intersection is basically [our current midwestern city, a northeastern city, a mid-Atlantic city, and a European city].

Cristina and Anthony jointly created a list of target cities that had opportunities for each person's career pursuits, thus ensuring that the couple would only make decisions in contexts broadly amenable to their dual-career partnership. Each partner compromised at this stage by forgoing career opportunities in places that would only work for one partner, preventing the couple from creating a power imbalance in their careers. For instance, Cristina, who wanted to work in international urban development, initially considered applying to positions in Latin America but tabled that idea because the graduate school opportunities for Anthony in that region were limited. At the same time, Anthony thought the PhD program at a large midwestern university was an excellent fit for his professional goals but did not put in an application because Cristina would not be able to find work in her field in the small city where the university was located.

Alex and Vanessa, who both received degrees in environmental science, described a similar process of coordinating their job searches. Alex was completing a postdoctoral research appointment and was looking for professor jobs. Although he put in a few applications to institutions located in various cities across the country, he focused mostly on applying to positions in and near the mid-Atlantic city where Vanessa had been working as a scientist for the past few months. Vanessa described how they chose to target their applications there:

> What I really want to do is climate change consulting in the U.S. I knew it would open more doors, working in [this mid-Atlantic city]. I wanted to be in [this city]. [This city] is kind of a hotspot for environmental science. Plus he wants to be a professor. There are a lot of good opportunities [for him] in [this city]. [This city] was kind of like this perfect middle ground—all roads led to [this mid-Atlantic city].

Alex and Vanessa considered each of their individual career goals as they prepared to enter the workforce and jointly strategized how they could bring them into alignment as a couple. Like Cristina and Anthony, Alex and Vanessa collaboratively constructed a couple-level plan in which each person could pursue their career alongside their significant other.

Consistent compromisers' process of making shared plans was shaped by their marital status. Five of the seven consistent compromiser couples were married, and the other two had clear intentions to marry in the near future. Yet marriage did not indicate a commitment to traditional gender roles for these couples. Rather, marriage represented a mutual agreement to sustain a dual-career partnership in which all responsibilities were shared. For example, Alex explained that his engagement to Vanessa symbolized a joint promise that each partner would support the other's career:

> The engagement is kind of a way of saying we should plan a little bit around each other in our job searching and things like that, and kind of coordinate our priorities so both of us can be employed and happy in the same place in the nearish future. And so my job search was both for me to get an awesome job, but also to have my future wife have a job in the same place as me.

For consistent compromisers, engagement and marriage provided assurance that each partner could pursue their professional ambitions with active support from the other. The promise to account for one another's career aspirations meant that each partner often had to make compromises in their own careers, namely by forgoing potentially lucrative professional opportunities, to ensure that the other person could continue their career. For example, after explaining that "all roads led to [this mid-Atlantic city]" for her and Alex's job searches, Vanessa continued:

That being said, not everything in the world is in [this mid-Atlantic city]. I had a lead in [a southern city] and I had a lead in [an East Coast city] and I had a lead in [a northeastern city]. I was like, "okay, those are backups."

Vanessa did not consider options in other parts of the United States as seriously as those in their targeted mid-Atlantic city because she and Alex promised to account for one another's job searches and prioritized being together in the same geographic location. Like two other consistent compromiser couples who were in long-distance relationships at Time 1, Vanessa and Alex hoped to move to the same city soon, so the availability of jobs for both partners in the same place was a major emphasis as partners identified the contexts that could support their dual-career relationship.

The small number of target cities available to Anthony and Cristina and the single city identified by Alex and Vanessa highlighted a major work-related challenge facing many dual-career partners: the limited locations with job markets that could work for both partners' careers. Yet compared to autonomous actors and tending traditional couples described in later chapters, consistent compromisers were relatively advantaged in this respect by being in similar fields. For example, although Alex and Vanessa wanted different kinds of careers, they were both environmental scientists, so they knew the labor market in their targeted city would generally support both partners' professional endeavors. Even so, couples often felt like they had very few options regarding the locations that would support their dual-professional partnerships.

Consistent compromisers also outlined the conditions necessary for partners to share the work of nurturing their relationship and building a family as they considered their two careers. Beyond the immediate goal of finding two jobs in the same city, these partners also had goals for sharing childcare responsibilities, given their professional demands, when they eventually became parents. Their deliberate planning to avoid uneven effort in unpaid work helped to keep power imbalances in check. Alex provided a metaphor for how he and Vanessa imagined their path to parenthood:

> We talk about stages of children. Step one is having cats. Then you upgrade and you get a dog. Then, five to seven years from now, that's when we'll start maybe child planning. We talk about it all the time because I like kids. She worries about whether she'll be a good mom, but she's being a good mom to the cat now and I think she'll figure it out in the future. One thing that set off a serious discussion at some point is when I jokingly, but not really jokingly, said I'd love to be a stay-at-home dad, [meaning] I would have the flexibility

to work from home and also raise children. She really does seem to want a nine-to-five job so if I am in a flexible situation, I was like, "she can continue her career and I can raise the baby."

Delaying childbearing and having pets together was a way for Alex and Vanessa to practice sharing caregiving before children came into the picture. Alex's positive attitude toward adjusting his work to their future parenting responsibilities also set the couple's expectation that he would be highly involved in caring for their future children. His description of "jokingly, but not really jokingly" discussing his desire for high involvement in raising children revealed a mismatch between broader cultural norms about gender and family and Alex's personal attitudes toward childcare. Joking about being a stay-at-home dad signaled his recognition of broader cultural gender norms that men do not provide childcare, but his *not* joking about working from home in order to raise children allowed him to express a different attitude in favor of taking on more family responsibilities. Importantly, this egalitarian preference hinged on the availability of flexible working conditions for Alex, showing how supportive structures at work and cultural approval of egalitarianism were both necessary to make equal sharing of work and family responsibilities a realistic possibility for this couple.

This joint approach to parenting was also expressed by consistent compromisers who wanted to have children in the more immediate future. Rick and Nora were pursuing academic careers in the natural sciences together: a professor job for him and a postdoc and eventually a professor position for her. They both reported asking potential employers about parental leave policies because they knew they wanted to start having children soon. Nora said:

> [The mid-Atlantic university that interviewed both of us has] a parental leave policy that says you have eight weeks paid leave for a mother and a father. We can both take it, which I think is really good, but only for employees that have been working for one semester or six months. If we end up coming out of this [interview process] still thinking [this university] is going to be the place [for us], that's something I would really like to negotiate because there's a possibility that we'll arrive there and just have had a baby. I would like something in writing that we could use our parental leave from day one.

Nora's quote shows, again, that workplace resources, progressive cultural attitudes, and partners' collaborative actions had to come together to produce the possibility of having an egalitarian arrangement. In terms of workplace supports, the mid-Atlantic university where they both interviewed offered a parental leave policy. Regarding progressive cultural attitudes, Nora saw the availability of parental leave for both mothers *and* fathers as "really good." Finally, with respect to joint action, both partners' active efforts to ask for institutional support to accommodate their two careers to their parenting responsibilities brought these conditions together to lay the groundwork for an egalitarian equilibrium in which Rick and Nora could both pursue careers while raising children together.

All told, the consistent compromisers' overall approach to building their work-family ecosystem at Time 1 centered on identifying favorable structural contexts as a team and remaining in step with one another. As Cristina said:

> You need to be a team player. It doesn't work if you are selfish and are trying to play for yourself, and it doesn't work if you are trying to play [just] for him or [just] for her. You need to sit down together, have a strategy, plan something, and agree. I think [it's about] trying to give support and get supported. If you're quitting on something that you really want, then that's probably going to play against the couple afterwards. That doesn't mean that you cannot let something go. For example, Anthony really likes the program in [a large midwestern university] and I definitely don't want to go to [this midwestern state]. But that doesn't mean that he's not applying to good schools. I cannot just stop his dream, but I cannot go and live for five years in [this midwestern state] and be miserable. It's a fine line there, but I think you need to negotiate. I think "team player"—that's the key word here.

Remaining situated in professional contexts that worked for the couple as a unit—and not considering any situations that would disempower one partner by putting them at a disadvantage in their career—was key to building a foundation for consistent compromisers' dual-professional relationships. Given their available work-related resources, each partner gave a little and took a little, and neither partner gave nor took too much in identifying situations that could support them in the future.

TIME 2: MAINTAINING A DUAL-CAREER PARTNERSHIP

Despite consistent compromisers' careful planning at Time 1, professional realities did not always perfectly align with partners' ideals at Time 2, four to seven months into the partners' job searches. Yet partners remained steadfast in their attitudes toward having an egalitarian partnership and took action to match their career situations to their original goal. For instance, Alex's academic job search resulted in multiple interviews but no offers. He continued to receive requests for interviews and was invited to pursue an opportunity at an academic research institution in a southwestern city. However, those positions were far away from the mid-Atlantic city where Vanessa had just started working. Rather than take those interviews, Alex altered his job search strategy. He switched away from looking for academic jobs and doubled down on finding other kinds of jobs in the city he and Vanessa originally targeted:

> I didn't get any offers [near our targeted mid-Atlantic city] at all and so I shifted my attention completely to finding work in the private sector. I looked for nothing outside of [our targeted city]. [This city] is a large enough area, and there's enough stuff in environmental and energy science that I should be able to find a job here. It has the right kind of jobs, and Vanessa lives there. She already has a job there and we were planning to move in together and so it was just—I am not going to find something somewhere else because I don't want to.

Because Alex and Vanessa outlined the specific contexts that would support their two careers when they chose a location that had job opportunities for both of them, Alex was able to pursue other kinds of jobs in his field in their targeted city. In explaining why he had altered his job search strategy, Alex expressed consistency in his attitudes favoring a dual-career partnership. He emphasized his commitment to sticking with the couple's broader plan for their life together and prioritized joining Vanessa where she had just started her career. Although Vanessa offered to compromise at Time 2 by investigating possibilities for transferring offices within her company or starting a new job search if Alex had his heart set on pursuing his one promising lead in the American Southwest—both of which would disrupt her tenure in her relatively new position—Alex did not consider those compromises to be fair. He reasoned:

> [The southwestern city is] a tiny, tiny town. There's nothing for her to do there, at least not without driving an hour every day. [The research institution] pays very well and [the southwestern city has] a great cost of living. If I wanted to continue the academic thing, there are a lot of reasons that it could be awesome. But she wouldn't be happy there and therefore I would not be happy. If I expand even a little bit beyond academia, [our targeted city] is one of the best places I could be. I'm a little disappointed about academia, but in [our targeted city], we're together and that's so much better.

Alex's proposed compromise to consider nonacademic jobs in a city with ample opportunities for environmental scientists would not disrupt his professional trajectory. In contrast, Vanessa's proposed compromise to leave a job she had just started to relocate to a city without similar career prospects for her would threaten her workplace attachment and create a power imbalance in the couple. Thus, for Alex to compromise his career plans to pursue nonprofessor jobs in their targeted city would end the partners' long-distance relationship and preserve the two careers the couple originally aimed to have. This pattern of men taking action to adjust their career plans given their advantages in the realm of work at Time 2 distinguished consistent compromisers from the autonomous actors in chapter 3 and the tending traditional couples in chapter 4. As I show later, the men on these other pathways took different actions when unfavorable job market conditions prevented them from pursuing their ideal jobs.

Even when things worked out as well as couples could hope, with job offers coming through as the partners searched for two careers, men continued actively ensuring that women would benefit from the couple's ultimate decision. When Anthony received acceptances into the PhD programs at two universities, one in the couple's current city and one in a mid-Atlantic city, he felt torn in making a decision. The program in his current city was less ideal for his career but would allow Cristina to advance in the interview process with an organization she was excited to work for. The program in the mid-Atlantic city was a much better fit for Anthony's professional goals but would redirect Cristina to applying for jobs with organizations that she was less enthusiastic about. Cristina felt strongly that Anthony should accept the mid-Atlantic university's offer. She reasoned that the career opportunities available to him after he completed the program would ultimately benefit him and the couple. But Anthony was concerned about what that decision would mean for Cristina's career in the immediate term and consequently in the future. Eventually, he agreed to take the offer from the mid-Atlantic university but was staunch in ensuring that Cristina could find a good job:

> The priority for us as a couple right now is for me to get the best possible outcome from the PhD. I wanted to balance that somehow because the labor market in [the mid-Atlantic city]—I am afraid of the types of work she can actually get. My concern is that she doesn't like the jobs over there. So, one of the conditions that I asked, kind of demanded from her when we made the decision was: she needs to find a job in which she wants to be. We have been doing some research and there are some areas in which she would be happy to work. [I told her,] "I don't want to go to [this university] if you end up working at this institution that you don't like, and you will be unhappy." So, the agreement we reached was, "Okay, I understand [this university] was

the best decision [for me], but let's make an effort to find some jobs in which you will be happy."

Anthony wanted Cristina's first job after graduate school to support her professional trajectory, so he made a concerted effort to monitor job ads and edit her cover letters once the couple agreed they would move for Anthony's PhD. In this way, the couple maintained their initial commitment to fostering a relationship with two equally important careers.

In a more extreme example, Rick used his multiple job offers as leverage to benefit Nora's career. When the couple was deciding among offers at Time 2, Rick stated that their final decision hinged on the opportunities available to Nora at each institution:

> It boiled down to quality of life and opportunities for Nora, so we are going to [a southern university]. She can actually do a postdoc [nearby] at [a private university] or [a state university], so she's following up with [the private university]. My original inclination was [a mid-Atlantic university] because they gave me a lot more money, but you know, it was not the department for us because they didn't know what to do with the request that I made for a spousal hire [for Nora]. And that rubbed me the wrong way. [The southern university] specifically told her, and told me, that they are going to interview her for a tenure track [professor] position in three years. That was part of the commitment when I signed. When they called her and told her what the process was going to be, she was very happy with it. So we decided for [the southern university].

Because the southern university had formal structures in place for spousal hiring that would allow both partners to simultaneously pursue their careers, Rick and Nora chose to accept that offer. They gave up the better opportunity for Rick at the mid-Atlantic university to maintain an equal balance of career opportunities for both people in the couple.

Nora's pregnancy at Time 2 and Rick's response to it also highlighted how consistent compromisers took action to make the most of their supportive workplace contexts as they strategized how to equally share career and family responsibilities. Rick altered his current work activities and requested to defer his start date at his new job to ensure that Nora could take her time to finish her degree and transition into her postdoc on the right foot:

> I actually asked for a deferral for a year for two reasons. First, I want Nora to have enough time to finish [her PhD] properly here. Second, I want to finish the projects that I am working on in the lab. These days I'm working less because I try to help at home as much as I can. Nora can't be the one cleaning the house or getting the groceries—doing the laundry is all me. For the first

three months [of the pregnancy] she was just exhausted. All the time. She was actually working in the lab and she came home a lot because if you're feeling nauseous all day, working in the lab—I don't know how I would do it. We have until June of next year, so there's going to be almost ten months for her to finish and actually be ready to leave.

Making the most of an available deferred start date policy, Rick asked his new employer to accommodate a different rhythm of work and life initiated by the pregnancy, not just for himself but also for Nora. Enabling Nora to take an appropriate amount of time to transition from graduate school to her postdoc given her pregnancy ensured that she would not falter in launching her academic career. This decision did not harm Rick, either, since he was working in the lab less than before because he was doing more housework than he had done previously.

In sum, consistent compromisers stood out from other couples at Time 2 for actively leveraging their favorable structural conditions to set up an egalitarian division of labor. When concrete job offers were on the table, men and women chose the ones in locations with opportunities for both partners. Further, men incorporated women's professional plans into their own career decisions. They used workplace resources to benefit women's careers when decisions had to be made. When external workplace conditions came together with men's and women's desires for egalitarian relationships, these couples took action to solidify partners' equal attachment to careers. This configuration of structure, culture, and joint action helped couples resist gender inequality and power imbalances in work and relationships because couples avoided favoring men's careers over women's careers and men made compromises for the couple.

TIME 3: LAUNCHING TWO CAREERS AND LOOKING TO THE FUTURE

The actions couples took at Time 2 to maintain broader conditions amenable to a dual-professional partnership set men and women up to launch two careers as they began a new chapter of their shared life at Time 3, eight months to a year and a half after couples began their job searches. Cristina quickly found a job that suited her professional goals close to the university where Anthony began his PhD work. Alex also found a job in his field shortly after moving to Vanessa's city, where she continued to work as a scientist. Rick began working as a professor at a southern university, and Nora was scheduled to begin her postdoc at a nearby private university after some extra time at home with their new baby. By Time 3, these couples were learning how to navigate the demands of two professional careers as they set up their new work-family ecosystem together.

In contrast to the tending traditional couples in chapter 4, who established a neotraditional division of labor at Time 3, consistent compromisers solidified the power-balanced egalitarian structure of their dual-career relationship by equally participating in other daily activities aside from their paid work. The everyday rhythms they developed to accomplish household chores, nurture the relationship, and raise children established standards for how they would interact with each other given their two demanding professional activities. The self-reinforcing feedback between couples' work and home life and the partners' commitment to practicing egalitarianism on a daily basis set them up to continue maintaining two careers while sharing household, relationship, and family responsibilities in the future.

For example, couples found strategies to complete household chores together given both partners' paid work demands. Alex and Vanessa developed a habit of sharing housework as they adjusted to living together for the first time as a dual-career household. Vanessa said Alex did most of the housework while he was still searching for jobs, but that distribution of work evened out once Alex found paid work:

> He still does most of the cooking. I'm always the one doing the dishes, I'm always the one folding up clothes. He typically cooks and vacuums, and then everything else we kind of just split. He's wonderful about it and he never makes the argument that he's tired. He typically gets home before me and cooks dinner. Tonight, it's kind of an interesting night because he's coming home late and I'm making dinner. So [we have a] pretty good distribution of housework without either party complaining.

Alex and Vanessa's flexibility in doing chores meant that their household could run even when one person's job demands temporarily shifted. When Vanessa was working more than Alex, he took on more housework. When Alex had to work more, Vanessa stepped in to pick up the slack. But the couple's default as egalitarian partners was to share the chores.

On top of the physical labor couples did to run a household, partners shared the relationship work: the work of maintaining each person's emotional well-being and affirming the partners' sense of being a family unit.[2] Cristina and Anthony were both stressed out by their simultaneous major life changes: Cristina was adjusting to long workdays in a large bureaucracy, Anthony was juggling classes and starting a research project, and the couple was trying to establish a friendship network in a new city where they did not know anyone. Recognizing that they needed to support each other through these transitions, they took advantage of the proximity of their workplaces to spend time together as much as possible. Anthony used his flexibility as a PhD student to organize his work schedule to maximize his time with Cristina:

> I have class very late and [Cristina's] work at [her large organization] is very demanding, but usually we go to work together in the morning and then we come back at night—we take the same bus and we try to spend time together. We try to have lunch once or twice a week. I decided since I started [the PhD program] that my weekends were going to be only for Cristina, so I try to finish everything during weekdays. I mean, we both have had to work on weekends, so we try to work during the day and do some things [for fun] during the night. I think we have managed to spend quality time on weekends—we traveled, saw things in the city, now we are furnishing the apartment.

Cristina and Anthony leveraged the perk of working close to one another to nurture their relationship and provide emotional support to each other. They shared their commute, took time for lunch dates during the workweek, and made a conscious effort to schedule time on the weekends to do leisure activities as a couple and to accomplish housework (like furnishing an apartment) together. These activities solidified the partners' power-balanced routine of sharing the emotional and physical maintenance work required of living together as equal partners.

Finally, consistent compromisers shared childcare along with their paid work responsibilities. Nora positively described her and Rick's joint transitions out of school, into parenthood, and into new jobs, and reported satisfaction with the way they integrated work and family life as a couple:

> He is an absolutely great dad, and so accommodating when we were in [our previous city] and [I was] trying to finish up my dissertation. Rick and [the baby] had a little office on the fourth floor of the building where my lab was located. I would be working in the lab looking at a microscope and when she would need to be fed I would run upstairs or he would bring her down to me so I could nurse her. In that way I finished gathering all my data for my dissertation. That was really great. . . . [Y]ou can kind of see the give-and-take. The last few months in [our previous city] were really all about me getting finished [with my dissertation]. Now we're here and he had these grants due. . . . [T]he focus of our family shifted from getting [my] dissertation done to getting Rick's grants done. I think it's good to see how that give-and-take works.

Combining paid work and childcare and trading off whose work demands were prioritized over time without having anyone fully suspend their professional activities set a standard for equally sharing work and family activities among consistent compromisers. Bolstering these partners' ability to act out their relationship ideals on a day-to-day basis and reinforcing consistent compromisers' endorsement of egalitarianism were supportive workplaces offering the partners a great deal of flexibility. These workplace resources, cultural attitudes, and behavioral factors all came together to solidify a foundation for couples to continue equally sharing work and family responsibilities in the future.

Altogether, consistent compromisers were happy with their immediate outcomes. Despite some feeling overwhelmed by having made so many life changes in a relatively short period of time, they liked the way each partner contributed to paid work and caregiving and were optimistic about their future together. Vanessa, for example, said, "We're really loving our lives right now. We're just really having golden days right now." These "golden days" of working in professional jobs and maintaining a relationship and household as an equal partnership prompted her and Alex to set a wedding date after having a purposefully long engagement to ensure they could build a life together as equal partners. Vanessa said, "We set the date two weeks after he started his job," after they were certain they had the kind of partnership that supported both of them working and living together. But consistent compromisers also recognized that continuing to have such a partnership depended on each person giving a little and taking a little to maintain broader conditions that supported this equilibrium. Anthony said:

> If you don't see the big picture, it's a perfect combination for a disaster. So you set that goal and say, "What are the things that we have to do in order to enjoy the things we enjoy?" Well, we have to make tough decisions, we have to move to a city we don't like as much or sometimes you have to take jobs that in the short term you don't like or I have to go to the university that's not the one I would like, but [that's] the kind of big picture you have to see. Okay, I enjoy life with you, so what are the things I have to do in order to do that? Well, let's do it. Even though they're hard, that's the big picture.

The "big picture" for Anthony—and for the other consistent compromisers—was sharing a life in which both partners pursued careers and each person worked to maintain the relationship and the family. This "big picture" of partners' equal power at work and at home was only possible due to the alignment of workplace structures, progressive cultural attitudes, and partners' successfully coordinated actions.

TIME 4: CHALLENGES TO ADVANCING TWO CAREERS
AND SHARING CHILDCARE

Consistent compromisers' unwavering egalitarian attitudes and coordinated actions up to Time 3 solidified working conditions that reinforced their gender-equal attitudes and habit of collaboration over time. At Time 4, five years after consistent compromisers began their careers, men and women continued expressing egalitarian attitudes and continued actively collaborating to advance both partners' professional activities while sharing relationship maintenance, household work, and if parents, jointly raising children. What changed the most in these couples' work-family ecosystems was the partners' professional contexts. Cristina moved up from junior associate to development specialist at her organization and earned $120,000 annually. Anthony was in the final year of his PhD program and was planning to look for professor jobs. He earned around $50,000 a year teaching classes and doing part-time research at a nongovernmental organization on top of completing his dissertation. They were also raising a one-year-old child. Vanessa changed organizations three times and moved into an environmental analyst role making an annual salary of $87,500. Alex moved up from environmental analyst to senior analyst at a new consulting company and earned $133,000 yearly. Vanessa had recently found out she was pregnant, and the couple expected their first child later that year. Nora was finishing her postdoc at a private university and was scheduled to start an assistant professorship at Rick's university. Although she earned $50,000 a year as a postdoc, she would make $85,000 as soon as she started her new job. Rick continued as a professor at the southern university and was earning $100,000 annually. He was being reviewed for tenure and expected to receive a decision later that year. Their child was about to start kindergarten. The other consistent compromisers' five-year trajectories and Time 4 outcomes appear in table 2.2.

These positive outcomes in salaries, job titles, and family milestones masked gendered workplace pressures that posed a constant threat to these couples' egalitarian balance of careers and family. Although I show in chapter 5 that this pattern was not unique to the consistent compromisers, these couples' experiences highlight this issue especially well. The high proportion of men and women working in science, technology, engineering, and mathematics (STEM) fields on this pathway made it particularly clear that workplace conditions play a prominent

TABLE 2.2 CONSISTENT COMPROMISERS' FIVE-YEAR TRAJECTORIES AND TIME 4 OUTCOMES

Partners & occupations at Time 3	Five-year trajectory	Time 4 outcomes
Cristina, junior associate Anthony, PhD student	She moved up to development specialist, then took temporary special assignment for office of CEO He continued his PhD & worked as temporary researcher Remained married & continued living together Had 1st child & took 5 months' paid leave together	She continued as development specialist ($120,000) He planned to graduate next year & continued working as part-time researcher ($50,000) Remained married & continued living together Co-parented 1 child
Vanessa, scientist Alex, analyst	She started as scientist in 2nd firm, got laid off, then moved up to analyst at 3rd firm He moved up to senior analyst at 2nd firm Got married & continued living together	She started as analyst at 4th firm ($87,500) He continued as senior analyst ($133,000) Remained married & continued living together Expecting 1st child
Nora, postdoc Rick, professor	She slowly advanced in her postdoc He continued as professor Remained married & continued living together Co-parented 1 child	She was finishing her postdoc & had professor position lined up at Rick's university ($50,000) He continued as professor ($100,000) Remained married & continued living together Co-parented 1 child
Katie, postdoc Will, PhD student	She slowly completed her postdoc, then started as senior scientist He completed his PhD, then started residency program Remained married & continued living together after moving to new city for both of their jobs Had 1st child; each partner took 3 months' paid leave sequentially	She continued as senior scientist ($131,000) He continued as resident ($47,000) Had 2nd child; she took 4 months' paid leave while he took 2.5 weeks' unpaid leave

Ashley, postdoc Jake, teacher	She slowly completed her postdoc, then started as senior scientist He continued as teacher, then stopped working to get MA Remained married & continued living together after moving to new city for his MA program	She continued as senior scientist ($120,000) He was finishing his MA & applying for jobs Remained married & continued living together Remained child free
Joyce, software engineer Jeff, researcher	Her firm closed & she took software engineer job in 2nd firm; firm closed & she took data scientist job in 3rd firm; firm closed & she took data scientist job in 4th firm, where she moved up to chief data scientist He moved up to engineering director Remained married & continued living together Had 1st child; took 1 month's paid leave together	She continued as chief data scientist ($220,000) He continued as engineering director ($300,000) Remained married & continued living together Co-parented 1 child
Anna, postdoc Peter, postdoc	She slowly advanced in her postdoc He completed his postdoc, then started as engineer Got married & started long distance when he moved for his job	She continued as postdoc ($48,000) He moved up in rank as engineer ($140,000) Remained married & continued long distance Trying to have children
Hannah, consultant Jared, medical resident	She stopped working to complete MBA, then started as product manager before moving up to product director He completed his residency, then started as physician Got engaged, got married, then moved to new city for both of their jobs	She continued as product director ($290,000) He continued as physician ($280,000) Remained married & continued living together Trying to have children

role in partners' ability to maintain gender equality in work and family. On the one hand, working in elite science professions gave consistent compromisers access to institutional resources like high salaries, control over their schedules, remote work options, and generous parental leave policies to support their dual earner-caregiver relationships. On the other hand, these men-dominated workplaces that valorize overworking put women at risk for experiencing gender-based harassment and discrimination,[3] two forces that threaten to push women out of their careers.[4] Nearly every woman—but none of the men—reported some combination of job instability, subpar mentorship, and workplace harassment or discrimination that negatively affected their five-year professional pathways relative to their partners. These gendered workplace barriers put women at a disadvantage in their careers compared to men, challenging consistent compromisers' attempts to maintain equality in their careers and thus an equal balance of power in their relationship.

Although they both worked as environmental scientists, Alex's and Vanessa's career histories were striking examples of gendered careers on the consistent compromiser pathway over the longer term. In the five years between Time 3 and Time 4, Alex changed jobs once in order to move into a more senior role at a larger company that could provide better financial benefits. He described his career progression as "super successful":

> At the [first] small firm I had good quality of life, got to do cool stuff, [and] they gave me elevating levels of responsibility. Then this new job transition, I have moved up a level. Some of my research initiatives, they come out to tens or hundreds of millions of dollars a year in impact. Plus, I still have my quality of life. And my boss likes me. So I feel super successful.

Alex's trajectory was one of increasing responsibilities and impact plus a good balance of work and life. The structure of Vanessa's pathway, in contrast, did not include such positive markers. Despite Alex's report that he and Vanessa "both work in the [same building] together for different services doing almost the exact same thing," her trajectory, title, and salary differed dramatically from his, threatening the balance of power in their two careers. She said:

> I'm six years into my career, but just a midlevel analyst. It's fine, I've just decided that I'm never going to love a job. Alex now works for a [new consulting firm]. He loves it. What he's doing gets published in papers and affects policy decisions, and he feels very satisfied with it by the end of the

day. I am a bit envious because I saw Alex's success and I was like, "Well, I can do that too."

Even though Vanessa did similar work to Alex, worked to move up within a company whenever possible, and changed organizations to improve her prospects for advancing when her efforts at promotion were blocked, Vanessa remained in a midlevel position at Time 4. The experience of working hard but not seeing the benefits threatened to change her view of her career. She found it difficult to find meaning or potential for growth in her professional life like she had expected to when she began her career. Seeing Alex become a leader in their field and watching him work with others in a dynamic professional environment on issues she deemed important deepened Vanessa's sense that her profession did not want her despite her having skills and experience similar to Alex's. I show later in the chapter how consistent compromisers responded to these gender-unequal workplace conditions to maintain egalitarian partnerships, but first I detail the job instability, unsatisfactory mentoring relationships, and harassment or discrimination women faced at work that contributed to gender disparities in the partners' career trajectories.

Job instability was more common in women's work histories than in men's. For example, as shown in table 2.2, Vanessa experienced a layoff and two other job changes, whereas Alex changed employers once in the five years between Time 3 and Time 4. Switching between employers impeded Vanessa's ability to stay with one company long enough to advance professionally at the same rate that Alex had. One woman remarked that in the last five years she had "switched jobs many times—unfortunately, too many times." This woman's assessment of her job churning as "unfortunate" was accurate, given that frequent job changes have been associated with slower career growth.[5] Further, the reasons women gave for leaving jobs and starting new ones (escaping subpar working conditions) differed from the ones men gave for their employment changes (advancement opportunities).[6] These stories shed further light on why job churning can be negatively related to professional advancement for women.

Consistent compromiser women pointed to bosses and supervisors as key figures channeling them along their career trajectories. In particular, women, but not their partners, reported a mismatch between the mentorship they received and the mentoring they needed for professional growth. Nora, the scientist scheduled to start a postdoc at Time 3, was just finishing this research appointment five years later at Time 4. As a comparison, her husband Rick, who was also a scientist in a related field, spent three years as a postdoc before starting as a professor—and one of those years was an extra one he negotiated when their child was first born. Although Nora generally felt positive about her training and had recently landed a professor job at Rick's university, she recognized that her adviser contributed to the long duration of her postdoc:

> The one thing I wish I had done differently in my postdoc is recognize, and maybe push my adviser to recognize, that with the academic job cycle, [publishing] any paper at all before you send out your [job] applications is worth [more than writing] your dream paper six months later because six months from now, no biology departments are going to be hiring. That was something timeline-wise that I didn't manage very well. And partly, I think my adviser is comfortable with a longer time horizon for those publications. This is why I didn't think about going on the job market in the last cycle because I just knew I wasn't competitive. I didn't have the CV that I needed.

Nora delayed her search for professor jobs by at least one year because her adviser trained her on a very long timeline. The structure of her training also channeled her toward publishing research at a cadence that did not match the timeline of hiring in most academic departments. Although Nora received professional support in the form of research funding for five full years, she did not have the structural supports necessary to transition into a professor job in a timely manner.

Whereas some women received subpar mentorship along their professional pathways, others had unequivocally negative relationships with their superiors. Harassment and discrimination by those with decision-making power over work assignments and promotions played a prominent role in women's accounts of their professional pathways. For example, unlike Alex's boss, who treated him favorably, one of Vanessa's bosses treated her so poorly she felt forced to leave her company before she was ready to do so:

> [My boss would] email me in the middle of the night, and then I can't sleep and I wake up, and I'm all stressed, and it was over nothing. Even if she made a mistake, somehow it's my fault. A lot of energy at that point was spent negotiating her. This culminated in a 2,500-word email about how incompetent and unprofessional I am, and she cc'd our mutual boss. . . . How does this woman expect me to work with her productively? It was so deeply insulting. It was almost abusive. I decided to muscle through the majority of the rest of the year, so that I can just help get all the work done and then leave. I hit the two-year mark. I wanted to stay five, but I just couldn't work with her.

Managing this emotional abuse on a daily basis drained Vanessa's energy and impaired her productivity. This mistreatment further hampered her advancement because Vanessa had little choice but to leave the company and forgo promotion opportunities within her organization.

Harassment was common in women's stories even if they reported positive growth in their careers over time. Cristina, who moved into a higher position as a development specialist in her large organization during her five-year tenure, actually looked for a more senior role partly to escape a bad relationship with her first boss:

> I was tired of my entry-level assignment. I was also experiencing a lot of harassment in the workplace so I wanted to switch to whatever I could and escape that guy. I applied to several positions [within my organization], including this one, and I actually got a job offer on another team [first]. So, my two options [at that point] were staying with this boss that was not good and the offer that I got with the [other] team. That [other] boss was known for being a harasser as well. . . . [S]o when I got the offer that I ended up taking, which is the one that I'm in now, the manager of that position was someone that I looked up to and she would mentor me. That was a huge weight in the decision on working with a team that I felt comfortable with.

Cristina's professional growth as measured by job titles and salaries did not capture her experiences of harassment at work. Even though Cristina was able to advance professionally, hostile working relationships riddled her path forward before she found a less contentious context in which to continue her professional development.

In addition to harassment, women reported more subtle forms of discrimination that their partners simply did not face. For instance, Vanessa told stories about not getting included in meetings, not getting sent on business trips, and not getting work assignments despite her expertise—all of which are well-documented forms of gender-based discrimination.[7] Cristina worried that the timing of her maternity leave would disrupt her integration into a new work team, and Nora constantly questioned whether keeping strict work hours because of her childcare responsibilities stigmatized her as less than an ideal worker.[8] All these experiences added up to negatively shape women's professional pathways relative to their partners even if they appeared equal to, or even seemed to be outpacing, men in their job titles and salaries.

In the face of these gender-unequal workplace circumstances, partners maintained their cultural support of egalitarianism and continued endorsing equality in sharing all responsibilities. Cristina, for instance, described a moment in which she considered having a more traditional division of labor to ease the competing demands of work and family:

> I did struggle at the beginning [of my parental leave] with whether I wanted to return to work when I had the baby. I told Anthony, "I'm not going back." And he's like, "We don't have an option. You have to go back—and I'll support you."

Because the demands of intensive mothering conflicted with the demands of an ideal worker,[9] Cristina contemplated giving up work to stay home with the baby, which would have changed the couple's division of labor from gender egalitarian to gender traditional. Anthony, however, responded by encouraging Cristina to return to work. Of this incident, Anthony said: "She doesn't have the personality of a stay-at-home mom. She will get bored. I don't think that's what she likes. I wouldn't like her to do that either. She really enjoys working." Anthony recognized that Cristina wanted to both work and parent when he said she did not have the "personality of a stay-at-home mom." Cristina's concern actually stemmed from the incompatibility of the structure of her professional duties and the culture of intensive mothering, not an idiosyncratic preference for a gender-traditional arrangement. Further, Anthony stated his commitment to egalitarianism in saying he "wouldn't like her to do that [be a stay-at-home mom] either." His remark differed from what has been found in previous studies of men in dual-career families.[10] Prior research suggests that men "allow women" or "give women the option" to stay home when balancing work and family becomes too difficult. Such a response from men depends on a cultural logic that assigns men the task of financially providing for the family and assigns women the work of both completing all family-related duties and resolving the couple's work-family conflicts. Anthony showed instead that he saw working and parenting, as well as strategizing how to share both, to be both partners' responsibilities.

Given the mismatch between couples' egalitarian attitudes and women's unfavorable workplace contexts, consistent compromiser men took action by using their workplace resources and supports to facilitate women's continued career advancement. First, men provided women emotional support and professional advice as they discussed women's concerns at work. For instance, each time Vanessa had to start a new job search, Alex discussed her professional goals with her to help direct her applications:

> When we talk about jobs, she's going through [a list of questions]: What elements of self-fulfillment is she getting from that job? Does she feel like she's being paid appropriately? Is she bored at work? Is she challenged at work?

Does she like her co-workers? Does she like her boss? Does she feel like she's doing something important? So, we kind of go through each of these things. Because a job is so important to her. We talk about it a lot because it affects [her] mental health a lot.

Alex took Vanessa's professional identity seriously and recognized that having a fulfilling career supported her emotional well-being. Therefore, he put conscientious effort into helping her figure out what she wanted from her job and what positions were appropriate for her to apply to.

Second, some men went as far as pursuing other career opportunities in different cities to find conditions that could enable women to move up in their careers. Five years earlier at Time 2, Rick had accepted the job at his university specifically because they offered to interview Nora for a professor position when she finished her postdoc. A few years in, Rick realized that, despite the spousal hire arrangements written into his contract, the university would not begin Nora's hiring process unless he aggressively pursued the matter:

> We had been trying for [my university] to hire her, or at least interview her, as it was in my contract, for about two years. And they kept bumping the ball down. I kind of got fed up with that. But when [my grant] money started coming, I started realizing I had leverage. I knew that at least [getting] an interview [at another university] was going to be good in terms of negotiations with [my current university]. . . . When I told [the department chair] that I had interviews, that I was considering the possibility of leaving [and taking my grant money with me], and that I had been approached by [another institution], they actually started the process of hiring Nora.

Continuing the pattern from Time 2, Rick used his marketability as a job candidate to hold his employer to its promise to create a professional opportunity for Nora. Without Rick's diligence, his university would not have been proactive in supporting Nora's professional advancement. Again, Rick's actions were only possible because of his work-related advantages: he had grant money and job interviews he could use as leverage, and his university had mechanisms in place to hire spouses of current faculty members.

The third and most prominent way men supported women's careers was by leveraging their own flexibility and seniority at work to fulfill the couple's childcare responsibilities—a factor that has historically put women at a disadvantage in their careers relative to men. Again, this pattern differed from those found in previous research, in which couples adopted neotraditional roles when men's careers took off and women's careers stalled.[11] The couples in this past research reasoned that if women were not growing professionally, their energy was better spent caring for the household and the children. In this gender-traditional arrangement, men would be free of these unpaid responsibilities, could devote more energy to work, and could earn more money for the family. Yet this arrangement would result in a gender imbalance in power, as men would gain more access to the socially valued resources of income and job prestige while women would get burdened with the socially devalued work of unpaid domestic labor. Consistent compromisers used a different logic that prioritized maintaining both partners' equal involvement in work and at home—and therefore both partners' equal power. As a result, men equally shared and sometimes took the lead in parenting to maximize women's time and energy to complete their paid work. That way, women would not be further penalized in their careers by being overburdened by unpaid care work.

Anthony and Cristina established a precedent of doing childcare tasks together during their simultaneous parental leaves when their first child was born. As noted previously, when Cristina questioned whether she would return to work after having a child, Anthony responded by expressing his desire for her to return. He told her, "I'll support you." Cristina explained that Anthony's support came in the form of being a highly involved father:

> He is really, really, really an active dad. Like, he does everything. Everything. From feeding the baby—everything. He spends quality time with him. He takes him to and from daycare every day. He puts him down to sleep. He does a bunch of things.

Cristina was emphatic about the amount of work Anthony did to care for their child as both partners finished up their parental leaves and returned to work. Anthony's work-related resources—namely his flexibility as a PhD student—allowed him to accommodate Cristina's more rigid work demands with respect to childcare. In addition to feeding the baby, putting him down to sleep, and shuttling the child to and from daycare, Anthony was primarily responsible for their one-year-old's emergencies:

> We pretty much share. It is my feeling that I have had the heavier burden, but by a small margin. I don't think it's that different. Just the nature of my work and that Cristina was in this program [at the office of the CEO of her organization] so basically, she was in two jobs at the same time. I had to take on more [childcare]. If [the baby] gets sick, he cannot go to daycare, so someone has to stay here, and given the nature of my work, oftentimes that is me.

As Anthony asserted several times, his access to autonomy and control over his work schedule made it easier for the couple to divide childcare such that he assumed somewhat more of the work, particularly in response to unforeseeable circumstances like their child's illnesses.

Importantly, because men's jobs often afforded them control over when, where, and how they completed their work, equal parenting did not meaningfully hamper men's career advancement. The favorable workplace conditions that allowed men to move up in their careers while still being highly involved parents, when paired with the hostile workplaces that women faced, therefore posed an additional challenge to consistent compromisers' aim to have equally successful careers.

Nora and Rick also split their childcare duties, but Rick did a significant amount of childcare in the mornings and afternoons because his professor job offered him more freedom than Nora's postdoc job did on a day-to-day basis. He did not think his childcare responsibilities affected his professional productivity:

> I spend a lot of time with [our child]. I wake up with her every morning and make breakfast and lunch for everybody. On Thursdays I pick her up at 1 p.m. and take her to a library, so I spend a whole afternoon there. On Saturdays and Sundays, I don't even open my computer, I spend it completely with her. I can do it because I don't have to write papers at this point. I am going to get tenure. Usually, one grant almost guarantees tenure. I got three.

For Rick, professional success supported by the structural conditions of his work, like generous lab funding, grant money, and the labor of his postdocs and research assistants, enabled him to be an involved parent. With a demonstrated record of professional output and the job security of tenure in sight, he felt that spending time with his child and enabling Nora to do her work were things he was not "willing to sacrifice."

In contrast, even with Rick doing his equal share of parenting and sometimes more, Nora expressed that parenting as a fixed-term postdoc who lacked the status of a professor with her own lab made her feel as if she was never doing enough:

> There are just some days in the lab where if you could stay an extra half an hour, you would save an overnight step. But you can't stay an extra half an hour if daycare pickup is in half an hour. So, I think that having that hard stop at the end of the day is the biggest thing that made my postdoc productivity slower than I hoped it would've been. The things that I don't do that I wish I could—go to more seminars and spend more time in a scientific community— I just can't take that time out of my schedule when I really need to be getting

things done in lab. So that's been difficult, not having control over my schedule and feeling like the limited time I have here, I have to invest in the research.

Nora felt that her multiple professional demands could never be satisfied. Her position as a postdoc working in someone else's lab meant that having a partner who was a committed, equal parent was still insufficient for a job that assumed a worker with no parenting responsibilities at all. The entire configuration of these conditions—women's workplace challenges despite having equal partners at home and men's workplace success despite doing more childcare—made complete equality in work and family across partners a constantly moving target at Time 4.

Additionally, managing two professional careers and parenting as equals was simply hard work for these men and women. Consistent compromisers talked about how little time and energy they had for other pursuits, particularly for having other personal relationships. First, as much as partners expressed satisfaction with the way they accomplished tasks as a team over time, they missed the way they used to spend time together as a couple. Cristina said:

> We're a great team. But I miss being a couple. We have a great relationship. We trust each other. But now, we're behaving more as a team than as a couple. It's like, "You do this. You do this. Let's do it! Great job! We managed!" But I want some of the romance back. I want some of the alone time, for us to do nothing, to be with each other.

In molding their relationship to fit the structure and demands of the workplace and to the responsibilities of parenthood, Cristina and Anthony lost some of the romance and intimacy that their relationship used to have.

Second, consistent compromisers had less time for other relationships outside of their families. Nora felt deeply fulfilled by her relationships with Rick and their child but noted:

> It's hard to make friends when you basically just do kid stuff and work stuff. I have work friends, but I never get to spend time with them outside of the workday. Now that free time is a limiting factor, you just want to use it more judiciously. But that also makes it hard to get to the point of being close friends with people. Sometimes I guess I feel a little bit lonely for the types of friendships that I had [before].

The limits around socializing in professional settings and the private, individualized nature of raising children in the suburban setting near their workplaces led to smaller friendship networks for Nora. In short, having an equal arrangement of two careers and sharing parenting was a lot of work for consistent compromisers that came with unforeseen costs to the partners' romantic relationships and friendships.

VARIATION ON THE CONSISTENT COMPROMISER PATHWAY

Although this sequence of events was emblematic of the consistent compromiser trajectory, some couples traveled slightly off this exact path. Yet these exceptional cases underscore the need for structure, culture, and joint action to come together perfectly to create consistent egalitarianism in couples' experiences of work and family. They also highlight a key characteristic that contributes to this pathway: men's active support of women's careers.

Long-distance partners Peter and Anna, both PhD students in the natural sciences, did not make deliberate couple-level job search plans at Time 1 as the other couples did. Instead, they agreed to each look for jobs independently without geographic restrictions, making them more like the autonomous actor couples in the next chapter. What put them on the consistent compromiser pathway was Peter's attitudes and actions at Time 2. Like the other consistent compromiser men, Peter altered his job search to support Anna's career. Anna landed a job first, and once the couple confirmed where she would start working, Peter targeted his applications to her city exclusively. Echoing environmental scientist Alex's sentiments about the importance of reuniting the couple and enabling his partner to establish herself at work, Peter said:

> When it was decided that she was going to [a southern city], I focused all my attention on [that location]. I said, "We've been away from each other for six years." There's no point in continuing [long distance]. So, I really wanted to be in [this southern city]. There was the chance that I would find a job somewhere else. She could try to move to that place, but it's not very good for her to leave her job right now.

Although Peter's attitudes supporting gender equality in paid work and men's equal responsibility for maintaining the relationship stood out, coordinated action and favorable workplace conditions factored into their trajectory, too. After moving to Anna's city and continuing his job hunt, Peter eventually found a position in his field, and the partners laid the groundwork for an egalitarian relationship at Time 3.

The couple stepped off the exact consistent compromiser pathway again at Time 4. Unlike the other couples, Peter and Anna were maintaining a long-distance relationship again. Peter's contract had expired after several years, and this time the couple lacked structural support for their dual-career relationship: Peter could not find another job in their current city. On the advice of his mentors and with Anna's support, Peter took a position on the West Coast where lucrative and cutting-edge research opportunities in his STEM field were abundant. The partners imagined it would not be difficult for Anna to also find a job out West—indeed, this region had a high concentration of research universities, medical facilities, as well as private industry—and to join him once she had wrapped up the major parts of her current project.

Though Peter's decision to move by himself to pursue better professional opportunities seemed out of step with the other consistent compromisers, this arrangement turned out to be temporary, and Peter had started making new plans to return to Anna's city. What prompted this change of plans was Anna's challenging work-related conditions and Peter's desire to support her professional growth.

The workplace barriers that plagued consistent compromiser women's careers also beset Anna's professional trajectory. Like the other women on this trajectory and like scientist Nora in particular, Anna reported very slow career progression due to inadequate mentorship. Her boss was not actively hostile toward her but was happy to keep Anna in an entry-level position rather than encourage her to seek advancement opportunities (as Peter's mentors did). As she enumerated the impressive level of work she did for her research group over five years, including making novel scientific discoveries and fostering international public-private collaborations, Anna also recognized: "It's been too long that I've been on a very, very low salary. I know that I'm worth more, and sometimes it's hard not to think about it." Anna's boss exploited her labor, paying her a pittance and getting credit for her work as the formal head of the research lab.

Yet Anna stayed on because she felt frozen in place. She loved the research but could not think of another position that would allow her to continue this work without further trade-offs. If she pursued an academic job that would enable her to run her own lab, she feared becoming "a sad overworked female professor, [of] which we see so many, unfortunately." Anna's comment points to the problem of women's underrepresentation in academic STEM fields. Too few women in academic science creates an environment in which women professors are overburdened with work like mentoring women students and serving on diversity committees, without additional resources or modified expectations of other professional duties.[12] These conditions did not appeal to Anna. Of searching for jobs outside an academic setting, she said:

> I haven't found a role model which I can kind of follow and say, "This is what I want to be.". . . Maybe something in industry would be good, but I just lack good relatable role models to help me see and envision those goals.

Anna repeatedly brought up a lack of professional role models in her natural science career, which led to her continuing in her present position and hesitating to more aggressively job hunt.

Peter recognized the exploitative conditions of her work and wanted Anna to find a new job that would make her happy and pay her what she was worth. He thought moving back to her city, taking any job he could find for the moment, and trying to find new jobs together would work out more favorably for the couple: "Anna needs my support and I feel like she will be more confident in her job search if we are together." This series of events put Peter and Anna back on the consistent compromiser pathway because the man deliberately made career decisions that would support the woman's career and keep the couple together.

CONCLUSION

This chapter showed that supportive workplace structures, cultural attitudes endorsing egalitarianism, and couple-level action aligning them all came together to produce the consistent compromiser pathway in which men and women both had careers and shared household and childcare responsibilities over time. On the whole, this trajectory pushed the gender revolution in work and family forward. Both men and women maintained their workplace attachment and grew in their professions while contributing equally to housework and childcare. Thus, the balance of power across men and women over time was fairly even in these relationships. Yet consistent compromisers' equal work and family outcomes in the short and long term masked gender-unequal processes and difficult trade-offs lying beneath them.

First, launching and advancing two careers while sharing childcare were different experiences for men and women. Even though partners generally experienced favorable workplace contexts, men systematically had more advantages in the labor market than their partners. They had more opportunities available to them during career launch; had smoother professional growth trajectories; and gained status in, and control over, their work activities such that equally sharing household chores and parenting did not hinder their careers. Even though men used their workplace power to benefit women's professional growth and to perform caregiving in their families as much as possible, couples could not change the relatively more challenging conditions of women's careers. Women had fewer lucrative job opportunities to choose from to start their careers; experienced inadequate mentorship and harassment from their superiors; and had less control over when, where, and how to do their work, making equal housework and childcare tougher for women to accomplish than for men. As much as these partners' attitudes and actions equalized the partners' power and pushed the gender revolution forward, especially at home, workplaces that devalued women but supported men posed an ongoing challenge to partners' efforts to maintain two equally successful careers and an equitable division of housework and childcare.

Second, professional careers greedily demanded all workers' time, meaning that having two equal careers while sharing unpaid housework and parenting took up most of men's and women's energy and wore on their personal relationships. This side effect of "having it all" in work and family revealed that partners were still missing parts of a holistic life with work, family, relationships, and other personal pursuits. Without more changes to the gendered and greedy nature of professional workplaces, and without additional public support for personal and family care, the gender revolution cannot move forward. I discuss potential solutions to the challenges the consistent compromisers faced in equally sharing work and family responsibilities in chapter 6. But first, I turn to the autonomous actor pathway to show how gender-neutral attitudes about men's and women's equal right to pursue their best individual career opportunities belied a gendered pattern of actions in which men took the best career opportunities for themselves without considering the relationship, while women were more likely to actively compromise their careers for the couple.

## CHAPTER 3

Autonomous Actors

I'm sort of still deciding what I want to do next year but I'm definitely applying to, like, thirty medical schools. Right now, I want to go to [a northeastern university]. Josh will probably only take three or four [years to finish his degree], in which case we'd be apart for a year or two. . . . So this will be perfect if I went to [the northeastern university]. He could work in industry there—or industry anywhere I go, because most places with medical schools are places with industry, too—so he could work there until I'm done with my MD and then there are a couple of possibilities of what could happen after that. . . . [I]t's just sort of like, we're really stressed and tense and we don't know what's going to happen and so we'll have these fights. He's like, "It'll work out. If we want it to, we'll make it happen." He's always the optimistic one and I'm the practical [one]. But it's hard when one person has to commit more than the other person. I had to jump in more than he did, as far as commitments and stuff, just by moving here. He's here because he's doing his PhD. That's what he would be doing anyway, but I could be doing other stuff. . . . I don't know, it's always the girl who ends up doing more long-term [planning], and making the initial first steps, which is frustrating.

—Samantha, Time 1

Samantha and her partner Josh were likely to start a long-distance relationship to set up their two careers. Whereas Josh thought "it'll work out" without making any specific plans to realize that goal, Samantha felt that she "had to jump in" to actively map out how a long-distance relationship would work for them and how long they could or would live apart while each person launched their career. The mismatch in the level of effort Josh and Samantha each put into building two careers while sustaining a relationship was characteristic of the work-family equilibrium on the *autonomous actor* pathway and set it apart from the consistent compromiser (chapter 2) and tending traditional (chapter 4) pathways.

Regardless of whether partners had work-related resources to support their dual-career relationships, attitudes favoring men's and women's "equal right" to make individual choices and men's and women's "equal responsibility" to allow each partner to maintain autonomy led to gendered actions within the couples. Men on the autonomous actor pathway consistently focused on their own career plans without considering the relationship and encouraged women to do whatever they thought was best. Women responded to men's invitation to do whatever they wanted in various ways. Some women "chose" to compromise, or even give up, their careers to maintain the partnership. Other women acted like men and did what was best for their careers without accounting for the relationship. This combination of gender-neutral attitudes and gendered actions, regardless of the partners' workplace contexts, contributed to gender inequality in autonomous actors' work-family *processes* even when these partners achieved gender equality in some work and family *outcomes*, as women did more work than men did to maintain the partners' careers and their relationship. This power-imbalanced equilibrium in which men and the couple benefited from women's invisible work was not set in stone, however. Over time, autonomous actors came to make career, relationship, and family decisions more interdependently—though not always with the same partners they had at the start of the study.

The stories of Julie and Max, Janelle and Stephen, and Cassandra and David highlight the key features of this pathway. These couples also showcase the variation across autonomous actors' outcomes despite the similar process that led them there. Although Max, Stephen, and David had similar work-related resources, held similar attitudes about autonomy, and took the same kinds of actions on this pathway, their respective partners, Julie, Janelle, and Cassandra, had differing levels of workplace constraints, thought of different solutions to resolve their dual-career dilemmas, and took different actions to implement these solutions. Details about the other autonomous actors appear in table 3.1.

THE COUPLES

Julie and Max were introduced in the first chapter of the book. As a reminder, they met in college, and both wanted to be medical doctors. They maintained a long-distance relationship for five years while they went to medical school in two different cities. When they joined the study, Max had just started his residency, and Julie, a year behind him in her training, was beginning to apply to residency programs. Julie imagined talking more explicitly about getting married and having children once they were in the same city again, but Max cautioned that they did not know for sure whether Julie would be matched to the residency program at his hospital. Julie and Max's story demonstrates how men on the autonomous pathway pursued their own individual plans without considering their partners, but some women leveraged their workplace resources to ensure an equal outcome for both partners' careers and the relationship.

Janelle and Stephen met in high school. Janelle recounted that they were "best friends for about five years" before Stephen "convinced [her], finally, to date him" when they were both in college. At the beginning of the study, they had been in a relationship for over five years—much of it long distance as each person pursued their education. They had recently gotten married and were open to starting a family soon. Janelle had an MA in the humanities and was figuring out how to continue into her university's PhD program. She wanted an academic job in the future but was pragmatically prepared to fall back on her prior career as a teacher and professional musician if her PhD goals did not align with Stephen's professional plans and the couple's family goals: "I really am interested in getting my hands into this research, but if that doesn't happen, there are other options." Stephen was a few years away from completing his physical science PhD. He was "still waffling a little bit" between pursuing an academic or applied career but hoped to decide his course in the next year, depending on Janelle's PhD plans and what the couple decided regarding having children. Janelle and Stephen's story highlights how men's early independent pursuit of careers and their assumptions that women would do the same could result in some women "independently choosing" a traditional division of labor when they could not find a way for both partners to have careers while maintaining their family life.

Cassandra and David were both PhD students in the social sciences. They met in one of their graduate classes and had been in a relationship for three years. When they joined the study, they were living in different cities while David was away for the year collecting data at his field site. Both partners wanted to be professors in the future, though each person imagined slightly different career paths for themselves. David said, "I've always loved the classroom and that's what I want to do, I want to teach." Cassandra, on the other hand, loved conducting research and hoped to work at an institution that could support her future projects. Given the competitive nature of landing academic jobs—let alone two of them—both partners were applying to any and all academic

TABLE 3.1 AUTONOMOUS ACTORS

Partners & occupations	Relationship status at Time 1	Time 1 *Men made their own plans; some women applied to mutually beneficial cities, others made their own plans*	Time 2 *Men deferred to women to make decisions, shifting couple's fate onto women*	Time 3 *All men & some women pursued careers; women managed uncertainty for couple*	Time 4 *Men and women increasingly compromised for couple & family*
Julie, MD student Max, medical resident	Unmarried, long distance	Julie applied for jobs in Max's city	Julie made special arrangements to work in Max's hospital	Both employed in Max's city	Both advanced in their careers & started applying to new jobs together Got married Co-parented 1 child
Karen, STEM PhD student Jacob, lawyer	Unmarried, living together	Karen applied for jobs broadly Jacob planned to stay in their current city	Karen considered 2nd job search to stay with Jacob in their current city	Jacob continued his job Karen moved for work & couple started long distance	Jacob advanced in his career Karen advanced more slowly Started applying for new jobs together Ended long distance & got married Remained child free

Amanda, SS PhD student Louis, law enforcement	Unmarried, long distance	Amanda applied for jobs in Louis's city	Amanda pursued remote work to join Louis in his city	Both employed in Louis's city	Louis advanced in his career Amanda advanced more slowly as primary parent to 2 children Got married
Janelle, Hum. MA student Stephen, STEM PhD student	Married, living together	Janelle applied to PhD program in one city Stephen planned to stay in their current city	Janelle stopped pursuing her career plans to stay with Stephen in their current city	Stephen continued his program Janelle stayed home with 1st child	Stephen returned to school to pursue new career Janelle moved to new city for Stephen's graduate program & continued staying home with children
Cassandra, SS PhD student David, SS PhD student	Unmarried, long distance	Both applied separately for jobs broadly	Both chose best option for their respective careers in different cities	David continued applying for jobs in his city Cassandra moved for work & couple broke up	David advanced in his career alongside his new spouse Cassandra advanced in her career alongside her new spouse
Samantha, research assistant Josh, STEM PhD student	Unmarried, living together	Samantha applied to graduate programs broadly Josh planned to stay in his city	Samantha chose best option for her career in different city	Josh continued his program Samantha moved for school & couple started long distance	Couple broke up Josh advanced in his career alongside his new partner Samantha advanced in her career & stayed single

SS = social science; Hum. = humanities

job openings in their respective fields all over the country. They considered getting married and having children to be serious commitments, so they imagined that those life events would likely come in a few years, after both partners became more secure in their careers. Cassandra and David's story illustrates what happens when both men and women prioritize autonomous pursuit of two individual careers over making joint plans for the relationship.

TIME 1: GENDER-NEUTRAL SUPPORT FOR AUTONOMY; GENDERED ACTIONS IN WORK-FAMILY PLANNING

Men on the autonomous actor pathway approached their career launches at Time 1 differently than women did. Unlike consistent compromiser men in chapter 2, who incorporated their partners' careers into their own professional plans, autonomous actor men thought it would be best for each person to independently pursue the best opportunities available to start up their respective careers, even if it meant the partners would have to live apart.

Long-distance partners Max and Julie were both working toward careers in medicine, but Max graduated from medical school one year before Julie did. In picking medical residencies for his next step of training, Max explained that although he and Julie had discussed locations that could work for both of them, he ultimately chose the best option for his own career:

> We actually made a list of cities and compared them. We had a lot of the same cities on the list, like [this Mountain West city, my current city]. Then I applied to a bunch of places: West Coast, East Coast, some in the Midwest.... Out of all the places I interviewed, I liked [the Mountain West institution] the best. Knowingly, it wasn't ideal for our relationship because if I was to move to [Julie's city] that would have been simpler. But it would have probably been better to go to places like [the East Coast] where there would be more programs for her to apply to. I knew already that she was applying to [residency] programs this year, like now. My second choice on the list was [an eastern institution], and for example, [that East Coast city] has four or five [residency] programs [in her specialty] where [this city] has one. So, it was maybe not the best decision at that point, but it was the place I liked the best.

Even though Julie and Max listed cities in which both people could envision themselves living and working, as the consistent compromisers in chapter 2 did, Max ended up applying to residencies very broadly across the country. Ultimately, he chose a location that was best for his career. Compared to the other cities on the couple's list, the Mountain West city where Max wanted to do his residency offered limited options for Julie's career. Putting heavy consideration into what would be best for his personal career, Max's decision appeared to limit Julie's professional options as she began her applications. Yet Max insisted:

> It generally isn't a huge expectation for her to try to come [to my city]. She picked a lot in the West just because I'm here, but I think there's a lot of good programs out here as well. I said, "Yeah, I think those are fantastic choices." I don't think I have much to say, other than I'm supportive of her applying everywhere, and if she found a place she really wants to go more than anything, she should go and we would make it work.

Whereas Max claimed there was no expectation for Julie to restrict her application to his institution or region and assumed that each person would pick the best place for their own training based on their individual professional considerations, Julie put relatively more emphasis on being in the same location when choosing institutions for her residency:

> [Max's hospital] is at the absolute top of the places I wanted to apply to because Max had already matched there the year before. I kind of decided based on the fact that he was there and that we were trying to be in the same place, or at least the same geographic location. The frustrating part is that places like [this Mountain West city] only have one program in the entire state—it didn't give me a lot of options for applying to different programs. The East Coast [would have been] a little easier just 'cause it's a little denser with programs. So, would [Max's hospital] be number one if Max wasn't there? I don't know.

Although Julie reported making an "independent choice" to geographically restrict her applications ("I kind of decided"), both partners recognized it was Max's decision to train at his particular institution that led Julie to consider programs exclusively in one part of the country at Time 1. Julie and many of the other women on the autonomous actor pathway were more like the consistent compromiser women detailed in the previous chapter: they conscientiously considered locations that would support the couple when formulating their career plans. Because women more often considered their partners' careers and their relationships when making their own career plans than men did, women began making more compromises in their job searches at this early stage of career launch. This uneven compromising for the couple began tipping the balance of power in men's favor.

Notably, Julie called her *situation* "frustrating." She did not explicitly direct that frustration at *her partner* even though he contributed to creating this situation. Julie's use of the phrase "the frustrating part" aptly pointed to the external conditions that created this challenge for her dual-career relationship: the city where Max was completing his training only had one residency program in the entire state. However, this phrasing also excused Max from being responsible for choosing the circumstances that would frame Julie's career decisions. Given Max's explicit position that both partners should independently take their best career opportunities, though, Julie felt she could not really blame him for his decision.

Several factors can explain the autonomous actors' process at Time 1, as well as women's acceptance of men's independent decision-making. First, the individualized logic men used on this pathway mirrored the assumptions built into workplaces. Many professions and workplaces structure jobs for individual workers who have no outside responsibilities and are not attached to other workers.[1] Employers hire individual people, not their partners and families, and companies rarely consider workers' relationships with other workers and other people when outlining job duties. Further, the competitive and increasingly insecure nature of employment compels individuals to adapt their personal relationships to workplace demands; otherwise, they risk losing their access to economic security. In what Allison Pugh calls the "one-way honor system," workers feel as if they owe it to their employers to be accommodating and loyal without expecting the same in return from their companies.[2] Given these work-related circumstances, men's individual-focused approach to launching careers was practical and understandable.

Second, men's and women's unequal consideration for their relationships when planning their career launches aligned with cultural scripts that associate men with work and women with family.[3] According to dominant, White, upper-middle-class cultural norms for gender, work, and family, being a "good" man requires men to pursue careers that can financially support their partners and families. Women, in contrast, may experience more cultural support for prioritizing (or pressure to prioritize) their relationships and families relative to their careers in order to be "good" women.[4] Given these societal expectations around gender, work, and family, it comes as no surprise that Max would choose a residency opportunity based on his own professional advancement, but that Julie would mold her residency plans around her relationship.

Third, marital status may have shaped the starting point of this trajectory. Almost all the autonomous actors were unmarried at Time 1. Although these men and women insisted, as David did, that "marriage is just a piece of paper," and that they were not "thinking of [these career decisions] in terms of what's good for me and what's good for him in a different way than we would be if we were married," as one woman put it, past research suggests that marriage often changes people's behavior and the way partners think of themselves as a couple.[5] Perhaps being unmarried made it more likely that autonomous actors—especially the men—would support independent rather than joint career planning at this point. These cultural models for gender, relationships, and marriage created a gendered commitment gap in which men acted in their own interests, but women acted in the interests of their partners and the couple.

A final factor, and what was unique to the autonomous actors, was that they expressed a specific set of gender-neutral attitudes about work and relationships. They believed that men and women should both have the opportunity to pursue their individual careers and goals, and that equal partners should give each other space to do so. For these couples, preserving each person's autonomy within a relationship was key. Yet men and women had different ideas about how to act autonomously while supporting a partner's independence.

Janelle and Stephen were both graduate students—Janelle in the humanities with the hope of becoming a professor, and Stephen in the physical sciences with the options of becoming a professor or doing applied work in industry. Stephen was a few years away from completing his PhD, and Janelle had just finished her MA. She needed to formally apply to the PhD program at her university abroad to continue her research, so the couple began discussing their next steps. No longer interested in a long-distance relationship, the partners believed they could live together while simultaneously finishing their degrees. Because each person was done taking classes, it was conceivable that they could each write up their dissertation research remotely from anywhere. If either person needed to collect additional data, they could periodically spend a few weeks away from one another visiting a field site (for her) or a lab (for him). In describing how the couple could move forward, then, Stephen used vague, gender-neutral language that prioritized making space for each partner to make the best choices for himself or herself:

I'm not worried about the logistics of how it's going to work out, because it just will [laughs]. I don't know, there are enough degrees of freedom on both of our sides that we'll be able to find something that makes us both happy and be in the same city. There is no hard and fast, you know, "my career comes before your career because [your career] involves living [abroad], or your career [comes first] 'cause it makes more money" or anything like that, but we've both been really blessed to have some really awesome opportunities and [we're] trying to balance how to take advantage of the opportunities and support the other one without making them feel guilty.

Stephen expressed a gender-neutral belief in men's and women's equal freedom to pursue careers and equal obligation to refrain from imposing on the other person's plans. He rejected the idea that one person in the couple had the more important career, either for geographic or financial reasons—factors that generally favor men's careers.[6] He stated instead that the partners prioritized enabling each other to take the opportunities each person wanted without holding each other back. However, Stephen's laughter about not being worried about logistics working out because "it just will" revealed a level of absurdity in his faith that everything would come together without more specific planning or compromising to align the two careers.

Janelle used the same language of wanting to support a partner's personal pursuits. But she expressed more consideration for how her PhD plans, Stephen's career plans, and the couple's family desires needed to all be woven together:

It's really a priority for me that he's ultimately doing something that he really wants to do. It's probably not practical for me to say, "well, I want to do [my PhD] in this particular way." I'd have to compromise, maybe travel to [my field site] once every year, every summer or something. So, eventually we're going to hit a point where we have to decide [whether we live together near his university or mine]. Like, do we want to live [abroad near my university] right now? Okay, now what if we had a kid, what about grandma? Are we going to go somewhere because all of our family is there? That's something [raising children near family] I don't think we've gotten into very much, but we know eventually it's going to be part of it and I'm not really sure how me doing this PhD will fit into that.

Compared to Stephen's vague optimism that somehow all the logistics of coordinating two people's PhD programs on two different continents would work out, Janelle deliberately thought through how she could negotiate her career plans to support Stephen's work. She further discussed her next steps in relation to the couple's wishes to raise children near their parents, a topic Stephen waved to in the abstract without detailing specific plans for addressing the issue.

Altogether, despite the partners' matching gender-neutral endorsement of maintaining both partners' autonomy, men and women began taking mismatched, gendered actions to meet this stated ideal. Men believed that preserving women's autonomy while launching their own careers meant refraining from making women "feel guilty" about their goals. Women, however, believed that preserving men's autonomy while launching their own careers required them to make certain compromises regarding their own professional opportunities. The different levels of effort these men and women put into coordinating the couple reflects a gendered power imbalance—an imbalance rendered invisible by partners' use of gender-neutral language.[7]

In some autonomous actor couples, both the man and the woman endorsed autonomy above all else and believed that each person should work toward their individual career goals without accounting for each other's plans or the relationship. Cassandra and David, both PhD students in the social sciences looking for academic jobs, were applying widely to all available positions across the country. Cassandra explained:

> We are mostly doing our own thing [applying for jobs], together. You're more likely to solve the dual-body problem in the long term and have the kind of career you want if you are willing to tolerate [long] distance now and just pursue the best opportunities available, so we haven't really been trying very hard to be in the same place. I don't want one of us to totally sacrifice our career.

Because each person wanted a career and wanted their partner to fully pursue their profession as well, independently building up their careers now was ideal for these partners and their future. Following advice from a friend (who, perhaps not coincidentally, was a man) that Cassandra said "really changed the way I thought about this," she and David both agreed to compromise on the relationship for now. They accepted that the partners would "tolerate" the long distance now to autonomously set up careers that would give them the dual-professional relationship they wanted in the long run. We will see in the following sections how this approach ultimately worked out.

TIME 2: LEAVING DECISION-MAKING UP TO WOMEN

Autonomous actors' gender-neutral attitudes about work and relationships, paired with their gendered actions for achieving two careers while maintaining the couple, collided with a mix of favorable and unfavorable professional circumstances at Time 2, several months after partners began job searching. Regardless of whether the partners secured job offers or otherwise formalized their professional plans at Time 2, men took a "hands-off" stance and left it up to women to take whatever actions they believed would be best. Women reacted to men's invitation to do whatever they wanted in various ways depending on their access to external, professional resources. Women's wide-ranging actions in this ecosystem of workplace conditions, autonomous attitudes, and lack of coordinated action thus began channeling autonomous actor couples toward different outcomes at Time 2.

Let us return to Max and Julie, the aspiring medical doctors. Max had little to report at Time 2, when Julie was supposed to hear back about her residency applications. For the last few months, he had been doing what he would have been doing in his residency regardless of Julie's plans. For the immediate future, he said he would do the same because he felt he could actively do very little to support the couple while Julie was waiting to learn her match results. He simply said: "I mean, we didn't make any specific contingency plans other than we would figure it out, make it work some way or another."

In contrast to Max's reactive approach to "figure it out" once they heard back about Julie's applications, Julie proactively looked for workplace supports between Time 1 and Time 2 to allow both partners to have careers in the same place. Not only did Julie restrict her applications to the Mountain West region of the country to be as close to Max as possible, she also found out about, and made use of, a formal professional program that would increase her chances of matching to the residency program at Max's hospital:

> I went to [Max's institution] to do an away rotation there. If you really need to end up in an area, it's sometimes a good idea to do a rotation there so that the program knows who you are. If you go and work really hard and they like you, it can be a boost up. In [my specialty, away rotations are] not required unless you have a really good reason for why you want to end up at a certain place. So, because I had a really good reason why I would want to end up at [Max's institution] I ended up going out there.

Julie did extra work in arranging an away rotation at Max's hospital to "boost up" her application and increase her chances of reuniting the couple while still advancing the partners' two careers. This gender-unequal burden of compromising and taking action to achieve two careers while sustaining a relationship was not inevitable. Consider the actions that Max *did not* take compared to the actions that Julie *did* take to support their dual-career partnership. According to Julie, partners graduating from medical school together theoretically had access to "couples matching." This workplace accommodation allows hospitals to hire medical resident partners or spouses together. Because couples matching only works for partners applying to residencies at the same time, Max might have considered using another policy to defer his graduation by one year so that he and Julie could apply for residencies together at Time 1. Julie mentioned that it was common for MD students to extend their training by seeking additional certifications during medical school. Max did not think about this possibility and gave up the opportunity to take advantage of this professional resource for dual-career couples. Even with couples matching off the table, Max could have chosen a different location to do his residency to give Julie more options for her residency applications. Max did not do this either, so Julie ended up geographically restricting her applications at Time 1 and doing an away rotation before Time 2 to ensure that the couple could be together while pursuing their careers.

Julie's extra work paid off, and she was matched to Max's institution. She felt "excited and relieved" that things had worked out the way she hoped—she would get the egalitarian outcome she wanted, two careers and a relationship in the same place—but noted that the uncertainty leading up to the decision had made her anxious:

> I played so many scenarios in my head: What happens if I open my envelope and it doesn't say ["Mountain West institution"]? What is that going to be like? And it's not something I really talked to Max about. It was really stressful, and I don't know what I would have done if it hadn't had said ["Mountain West institution"]. It would have been really horrible.

In saying "I don't know what *I* would have done," Julie revealed that, had she not matched to the residency program at Max's hospital, she considered herself to be solely responsible for coming up with a solution for herself and for the couple. She did not say, "I don't know what *Max and I* would have done *together*," despite Max's insistence that "*we* would figure it out" if Julie's application had not worked out as they hoped. This subtle linguistic choice revealed that the work of keeping the couple on track to have two careers while remaining together was understood to be mostly Julie's responsibility. Further, that Julie did not talk to Max about her stress during this time indicated that managing the emotional burden of maintaining two careers and a relationship was also her responsibility rather than a shared one. In Max and Julie's story, we can see that gender-equal *outcomes* for autonomous actors can result from gender-unequal *processes* and mask a gender-unequal power dynamic in which women work harder than men to get an outcome both people want.

Men took this "hands-off" stance at Time 2 when couples had to make final decisions about their job opportunities because they wanted to give their partners freedom to make an independent choice. Men thought that taking specific actions before their partners had made their own career arrangements first would unduly influence their partners' decisions and compromise women's autonomy. And so, men continued working on their own careers independently until they saw an explicit need to change course. Women, however, did not ask men to coordinate their plans with them because women wanted to preserve men's autonomy and freedom to pursue careers.

Consider Janelle and Stephen's situation at Time 2. Janelle was living with Stephen in the United States for the summer and decided she wanted to formally arrange her continuation into the PhD program at her university abroad. Because the deadline to meet all requirements for entry into the program was fast approaching, she was actively planning an international trip to "meet with everyone and possibly put together a [dissertation] committee, and just feel everything out and see what my options are" for working remotely for most, if not all, of the rest of her time in the program. If she could make this arrangement with her university, Stephen would not have to change his PhD plans while she completed her own training, and she could satisfy the couple's desire to live together. With her situation still uncertain, she said, "depending on how that goes, we'll see if I'm here or there."

Stephen, however, had not taken any similar actions for the couple at Time 2. He described hypothetical arrangements he could make with his own program to facilitate Janelle's PhD work but stressed that he was waiting for her to come to a decision first:

> It's really going to depend on what she hears from [her dissertation adviser] 'cause I really have no idea [what she'll be doing]. I probably would be able to finish [my dissertation] from abroad and just come back and do my defense. I haven't mentioned that possibility to [my adviser], but yeah, I've seen it happen with some of the other students, so I'm guessing it wouldn't be that different or that much of a problem for me to be out [of the country].

Stephen *assumed* there were options for him to adjust his PhD work to support Janelle's plans but did not take concrete action to begin discussing any possibilities with his dissertation adviser. Taking the position that "we're just going to have to wait and see," Stephen did not think making joint plans was necessary at the moment and effectively excused himself from actively working toward the couple's goal of completing their PhDs in the same place. Because Janelle did not directly ask him to coordinate their plans, Stephen continued working on his own career and left it up to Janelle to make career arrangements for herself. In the next section we will see the outcome of Stephen's independent focus on his own PhD and passive rather than active support for Janelle's academic plans.

Sometimes when men stepped back to give women space to take independent actions in their careers at Time 2, women did so without considering the couple. Cassandra landed a postdoctoral research position at a university in a small midwestern city that would set her up to pursue her long-term professional goal. David, however, did not get any job offers. Without much discussion, Cassandra accepted her job offer, and David began making arrangements to spend one more year as a PhD student at his university, lecturing college classes to make ends meet while he continued applying for academic jobs. David explained that, given these job-related circumstances and the assumption that the partners would each take their best opportunities to advance their respective careers, an in-depth conversation was unnecessary:

> I feel like there wasn't really a decision to be made because it was the only [job offer] she got. The understanding was: if you only get one response then that's where you have to go. I don't think there was a talk—just kind of stating the obvious, you know what I mean? Like, for example, if I had gotten that postdoc at [a northeastern university] there wouldn't have been a talk. I would have just done it and she would have known I was going to do it.

Continuing their autonomous approach to decision-making, David was unsurprised that Cassandra accepted her only available opportunity without considering his plans. David applied these expectations to himself, too, stating that if he had gotten only one job offer, he "would have just [taken] it and she would have known I was going to do it." Now, however, he had to make other independent plans for himself.

Cassandra recounted the same series of events, and also revealed at Time 2 that she had vaguely known about policies to support partners at her new university. However, she had not thought about using these workplace accommodations:

I haven't looked into [the partner support policies] recently. This school has an affiliation [program] so if he came to [my new university] he could actually be officially affiliated with the university and have all these privileges that any student has, like access to all the buildings and libraries and housing and whatever. I haven't thought about it for a while [laughs]. I'm happy to explore that option more, but I'm not going to force it on him or anything.

Having adopted a fully autonomous approach to career decision-making to parallel David's approach, Cassandra had not considered using formal workplace policies that might support David's career and allow the partners to be together. Further, to avoid compromising David's autonomy, Cassandra had opted against exploring the university's affiliation program so as not to "force" anything on him. However, Cassandra's laugh suggests that she recognized that they were potentially missing an opportunity to advance their two careers in the same place.

Taken together, regardless of their external, work-related opportunities and constraints, partners' gender-neutral support for autonomous decision-making produced gendered, mismatched actions across partners at Time 2 when actual job offers were (or were not) on the table. By being "hands off" in order to make space for women to do what they thought was best, men effectively left all work-family decision-making, and the fate of the couple, to women. Some scholars might argue that autonomous actor men engaged in "strategic silence" because they shifted the responsibility of maintaining the relationship to women while preserving their power as the ones who did not need to change their own circumstances or behaviors.[8] In reacting to men's invitation to do whatever they wanted, women took a variety of actions given their workplace resources and constraints. These actions set the autonomous actors up to experience a wide range of outcomes at Time 3, a year after partners began job searching.

TIME 3: GENDER-EQUAL AND GENDER-UNEQUAL
WORK-FAMILY OUTCOMES

At Time 3, Julie moved in with Max and started her residency at the hospital where Max continued his own training. When women had access to, and proactively used, professional accommodations to support two careers, couples like Julie and Max could get an egalitarian outcome: two careers in the same place. Remember, however, that this gender-equal result depended on women's extra work to compromise their careers. Even Max recognized that Julie's choice to target his institution and her initiative to do an away rotation ultimately benefited his career and the relationship more than it did her career: "I'm happy about her matching here. I don't think there are any disappointments in the process—maybe for Julie. I don't know if she really would come here if I wasn't here."

Julie nonetheless rated her career and relationship outcomes positively at Time 3. She and Max both had jobs at the same hospital and imagined they could both be hired to fill physician openings there following their medical residencies. Living together for the very first time, she reported satisfaction with the new rhythm they had developed for completing chores together given their busy work schedules. They even bought a house together and began planning their engagement. This trajectory reveals how gendered power imbalances can be overlooked and allowed to persist within couples: as long as men and women got equal outcomes in the major areas of their lives, the process that got them there—women's extra planning, compromising, and work to fit into men's relatively autonomous plans—was coincidental, something that just had to be done.

Other couples got decidedly gender-unequal outcomes as a result of men's lack of actions and women's work-related constraints and subsequent reactions between Time 2 and Time 3. For example, Janelle, the humanities graduate student, had never made the trip back to her university abroad and was still in the United States with her husband Stephen. Although Stephen had progressed enough in his PhD program to begin planning his applications to postdoctoral research fellowships, Janelle felt at Time 3 that her own "window for [pursuing an academic career] is kind of closing." The couple found out they were expecting their first child shortly after Time 2, so the idea of a long-distance relationship became even less appealing to them than before. Wanting to keep the couple together, and unsure what her graduate program would say about her preference to work remotely with a newborn, Janelle explained that she simply stopped talking to Stephen and her program supervisors about her career plans. She assumed that her PhD studies abroad were no longer worth discussing:

> I kind of let this slip to the back burner because we had so much going on the last couple of months, and you know, the trip kind of fell through. I brought it up to Stephen and he was like, "Well, why haven't you gotten on this?" And I was like, "Well, I guess I just figured that we didn't have a whole lot of money and there were all these different reasons and it just wasn't going to be easy and affordable for us right now [with the baby coming]." And he was like, "Well, I thought you didn't want to do it because you weren't interested

in it." It was one of those things where it was like, "Oh man, I wish we had talked about this."

The combination of professional circumstances, attitudes about parenting, and the partners' mismatched actions came together to produce this gender-unequal outcome for Janelle and Stephen. In terms of the couple's work-related contexts, the partners were living in the United States where Stephen's PhD program was, not abroad where Janelle's university was, so Janelle deemed it easier to stay put than to travel internationally. Janelle's university also required her to formally apply to their PhD program, rather than having structures in place to facilitate MA students' continuation into the PhD program. An additional unspoken expectation that PhD students should be in-residence even if they could complete their research remotely discouraged Janelle from continuing her graduate school plans. At home, the structure of Janelle and Stephen's family was changing with their first child on the way. In terms of attitudes, the partners held certain ideas about what it meant to be expecting a baby: they believed parents should avoid a long-distance relationship and save money to prepare for the child. Finally, the partners' mismatched actions—Stephen's autonomous pursuit of his career and his hands-off, passive support of Janelle's career, paired with Janelle's challenges to reconciling her career plans with Stephen's career and the couple's family goals—culminated in Janelle's giving up her career pursuits to support Stephen's career and their growing family.

Stephen expressed some ambivalence about the couple's outcome as he reflected on the partners' career decisions over the previous year. Despite making progress in his own work, he noted that things had not gone as expected for Janelle's career:

> With Janelle and [her PhD plans], I wish we had been maybe a little bit pushier with that. My take, I guess, with her and those possibilities is that I really wanted her to be able to have more direct control with what was going on with that, like with her planning the trip. I didn't want to be pushing her 'cause I didn't want her to think that that was something I wanted for her as opposed to anything else. I would have liked to have seen more communication with [her advisers], but because that was something that she was more in charge of—I mean, we're both so happy with the way life is going and with the baby coming, it almost doesn't make sense to think of what would have gone differently.

Stephen never wanted to "push" Janelle into pursuing a career because he wanted her to choose what she wanted for herself. Yet he thought that being "a little bit pushier"—more actively providing Janelle with support for her career rather than passively giving her space to work toward her goals on her own—might have resulted in a different professional outcome for her. Still, he asserted that her career plans were "something that she was more in charge of." He brushed off his lack of "pushing," as well as the poor formal supports for continuing PhD studies at her university, to refocus on how excited they were to welcome a baby into their family.

Other autonomous actor couples began or continued long-distance relationships at Time 3 when women could not or otherwise did not take action to reconcile their careers with the relationship when men excused themselves from decision-making. Cassandra, for instance, started her postdoc at a new university, an eight-hour drive away from David, who was teaching classes at his university and continuing to apply for jobs. As we saw at Time 2, when Cassandra did not leverage the partner support policies at her new university, the partners concluded there were no options other than continuing to live separately while pursuing their two careers.

Neither men nor women liked this arrangement. One woman remarked, "Nobody wants to be [long] distance. It's not fun. It sucks and it's expensive—it just feels like you're in limbo." Her partner further noted that "things are very unstable at the moment" because neither person knew when or how the long-distance arrangement would end. To ensure that the partners still felt like part of a couple given their physical separation and the uncertainty about when they could be together again, women took on extra relationship work at Time 3.[9] Cassandra, for example, put in extra effort to arrange daily phone calls with David because living separate lives made it hard for her and David to relate to each other when they did visit each other:

> When our relationship is sort of on hold for six weeks, that feeling of really being in it decays a bit because day to day you're not engaging in the actual behaviors of a relationship. When he first [visited me], I just think that we were kind of alienated from each other and it took a couple days to feel normal again. It just didn't feel like my boyfriend entirely. We had just gone too long without seeing each other. So, we have a phone date every day 'cause I was like, "We don't talk enough. It's too much checking out."

As in Times 1 and 2, women did more work than men did to support the dual-career partnership. Men benefited from women's labor and gained a relatively more powerful position in the relationship. David remarked, "It's no fun doing long distance. But I don't think this is going to be a problem for us. I think we're going pretty strong right now." He could feel this way because Cassandra worked to ensure that this was the case. Although they successfully maintained their two careers, Cassandra and David's story raises the question of why *women* were more often responsible for making arrangements for the couple, rather than the relationship's being something men were equally involved in maintaining or something that workplaces could better facilitate for all people.

Managing this "limbo" eventually overwhelmed some couples and led them to break up. Cassandra and David ended their relationship several months after Cassandra moved away for her postdoc. She explained that the partners' seemingly endless long-distance situation as each person pursued their best career options created an excessive amount of disconnectedness that undermined their relationship:

> The distance was just starting to make things feel kind of detached and weird. The feeling of detachment was not really what relationships are supposed to be like. I think that our pursuit of our best opportunities did ultimately undermine our relationship. It's a really sad situation, but neither of us would have wanted each other to do things differently. It wouldn't have been an option for him to not go [away to collect data last year] and for me it would not have been an option to not come here [to my new university]. The alternative [to breaking up] was: he's just going to move here [to my city], and move into my apartment, and try to look for a postdoc and then hopefully he'd be here. But maybe he'd be leaving again [if he continued applying for jobs broadly]. So, you know, it was an imperfect choice.

The particular combination of unfavorable professional conditions ("it was an imperfect choice"), attitudes favoring men's and women's autonomy ("neither of us would have wanted each other to do things differently"), and both men's and women's independent actions to pursue their respective careers ("it wouldn't have been an option for him . . . and for me it would not have been an option") could take a toll on relationships and the people in them. As David put it when evaluating their breakup shortly after Time 3, "I'm pretty devastated." I discuss breakups among other couples in the study in further detail in chapter 5.

All told, autonomous actors' immediate work-family outcomes at Time 3 were highly variable. Although men were largely able to pursue their careers and ended up where they would have been professionally regardless of their relationship status, not all women were able to do the same. Some women, like Janelle, put their careers on the back burner while trying to bring together his career, her career, and the couple's relationship and family desires with a "hands-off" partner. Other women, like Julie, made major career compromises to maintain a dual-career partnership in the same place without there being similar compromises from their partners. Finally, some women, like Cassandra, fully pursued careers as their partners did, but had to do extra work to nurture a long-distance relationship. Sometimes achieving these gender-equal career outcomes by having long-distance relationships strained the partnerships to the point of ending them.

TIME 4: ABANDONING AUTONOMY?

The gender-unequal equilibrium in partners' interactions in Times 1 through 3 did not last. Five years later at Time 4, autonomous actors increasingly collaborated with their partners to maintain their careers and the relationship. This change from prioritizing autonomy to jointly making decisions was related to men's increasingly favorable career conditions and the couples' transitions to marriage and parenthood. Still, specters of autonomous attitudes and behaviors persisted, especially when it came to childcare.

Julie and Max both completed their medical residencies. They continued working at the same hospital as medical fellows, each earning $74,000 annually while pursuing additional training in their respective subspecialties. They got married a few years after they started living together and were raising a six-month-old baby. At Time 4, Julie and Max were actively looking for two permanent jobs at select hospitals across the country. Janelle continued taking care of her and Stephen's children—they had just had their third—as a stay-at-home mom. Stephen had finished his PhD and began working as an applied scientist. He then changed careers and started medical school to become a medical doctor. The couple had recently moved back to their hometown for Stephen to pursue his MD. Cassandra decided not to pursue a professor job after completing her postdoc and was working instead as a researcher for an educational organization earning $75,000 a year. She married and lived with a new partner who had two young children. David taught college classes as a lecturer, where his new spouse was also a professor. They were living together in the same city after dating long distance for a short time. The other autonomous actors' five-year trajectories and Time 4 outcomes appear in table 3.2.

These work and relationship outcomes hinted at, but did not fully capture, the increasingly coordinated actions partners took together to maintain two careers while nurturing a relationship. Even autonomous

TABLE 3.2 AUTONOMOUS ACTORS' FIVE-YEAR TRAJECTORIES AND TIME 4 OUTCOMES

Partners & occupations at Time 3	Five-year trajectory	Time 4
Julie, medical resident Max, medical resident	She completed her residency, then started fellowship He completed his residency, completed 1st fellowship, then started 2nd fellowship Got engaged, then married Had 1st child; she took 6 weeks' paid leave, while he took 1 week's paid leave	She was finishing her fellowship & applying for jobs ($74,000) He was finishing his fellowship & applying for jobs ($74,000) Remained married & continued living together Co-parented 1 child
Karen, postdoc Jacob, lawyer	She started 2nd postdoc at new university He finished his contract, then became lawyer for new city Got married after moving to new city for her 2nd postdoc	She was finishing her postdoc & choosing between professor offers ($48,000) He continued as lawyer & was applying for jobs ($76,000) Remained married & continued living together Remained child free
Cassandra, postdoc David, PhD student	She completed her postdoc, moved to new city to start as research analyst at 1st institution, then moved up to researcher at 2nd institution She met, then married, her new partner He completed his PhD, started as temporary professor at 1st university, changed to senior fellow at 2nd university, then changed to lecturer at 3rd university He met & married his new partner, moving wherever she started new jobs	She continued as researcher ($75,000) She remained married & continued living with her new partner She co-parented stepchildren He continued as lecturer (salary not given) He remained married & continued living with his new partner

Samantha, MD student Josh, PhD student	The couple broke up She completed her MD, then moved to new city to start MPH program She remained single He finished his PhD, then moved to new city to start postdoc He started long-distance relationship with his new partner	She continued as MPH student (no salary) She remained single He continued as postdoc ($51,000) He moved in with his new partner & got engaged
Amanda, freelance researcher Louis, law enforcement	She changed to temporary researcher at new university, changed to temporary lecturer, then changed to permanent lecturer He continued in law enforcement & moved up in rank Got married & continued living together Had 1st child; she took 6 months' paid leave, while he took 5 days' paid leave	She continued as lecturer ($56,000) He continued in law enforcement ($55,000) Remained married & continued living together Had 2nd child; she took 6 months' paid leave, while he took 1 month's paid leave
Janelle, at-home parent Stephen, PhD student	She continued as at-home parent He completed his PhD, completed his residency, then started MD program Remained married & continued living together after moving to new city for his MD program Had 2 children	She continued as at-home parent (no salary) He continued as MD student (no salary) Remained married & continued living together Had 3rd child

MPH = master of public health

actors who formed new relationships described greater "we-ness" and better-coordinated actions with their new partners at Time 4. Cassandra, for instance, thought her new relationship was very different from the one she had had with David. She and her current husband thought about themselves as interdependent parts of a larger whole in their family, rather than as autonomous actors who happened to be together:

> It's framed a little differently. It's more like, "Okay, we're family. We're attached now." We are each other, so to speak. I don't think about it in a transactional way at all anymore. We have had, in the past, sort of, transactional domestic labor—"I do some, you should do some," that kind of thing. But most of the time now, it's more like, "Let's do what's best for everyone, together."

In contrast to the approach Cassandra and David had taken in the past to independently pursue each person's separate goals without holding each other back, Cassandra and her current husband did "what's best for everyone, together." A joint outlook on all matters concerning any family members replaced the "transactional" logic that had characterized Cassandra's past relationship. David shifted from autonomy to interdependence with his new spouse, too. After a short period of a long-distance relationship with his new partner, he began following her to different universities as she navigated the tenure track as a professor. David was able to support his partner's demanding research career while pursuing his teaching career by taking college lecturer or instructor positions (which were relatively more abundant) wherever his spouse was working.

These couples replaced autonomy in their work-family ecosystems with interdependence over time partly because of men's increased professional security and workplace flexibility—and men's growing recognition that their work-related resources could be leveraged to actively support women's careers and their families. For example, unlike in the past, Max explicitly took Julie's career into account when he finished his residency and began applying to fellowships for his subspecialty training. Because Julie needed to remain at their current hospital to finish her residency, Max only applied to the fellowship program at that institution even though he risked not getting in:

> At that time Julie had two more years left in her program, so we would have had to be apart if I went anywhere else. I pretty much knew I was going to only [apply for the fellowship here], and that there was a decent chance I wouldn't get it. So, I talked to my adviser, who was also the director for the program of the [second-choice] fellowship, and said, "If I don't get this [first-choice fellowship] could I potentially do that [second-choice fellowship]?"

And they said yeah. Once you're done with the residency you can always get a job and I could have pretty easily gotten a job doing general internal medicine in the area. That's what I would've done if I hadn't been able to do the [second-choice] fellowship.

Max used his professional resources—his established working relationship with a mentor—to line up a secondary fellowship at the hospital in case his application to his preferred fellowship was unsuccessful (it was, so he took the backup fellowship). Knowing he had additional workplace advantages in the form of hirable skills as a physician gave him further confidence to restrict his application to his current institution rather than apply widely. If all else fell through, Max felt certain he could get a job practicing medicine to allow the couple to stay together while still advancing both partners' professional development.

Max's confidence in his professional trajectory similarly shaped the couple's active job search for two permanent positions in the same place at Time 4. With both partners scheduled to complete their respective fellowships in the upcoming months, the couple started a joint job search like the ones consistent compromisers undertook in chapter 2. Max and Julie targeted specific hospitals, and both partners asked about opportunities for their spouses if either one of them learned about an opening in their respective medical specialties. Max's description of his job search at Time 4 was strikingly different than his job search at Time 1:

> We have to find jobs for both of us. So, we're weighing what each of us wants, and what sacrifice each of us is willing to make. I'm more flexible on whether it's an academic job or if it's private [practice] with some academic opportunities or some teaching opportunities. [Julie] definitely wants to do academic [medicine], so it narrows it down pretty quick to a handful of places. She started reaching out to the places, talking to their program chairs. Then I went based on those locations, just started applying. [A midwestern institution was] hiring [in my specialty] so I interviewed there. They were pretty enthusiastic about hiring me and I asked if they could hire anyone in [Julie's specialty]. They said no, so it wasn't going to work [for us]. The people she works with here have been enthusiastic about hiring her to stay, but I haven't had a definite option [in our current city] until recently. Now it looks like they would hire me at [a nearby hospital]. I mean, there's demand for physicians so there's always a chance that one of us could take a job and the other one could just wait and see, but right now it's looking pretty good that we'll have an opportunity to stay here for both of us.

Whereas at Time 1 Max pursued career opportunities that benefited him regardless of the impact on Julie, at Time 4 Max actively considered Julie's career. He sent applications wherever she had professional leads and asked about job openings for her if he found a good opportunity for himself. Further, given Julie's strong commitment to pursuing a particular type of career, Max used his own flexibility regarding the types of jobs he would be willing to take to support Julie's narrower job search. Finally, Max stressed that "there's demand for physicians" and felt certain that he could find a job eventually if Julie found a job first.

On top of men's increasingly favorable conditions at work, men's increasing focus on their families shaped their attitudes toward work vis-à-vis their personal lives. When Stephen began the process of changing careers—he was working as an applied physical scientist before he became interested in pursuing medical school—he noted that Janelle played an active role in determining whether he would pursue more schooling and then in choosing the specific degree program that would work for their family:

> Janelle was actually pretty central to a lot of that decision-making process. It was kind of a perfect storm situation—I would only [change careers] if it was the right institution, with the right kind of program, and the right financial situation, and we had a place where we had good social support. One asset of [going to medical school at this southern university] would be [that] it would give us a several-year window to see what life was like living in [our hometown]. By that point, we had two kids and it would also give our parents time to be around them when they were really young.

Although Stephen still kept his career in mind ("the right institution, with the right kind of program") as he had in his past interviews, at Time 4 his career decisions were more explicitly contingent on having "good social support" for Janelle and his children. He also considered his and Janelle's parents' ability to see their grandchildren if he chose to pursue an MD in their hometown. Getting married and having children therefore also changed the way autonomous actor men approached their careers.

Still, Stephen and a few other autonomous actor fathers retained their initial "hands-off" approach specifically when it came to sharing childcare. At Time 4, Stephen expressed surprise and a hint of concern that he and Janelle had ended up in gender-traditional work and family roles. Yet in a familiar pattern of action, Stephen stepped back to give Janelle space to make the family choices she wanted:

> Janelle had settled into a decision of just wanting to do "stay-at-home mom" for a while. It was just an easier alternative. I feel like she's had to compromise a ton in terms of her career ambitions to make family life work. I would periodically bring it up to her, because I didn't want her to feel—but she was always really emphatic that, no [she's not compromising].

Stephen resumed a "hands-off" stance regarding Janelle's decision to "do 'stay-at-home-mom'" in reaction to the family devotion—a single-minded commitment to intensive motherhood[10]—that Janelle developed between Times 3 and 4:

> Well, we had [our first] baby, and it turned out to be really great and totally wonderful. I was getting to the point where it was time to choose to go back to work or to stay with the baby. And I just really felt called to stay with the baby. I just decided, I kind of don't want to do both, and want to just do the kid thing. And I never would have thought that I would be a stay-at-home person or have more than two children. But it's been such a beautiful, enlightening experience.

Janelle's immersion in full-time motherhood changed her attitudes toward work and family such that she came to see parenting as a desirable primary activity for herself. She was in charge of family life, and Stephen stepped in to help if Janelle told him, "I really need you to plug in this moment." Yet Janelle might not have made these choices and arrived at this outcome if she had initially had more support from her university to smoothly transition into a PhD program and if Stephen had been more proactive to jointly make career plans with her.

In sum, Julie and Max, Janelle and Stephen, and Cassandra and David in their new relationships came to make career decisions more jointly with their partners, rather than independently, over time. Autonomous actor men in particular grew more interdependent and apt to actively empower their partners to pursue their careers as their workplace circumstances improved and as they became husbands and fathers. These work- and family-related changes shifted some autonomous actors' ecosystems to be more gender egalitarian with respect to careers. However, this logic did not always also apply to parenting. Some men passively "allowed" women to take the lead in raising children. This pattern indicates that people—perhaps especially men—might see gender egalitarianism in careers to be separate from gender egalitarianism in the family.[11]

CONCLUSION

The autonomous actor trajectory complicates what it means to have "gender equality" in work and family. A gender-neutral endorsement of men's and women's equal right to autonomy—freedom for each person to make independent career decisions paired with the expectation that each person would refrain from holding their partner back—still led to gendered, mismatched actions across partners. Women made more career compromises and did more work to ensure that both partners could have their careers while sustaining a relationship. These gender-unequal actions then led to highly variable short-term outcomes for autonomous actor couples.

Sometimes this gender-unequal burden of work still resulted in gender-equal outcomes in the short term. When outcomes were equal—if both partners had careers and the relationship remained intact—couples could disregard the gender-unequal power dynamics and processes that got them there. This selective attention on outcomes allowed gender inequality to persist unquestioned in men's and women's *experiences* in attaining these outcomes.

The autonomous actor pathway further complicates the idea of "gender equality" in work and family by highlighting that egalitarianism is not a static trait that is fundamental to individuals or couples. Egalitarianism is a state of equilibrium that people can move in and out of over time depending on workplace circumstances, cultural attitudes, and how coordinated or disjointed partners' actions are. Although men initially did less work to support the couple than women did, over the long term, men came to make more compromises in their careers and took actions like those women did to support their partners' careers and their families. The autonomous actor trajectory demonstrates that examining both partners' actions and how well they align matters for understanding the gender revolution in work and family. Scholars repeatedly point to work-related challenges that bar men and women from having equal partnerships. This pathway shows that the availability of workplace supports for egalitarianism may not be enough if partners do not make use of their professional resources to benefit each other.

That couples broke up on the autonomous actor pathway suggests that autonomy in career and family decision-making (compared to sharing all decision-making, as the consistent compromisers in chapter 2 did) can put relationships at risk of dissolving. This pathway included other risks, too. Women who "independently chose" to compromise their careers without equal compromises from their partners put their professional trajectories at greater risk relative to the men in the relationships. If women compromised their careers to support the relationship but ended up breaking up with their partners, they could lose out on both career advancement and their partnerships. Men who took an autonomous approach may have achieved what they wanted in their careers but were also at risk of losing out in their relationships. A final risk on this pathway was that men's "hands-off" approach to career-related decision-making meant that couples' outcomes hinged on what was possible for women given their professional resources. Women's relatively constrained workplace opportunities made it harder for them to keep both partners together while moving two careers forward on their own. If men did not draw on their own workplace resources to support the couple, they could end up in unwanted long-distance relationships because women had no other options if they wanted to continue pursuing their careers.

In the next chapter I detail the stories of the tending traditional couples. The partners on this trajectory encountered a perfect storm of workplace challenges to having two careers, cultural attitudes accepting gender traditionalism in work and family, and gender-complementary joint actions. These factors came together to push men and women into a more gender-unequal division of labor than they ever expected for themselves.

## CHAPTER 4

Tending Traditional Couples

I started applying for teaching positions in [this southern city] because
Thomas got an offer at a big firm [there]. I never thought I would
be in [this city], but there's a lot of good history going on right now
in the public arena. Working in the history center there would be
awesome. . . . When it came up, like, "how am I going to find a job in
[this city]?" he did say after a year it would not be a problem to look
at other firms 'cause he knows that it's not fun to just follow someone
somewhere. [But] I mean, he's got an offer from this big firm already
and unless things are horrendous, I don't think that we'll be moving
again and I think it would be nice to be near family if we do decide to
have kids. . . . I'd like to have kids in the next three years, and I think
that, at least for a couple years, you kind of have to take time out and
do that. When I was working in [university administration] we did a
lot of projects about women in science and how they drop out because
they've got to take time out for babies and that's just it. There's just no
way around that, even if you have a very supportive husband. He'd
rather see me in a PhD program or working at something I really
love and not being a mom solely, and I mean, I'd like to be able to do
everything, but it's just not possible. So next year I would be possibly
teaching or working in a museum or a foundation in [our new city]
and Thomas would be working [at the firm that offered him a job].
Then there's more pressure to have children and it's going to push
other things to the back burner. But it's never too late to go back
to school, to get a new job, to re-create your life.

—Lauren, Time 1

Lauren and her husband Thomas both had professional ambitions,
but Thomas had more narrow career preferences than Lauren did and
landed a permanent job first. Taking for granted that "he's got an offer
from this big firm already," Lauren targeted her own job search to a city
she had never considered for herself. She thought it was possible to find

work there that was related to her graduate training but assumed it was inevitable that she would leave the workplace to have children in the upcoming years. Still, both partners imagined that Lauren could restart her career when their children got older. Beliefs that men's careers were less negotiable than women's careers, and that women, but not men, would temporarily leave work to care for infants, shaped the experience of couples on the *tending traditional* pathway.

Greater acceptance of cultural norms surrounding gender, paid work, romantic relationships, and caregiving among tending traditional couples, compared to consistent compromisers (chapter 2) and autonomous actors (chapter 3), channeled these men and women toward a power-imbalanced, husband-earner/wife-caregiver arrangement during the six-year study period. These couples were open to women pursuing careers if they wanted to but took men's continuous career attachment as a given. They praised men's interest in active parenting but believed it was necessary for women to take time off work to care for young children. Labor market conditions that threatened men's professional identities made these cultural norms especially salient to couples, leading partners to act in more starkly gender-complementary ways than they anticipated.[1] When men could not land the jobs they wanted, they pressed the importance of setting up their careers in a specific way at any cost. Women responded by pausing their own work activities to support men's intensified career pursuits. They established a gender-traditional work-family equilibrium that was hard to disrupt even when partners eventually found this division of labor and their gender-unequal power dynamic less desirable. Some couples did not want to risk giving up their high standard of living and contend with the unknowns of a wife-earner/husband-caregiver or even a dual earner-caregiver arrangement. Other partnerships dissolved when women no longer wanted neotraditionalism and ended their relationships.

This chapter showcases the trajectories of Rebecca and Joseph, Emily and Brad, and Liz and Hank. Their stories illustrate what gender traditionalism looks like when couples do not necessarily aspire to a strict husband-earner/wife-caregiver division of labor. Information about the other tending traditional couples appears in table 4.1.

THE COUPLES

Rebecca and Joseph met in graduate school, where she was completing a master's degree and he was pursuing a PhD, both in the same natural

TABLE 4.1   TENDING TRADITIONAL COUPLES

Partners & occupations	Relationship status at Time 1	Time 1 *Men & women applied for jobs sequentially*	Time 2 *Men prioritized their careers; women paused their careers*	Time 3 *Men launched careers; women were unemployed or underemployed*	Time 4 *Men continued careers; women tried relaunching theirs*
Emily, editor Brad, SS PhD student	Married, living together	Brad led their job search in select cities	Emily quit her job so Brad could take his offer	Emily stayed home with their child after moving to new city for Brad's job	Brad advanced his career Emily worked part-time from home with their 2 children
Mindy, teacher Bryan, SS PhD student	Unmarried, living together	Bryan led their job search in 1 city	Mindy quit her job so Bryan could take his offer	Mindy remained unemployed after moving to new city for Bryan's job	Bryan advanced his career Mindy returned to school Got married Expecting 1st child
Rebecca, scientist Joseph, STEM PhD student	Married, living together	Joseph led their job search in select cities	Rebecca quit her job so Joseph could take his offer	Rebecca remained unemployed after moving to new city for Joseph's job	Joseph advanced his career Rebecca advanced more slowly Co-parented 1 child
Leslie, SS MA student Andrew, defense professional	Married, long distance	Leslie applied for jobs in Andrew's city	Andrew convinced Leslie to move to his city without job	Leslie remained unemployed after moving to Andrew's city	Andrew returned to school & started new career after moving to new city for Leslie's graduate program

Liz, MPP student Hank, finance professional	Unmarried, living together	Applied together for jobs in select cities	Hank convinced Liz to return to her former job so they could stay in their current city for his job	Both employed in same city	Couple broke up Hank advanced his career & stayed single Liz changed careers & began dating new partner
Cheryl, SS PhD student Gordon, library clerk	Unmarried, living together	Applied together for jobs in select cities	Gordon convinced Cheryl to take unpaid position so he could take his offer	Both employed in new city, but Cheryl was underemployed	Got married & then divorced Gordon advanced his career & stayed single Cheryl slowly advanced her career & started dating new partner
Lauren, SS MA student Thomas, JD student	Married, living together	Lauren applied for jobs in Thomas's preferred city	Thomas convinced Lauren to move without job	Lauren remained unemployed after moving to new city for Thomas's job Couple divorced	Thomas advanced his career & stayed single Lauren moved to new city for PhD program & started dating new partner

SS = social science; MPP = master of public policy

science field (these characteristics make Rebecca and Joseph similar to consistent compromisers Vanessa and Alex and Nora and Rick; a detailed comparison of these couples appears in chapter 5). They dated for a year and a half before getting engaged and had been a married couple for just about two years when they joined the study. Although each person pursued graduate training to expand their professional opportunities, Rebecca surmised that she "didn't like science to the extent that Joseph did," whereas Joseph described himself as always looking for an "opportunity for advancement" in his field. At the time of their first interviews, Joseph was finishing his dissertation and doing a geographically targeted search for a specific set of industry jobs. Rebecca had been working in a research lab and was prepared to search for new jobs in these cities, too. They wanted to wait a few more years before having children, mostly so Rebecca could establish a longer work history before taking time out to care for an infant. Despite both partners' ample access to lucrative jobs all across the country, Rebecca and Joseph's experience shows that dominant cultural narratives around paid work and masculinity could lead couples to consistently prioritize men's careers over women's careers, even when it did not make financial sense to do so.

Emily and Brad were anticipating Brad's graduation from a social science PhD program and were navigating his job hunt when they joined the study. They had met as teenagers and had been together for a decade, nearly half of that time as a married couple. Emily's "family are all writers and historians," and she followed in their footsteps when she earned her doctorate and began working at a museum. Brad wanted an academic career and was doing a geographically targeted search for postdoctoral research positions and professor jobs. The partners understood that the academic job market was extremely competitive and that the chances of Brad landing a good position in a place they wanted to live were slim. Still, Brad said they were approaching his applications as "a team," while Emily stated they would "stick it out together" to give Brad a shot at pursuing his ideal career. They wanted to have children soon and believed their desired careers in the academic and museum worlds offered a great deal of flexibility for being active parents. Emily and Brad experienced the most traditional trajectory of these couples. Their story reveals how powerful cultural norms linking relationships and childcare to femininity, in combination with cultural imperatives about professional-class manhood, could push couples to abandon women's career pursuits in favor of women's full-time caregiving.

Liz and Hank had been dating for seven years when they joined the study. Liz was a data analyst who returned to school for an MPP. Her immediate professional goal was to move into a managerial role, and she hoped to one day direct an organization. Her partner Hank was a finance professional who was steadily working his way up in his firm. Liz remarked that she went back to school, and that Hank was interested in completing more education as well, because they both wanted "to have more professional and financial options afterwards." At the beginning of the study, the couple was considering a national job search to help advance Liz's career. They wanted to establish their careers in the next few years and imagined talking concretely about getting married and becoming parents after that. Liz and Hank's trajectory highlights how men's career attachment could prompt women to put their professional pursuits on hold, even when women had equally strong career ambitions. Their story also shows what can happen when women tire of forgoing their own professional opportunities to support men's careers.

TIME 1: SHARED PLANS FOR A DUAL-CAREER PARTNERSHIP (AS LONG AS HE IS WORKING AND SHE HAS NO CHILDCARE OBLIGATIONS)

Like the consistent compromisers in chapter 2, tending traditional couples assessed their work-related opportunities and constraints at Time 1 as they began searching for two jobs in the same place. To account for each other's careers, partners focused their job searches on certain locations that would professionally support both people. Finance professional Hank, for example, pointed to two cities that were especially likely to work for him and his partner Liz, a data analyst and MPP student who was looking for a new position in order to move up in her career:

> She has connections through her job to [a West Coast city] and [an East Coast city]. My company has connections in [the same two cities]. It might work if I move there—in fact I'm going there this Friday and I'm going to try to work in [the West Coast office] for the day so I'll test it out. So that'd be awesome, I'd love to live in [that city]. But if she gets a great offer in [the East Coast city], I'd go to [that city].

Hank and Liz had formal support from their companies—the option to transfer to different offices in the same two cities—to facilitate at least lateral, if not upward, movement in both of their careers. They also both took concrete actions to make use of their workplace advantages. Hank made plans to work from a different company office to test the possibility of transferring, and Liz tracked job ads for more senior roles across all her company's offices.

Yet unlike the consistent compromisers, tending traditional couples prioritized men's job searches because they considered women's careers more portable and less lucrative than men's careers. Even as they identified themselves as being in a dual-professional relationship, imagined that both partners would have careers, and took women's professional goals into account, couples sequenced their two job hunts such that men's searches came first. Women explored potential leads but did not start applying until men agreed that the location would be viable for their careers, too. This logic reinforced a subtle power imbalance in which couples granted men greater access to employment opportunities than women.

Rebecca and Joseph both worked in the same natural science field and had a similar skillset, but Rebecca had a master's degree and work experience, whereas Joseph would soon have a PhD. Joseph explained that although they hoped to land two jobs in the same city, they thought it was important for him to find a job in his desired sector of industry research first:

> The plan would be for me to get a position first so we know the area [she should target] and then she is going to start applying. Rebecca has actually compiled most of the job stuff—we have a huge spreadsheet we go through and I make cover letters—so in perusing [job ads for me] she kind of sees what's available for her. Her position is probably easier to get, is what we're thinking, because she has her degree and two years' experience in a position, which is really important . . . and in terms of financial sense, it does make more sense for me to go first. It is expected that I should make more money in any comparable position because the PhD level will start at a higher pay scale. But it also means it's harder to find a position 'cause they don't want to pay you, so that's the double-edged sword.

Regardless of whether Joseph's professional qualifications were a "double-edged sword" for his job hunt, they were certainly a one-two punch for Rebecca's career prospects. Even though the partners worked in the same field with strong labor markets in private industry, government, and academic research across various American cities—a major professional advantage for this couple—and maintained a shared spreadsheet that each person could populate with job ads, neither partner thought it made sense for Rebecca to send applications ahead of Joseph, nor did the couple consider applying for jobs simultaneously. Instead, both partners insisted it was "practical" for Joseph's job search to direct Rebecca's search.

Certainly tending traditional couples' prioritization of men's "more constrained" job searches and higher earning potential could be considered a reasonable response to professional realities. For instance, it is true that professional occupations dominated by women (like human resource management) tend to be available in a wider range of cities than those dominated by men (like engineering).[2] It is also true that men tend to have higher earning potential than women due to the gender pay gap.[3]

Yet tending traditional men were not restricted to geographically constrained careers, nor were women concentrated in more mobile careers. Remember, for example, that scientists Rebecca and Joseph both had research skills that qualified them for careers in multiple sectors available across the country. Further, these men and women were highly educated, meaning both partners could access jobs that pay more than what is available to most Americans. These couples would likely be financially sound even if they did not maximize men's earnings. In fact, chapter 5 reveals that consistent compromisers who invested equally in both partners' careers earned the highest family incomes by the end of the study. In using degendered reasoning that "whoever has the harder job to find can go first" or "whoever is the higher earner can go first" when these couples' material conditions did not make it necessary,[4] tending traditional partners ignored and reproduced gender inequality in their career prioritization strategy.

Still, it was not the case that tending traditional men opposed women's professional pursuits. Neither did tending traditional women aspire to be full-time homemakers without paid employment. These couples just definitely wanted *men* to pursue careers. Between listing pragmatic reasons for prioritizing Joseph's job search, for instance, Rebecca revealed that cultural norms emphasizing the importance of paid work for men also motivated their approach: "I guess Joseph being the guy in the relationship, he would definitely want to have a job so we would focus on making sure that was accomplished first."[5] Though couples rarely explicitly said that they prioritized men's job searches due to these cultural scripts—partners were more likely to note men's stronger desires for a specific career path compared to women's greater openness to a range of professional options[6]—these ideas certainly shaped the partners' actions at Time 1.

Subtle gender traditionalism in these couples' thoughts about child-care also shaped the prioritization of men's job searches. Married couple Emily and Brad both had social science doctoral training and were looking for work together in Europe, where they each had professional ties. Brad said the kinds of careers they could have there—he wanted to be a professor and she worked in museums—would provide them better work-family balance:

> There are more posts that I would be interested in taking, and if we start a family they won't ask me to work seventy hours a week and I'm going to have time to see my kids. And it's easier for her to have kids and get work at a museum.

Though Brad, like other tending traditional men, talked about his desire for both partners to be involved in raising children, Emily clarified that the mix of paid work and unpaid childcare each person expected to do once kids became a part of their lives was not completely equal:

> I'd like to go part-time for a few years because it's free childcare. The idea would be to go part-time and maintain enough of a career that I could go back to full-time. It might be easier for me to find part-time work there [in Europe] because their economic system is predicated more on part-time work and on flextime.

Whereas Brad wanted to avoid overwork to spend time with his future children, Emily envisioned working less than full-time for a little while so she could provide the couple with "free childcare."[7] Because the couple hoped to have children soon, and because they thought Emily could more easily find part-time work in her field than Brad could find full-time work in his, they thought it prudent to prioritize Brad's job search in a mutually agreeable location.

Again, there were pragmatic reasons for couples to prioritize men's job searches when women imagined temporarily scaling back their careers to raise children.[8] Scientist Rebecca, for instance, pointed to the financial necessity of establishing men's careers: "I don't have any intention of *not* working if I don't have kids to raise. But I would not work while the kids are very young, so then [Joseph] would *need* to have a job if he was the only one working."

This logic falls apart, however, when considering professional men's and women's access to paid parental leave and incomes that can cover childcare costs.[9] Indeed, the consistent compromisers' stories in chapter 2 show how partners used these resources to maintain two careers while sharing parenting responsibilities. Gendered cultural norms linking women to caregiving better explain why tending traditional partners deprioritized women's careers in response to couples' expected childcare needs.[10] Rebecca's husband Joseph indicated that it was socially acceptable for mothers, but not fathers, to temporarily stop working to care for children: "If we have kids, she probably would not want to work and that's fine. I probably couldn't do that. I couldn't be the stay-at-home dad." Given these prevailing cultural scripts, men expressed interest in raising children, but women expressed stronger feelings about parenting and greater comfort with scaling back paid work to do so. Recall, for example, that social science PhD student Brad wanted to work in Europe partly because he wanted "time to see my kids." Brad's wife Emily, on the other hand, saw herself going part-time for a while because "I like kids. I've always liked kids. I love kids." Thus, tending traditional couples imagined *women* prioritizing family caregiving, at least for a while.

These culturally patterned, gendered desires for work and family would not be a problem if caregiving were not relatively devalued compared to paid employment and systematically assigned to less powerful social groups in American society.[11] The work of raising children, though necessary to society and no easy task, is largely unpaid or poorly paid in America. The devaluation of care work is apparent in America's lack of investment in robust infrastructure to support caregivers.[12] Even though professional workers may have access to paid parental leave that is adequate in length and flexibility through individual employers, there are few viable part-time working options that facilitate caregiving over the long term. There are also few formal channels that allow people to move back and forth between full-time paid work, part-time paid work plus caregiving, and full-time caregiving without risking their job security. In a capitalist economy without additional forms of life support, a person's workplace attachment is key to survival.[13] Scaling back at work or leaving the labor force altogether is a risky choice—one that women disproportionately make, given cultural scripts for gender, work, and family.

Without explicitly acknowledging this inequality, trending traditional couples still recognized a power imbalance in having men lead the couples' job searches. Their understanding of marriage, however, helped partners maintain a sense of fairness (but not equality) even as men's job searches constrained women's job searches. Four of the seven tending traditional couples were married, and the other three described themselves as functionally, if not legally, married. For these couples, being (functionally) married meant two things. First, the partners expected each person's investments in, or compromises for, the other person's career to even out over time. If the couple focused on one partner's professional goals right now, the couple would focus on the other partner next. For example, finance professional Hank was helping Liz pay for her MPP degree even though they were not married because Hank thought "we'll probably be together forever," and the partners felt confident that Liz would repay Hank for his investment in her career in the future. Liz confirmed this:

> When we first went into this [arrangement], the deal was, "you're going to help me through these two years [of graduate school] and if you want to do something—a career change or go back to school—I'll be able to support you in that decision."

Being functionally married meant that Liz and Hank expected and assumed that they would take turns prioritizing each other's professional projects. Hank built up what Claudia Geist and Leah Ruppanner call "relationship capital"[14]—credit within the partnership for helping Liz through school. Hank could use his relationship capital to hold Liz accountable for repaying him in the future. She would be obliged to take a turn supporting Hank (financially or otherwise) so they could both build careers. Liz and Hank represent a more atypical case, as most tending traditional couples focused on men's careers now and expected to reprioritize women's careers later. We will see how tending traditional women like Liz fare later in the chapter.

Second, being (or feeling like they were) married provided the couples assurance that each partner had the other person's, and the relationship's, best interests in mind. Partners assumed and expected each other to act on behalf of the couple without needing to actively negotiate these terms. Emily said being legally married to Brad made making the big decision to look for work in Europe together easier for her:

> If we weren't married, I would not feel as secure in my decision to let him assemble our life. To have him be the person who chooses that place—I wouldn't feel okay about it. I wouldn't think of us as a family if we weren't married. He's my husband and he's such a good husband. He knows where I want to move. He's making lots of effort to get to where we want to move. He's focusing his applications there. If he wanted me to say "I'll move anywhere, it doesn't matter as long as your career is being fulfilled"—he realized it's probably not a good idea. It [has to be] mutually good. There's always balance.

Being married helped partners feel secure that each person would make choices that were "mutually good" for all parties and for the relationship. Marriage ensured that if one person was taking the lead in making major decisions that would affect them both, they could assume that this person would account for the other without needing to actively and constantly ask for this behavior. As we will see later in this chapter, however, the assumptions these partners made to reduce their interpersonal negotiation costs also restricted opportunities to renegotiate their work-family arrangements when circumstances were no longer "mutually good."[15]

These cultural beliefs about gender, work, relationships, and family came together to produce a gendered pattern of joint action among tending traditional couples at Time 1. Partners collaboratively planned for both men and women to participate in paid work and childcare but took special care to establish men's full-time careers now and prepared for women to scale back or pause theirs to have children in the future. The partners imagined they could trade off investing in, or compromising for, each person's career to even out the imbalance later.

TIME 2: LEANING INTO NEOTRADITIONALISM

Tending traditional men's unfavorable job prospects at Time 2, four to seven months after they began their job searches, contrasted with the couples' hopes for sequentially landing two jobs in the same place. Whereas at Time 1 they expected men to find work in their target cities so women could start and complete their narrower job searches, the reality at Time 2 was that men had not secured their ideal jobs in the couple's desired location. Although this experience was not unique to tending traditional men, as we have seen in chapters 2 and 3 and as I further detail in chapter 5, men who faced unemployment on the tending traditional pathway responded differently to these circumstances than consistent compromiser and autonomous actor men did.

Tending traditional men's suboptimal employment conditions threatened their professional identities, making dominant cultural models for gender, work, and family even more salient to them. The inability to live up to cultural ideals of professional-class manhood led tending traditional couples to abandon "Plan A" for two careers.[16] They devised a new "Plan B" that centered on ensuring *men's* employment only, no matter the cost. Any support for women's professional plans dissolved as men emphasized the importance of getting the exact job they wanted over both partners pursuing their careers in the same place. To boost men's morale and keep the couple together, women took more starkly gender-complementary actions. As men intensified their job searches, women redirected energy from their own applications toward encouraging men's career pursuits. At Time 2, these couples tended toward gender traditionalism, rather than toward egalitarianism as the consistent compromisers did or toward independence as the autonomous actors did, in the face of challenging employment landscapes. At this time point, the balance of power tipped clearly in men's favor, as women labored to prioritize men's professional goals.

After months of applying to and interviewing for natural science industry jobs across the nation, Joseph remained unemployed and would soon have to graduate from his PhD program. Rebecca initially sent out targeted applications as Joseph got interviews but gradually slowed down her own search when neither of their leads came through. At Time 2, Rebecca arranged to quit her job at the academic research lab to double down on supporting Joseph through the interview process at a large biotechnology company in a West Coast city:

> I told my boss to make my last day [in a few weeks]. I was thinking by this point [Joseph] might have something so it wouldn't feel strange, just leaving a paying job and benefits [chuckles]. . . . But he doesn't want to stay [and move up] as a postdoc in the same lab because he's not super happy with the structure of the lab and you're not necessarily going to progress or learn any new skills just staying in the same lab. So he kind of wanted to push himself out, intensify [the search], at least have something, one job, and then [we] move to the area, and then I would look for a job.

Even though Rebecca said at Time 1 that she did not "have any intention of *not* working" unless she was raising young children, she made plans at Time 2 to leave the job she already had to demonstrate her endorsement of Joseph's intensified out-of-state job search. This couple's story shows that childcare responsibilities are not the only factors that can interrupt women's career progression; men's careers also play a role in shaping women's professional trajectories.

This option was not the only one the couple had. Rebecca could have kept her position and financially supported both of them while the partners continued a joint job hunt. Or even if he did not want to advance into a postdoc role in his current lab, Joseph could have altered his job search strategy to target his applications to their current city. That way, Rebecca could continue working. Yet Joseph revealed that his ideas about work and masculinity led the couple to focus solely on his job search:

> We had thought about that [other job search strategies], especially when I applied to a bunch of jobs and hadn't heard anything. Like, "you [Rebecca] apply and I'll go wherever," but it doesn't seem like it's going that way. I wouldn't want to *not* work—I couldn't do that. I don't know, there's sort of the breadwinner mentality, like, "males make the money" [whereas] she's completely fine about not having work.

In a society that links White, upper-middle-class masculinity to having a full-time, high-paying professional job, Joseph's lack of suitable employment at Time 2 activated explicit statements of gender traditionalism.[17] Although Joseph had cited his higher earning potential as a reason for prioritizing his job search at Time 1, economic rationality no longer mattered at Time 2 if Joseph could not live up to his "breadwinner mentality." The continued prioritization of Joseph's job search even when it was not financially reasonable suggests that cultural scripts for men and work led the partners to focus on Joseph's career at the expense of Rebecca's career. Such scripts help men maintain power in a capitalist society, as partners accepted that access to paid employment "belongs" to men.

In addition to men's unemployment, women's pregnancies also triggered stronger gender-traditional attitudes among these men. At Time 2, Brad's academic job search in Europe failed to produce job offers. Like Joseph, Brad would soon graduate from his PhD program but had no job to go to. Emily was still working at the museum but was pregnant and preparing to take parental leave before trying to negotiate a part-time schedule upon her return to work. Without a job lined up for Brad and with a baby on the way, the couple decided Brad should redirect his applications to target lucrative technology sector jobs on the West Coast, and Emily should quit her job and follow him. The couple came to this new plan because Brad changed his mind about the feasibility of a dual-earner partnership in Europe and rejected the idea of taking on the primary parent role while staying in their current city:

> None of that worked out, so we were talking about the possibilities for when we have the baby. We could live in [our current city] on not very much money because it's cheap. She could go to work while I stay home with the kid. I didn't really want to stay at home, and she could probably do more good with the child, for the first six months especially, than I could. If I had the choice, I'd go to work. . . . It turns out there's this whole world of data science. So we looked into doing that, and there's work [for me on the West Coast].

The extremely constrained academic job market characterized by few positions relative to the number of qualified candidates and the timing of Emily's pregnancy created a discrepancy between the couple's reality at Time 2 and their hope at Time 1 to find him a job first, find her a job second, and then start a family.[18] In response to these circumstances, Brad advocated following a traditional cultural model for gender, work, and family. In line with cultural norms that pair men with work, he stated outright, "If I had the choice, I'd go to work." Because gender norms associate women with family, a nontraditional arrangement in which Brad stayed home with the baby was unappealing to him despite its financial feasibility. Instead, and consistent with these cultural scripts, he reasoned Emily "could probably do more good with the child."

Recall that tending traditional couples viewed being (functionally) married partly as a promise to keep the relationship's best interests in mind. As cultural ideas about gender and family call women, especially, to follow this tenet,[19] women felt compelled to show solidarity with their partners when men's employment conditions challenged their professional identities. Though at Time 1 women expected to fit their careers within the parameters of men's job searches, at Time 2 women went as far as to completely abandon paid work to help prop up men's "breadwinner mentalities." At Time 2, whatever was best for men's careers became the best interest of the relationship.

Women regulated their own uneasy feelings to convince themselves of the merit of these power-imbalanced neotraditional career plans.[20] Rebecca, the scientist who quit her job to show support for her husband Joseph's interviews with an out-of-state employer, de-emphasized her emotions to justify the couple's sole focus on Joseph's career. She acknowledged that it felt "strange, just leaving a job and benefits," but chuckled to dismiss the economic risk of their decision to invest in Joseph's job interview over having her keep the job she already had. She further privileged Joseph's emotions over her own by highlighting that he was "not super happy" with his option to stay (but still move up) in his current lab. Joseph's unhappiness with a position that was not *ideal* for him was enough to propel Rebecca to quit her job so Joseph could pursue his. These gender-complementary actions reveal the role that women play in helping men achieve masculinity in the context of an upper-middle-class, different-gender partnership.[21]

Dominant cultural narratives around pregnancy, work, and womanhood also helped women process how they felt about quitting their jobs to allow men to pursue the exact careers they wanted. Emily, the woman who worked in museums, felt "sorry" at Time 2 to give up the idea of working in Europe. She admitted feeling "really uncomfortable" that she was "putting [her] husband's career first." But being pregnant changed how she felt about leaving her job to follow Brad's career pursuits on the West Coast:

> [Then] we found out [I was pregnant]. . . . So that changed the way I was thinking about moving [to the West Coast]: the option of staying home and working from home became realistic. Financially it makes much more sense. In terms of the baby's health, having someone at home makes much more sense. If I stay home and take care of the baby—I wouldn't have to get some kind of position to do the sort of research I like to do. I could stay at home, and instead of working . . . I could work part-time on my [research].

Although at Time 1 Emily imagined working part-time as a new mother to "maintain enough of a career" so she could later "go back to full-time," at Time 2 Emily insisted that full-time at-home motherhood was best "in terms of the baby's health." Despite feeling "really uncomfortable" about moving to a part of the country with few museums specializing in her research to support Brad's continued job search, she argued that it was a rational financial decision for her to not work at all when their newborn arrived. Because existing frameworks for upper-middle-class working motherhood include working reduced hours independently from home while caring for children,[22] Emily was able to envision a new arrangement for herself that supported Brad's career, kept her (just barely) connected to her own career, and covered the partners' anticipated childcare needs. Women's pregnancies at Time 2, combined with men's unemployment, amplified gender-traditional cultural frameworks that directed women toward a fully domestic role.

These cultural and interpersonal dynamics played out even when both partners of a tending traditional couple got jobs in their respective professional fields at Time 2. Men still emphasized the relative importance of their careers to them, so women gave up better opportunities for themselves to allow their partners to pursue the specific jobs they wanted. Liz, the data analyst who was completing an MPP, and her partner Hank, the finance professional, halted their joint job search by Time 2. Their vision of both transferring to their respective companies' East or West Coast offices to give Liz a chance to move up in her career would not become reality. In explaining what happened, Hank said, "There are a lot of opportunities for me here. I want to stay. I think that's the best option." Hank did not want to miss advancement opportunities with his current team. He further added, "We have good jobs now," to convince Liz that pursuing a more advanced role was unnecessary and that she could stay in her same position and negotiate a raise with her new degree.

Remember that these couples believed that being married (or in a marriage-like relationship) meant partners should trade off being the career leader. This understanding of commitment led tending traditional women to give men "their turn" to have the focal career at Time 2. As Hank's preference to continue working in his current finance office grew more pronounced over time, Liz worked to change her feelings about the importance of her career:

> Three years ago when I was applying for school, Hank and I were at the phase in our relationship where I thought, "Well this is going to be fun until I want to make this big decision [to move for work], and I'm going to make that decision and Hank's either going to come along or not." Or I just imagine he can hitch his wagon to my star and I can just drag him along, just pop him on my back and live the life I want to lead without actually thinking about him, and I definitely wish that was not the case. That was completely unfair to even imagine that, and that was really immature of me, and now I've come to realize that. Going through [this process has] just made me think about "what [do] I want my life to look like?" more than "what do I want my professional career to look like?" and the rest will follow.

Hank cashed out his accrued relationship capital at Time 2 when Liz reframed her pursuit of career opportunities as "completely unfair." He had helped her pay for school. Now Liz was obligated to support Hank's desire to stay with his current team. Drawing on cultural models for gender and family that press women to consider their relationships and families above all else, Liz reoriented her attitude from "what do I want my professional career to look like?" to "what [do] I want my life to look like?"

Asking this question is neither wrong nor bad; perhaps American professionals could disrupt the culture of overwork if more workers asked this question of themselves, their workplaces, and their governments.[23] The issue is the gendered pressure on *women* to ask and answer this question. The work of considering relationships and families becomes women's responsibility, rather than a responsibility that partners share and that larger societal institutions facilitate. Given these existing cultural norms, women saw few options other than prioritizing their relationships and families over their careers. In turn, these actions reinforced gendered cultural understandings of work and family and reproduced gender-imbalanced power dynamics.

Tending traditional couples gave up their sequential, joint job search at Time 2 and shifted any attention they gave to women's professional goals toward establishing men's careers only. When men did not get the jobs they wanted, their tending traditional attitudes about work and masculinity became stronger, leading them to emphasize the importance of their own careers over women's careers. With these cultural attitudes made explicit, women turned to more traditional scripts about relationships, family, and femininity to revise their own feelings about working. As a result, partners took more starkly gender-differentiated actions—women gave up their career pursuits to support men's careers—to solidify the partners' neotraditional "Plan B's."

TIME 3: ACCEPTING NEOTRADITIONALISM

The actions couples took at Time 2 set men up to launch careers but positioned women to stall in, or disconnect from, their professions. Women who left their jobs were also poised to be financially dependent on their partners if they could not line up work in their fields at Time 3, approximately one year after couples began their job searches. Rebecca moved with Joseph to the West Coast after he secured a job with the large biotechnology company. She remained unemployed while she coordinated their cross-country move and set up their new home. Emily moved with Brad to the West Coast when he was offered a position with a technology company. She refrained from searching for work when they arrived to stay home with their newborn. Liz and Hank remained at their original jobs in their original city. They agreed to table any conversations about Liz changing jobs or Hank returning to school for at least a year.

At Time 3, tending traditional couples did their best to live their lives within a gender-unequal and power-imbalanced work-family ecosystem. They made peace with their decisions and tried to express contentment with their neotraditional outcomes even though they had not set up or advanced both partners' careers as they had hoped to do at Time 1. This process was straightforward for men, who felt positively about their careers and relationships, but was more complex for women, who continued to rationalize pausing their careers to support men's careers while keeping the relationship together. Men's and women's commitment to making their relationships work, despite their neotraditional division of labor or imbalance in career importance, contributed to the persistence of gender inequality in work and family.

At Time 3, men expressed satisfaction with their professional outcomes. Social scientist Brad, who changed fields and got a job with a technology company, said, "This is great. It's stimulating work." Joseph, who found work with a biotechnology company, said, "I'm very happy. There's a lot of things to learn about the biotech industry and there's definitely room for advancement. It's definitely a good place to be, straight out of grad school." Such comments were unsurprising, as men launched professional careers at Time 3, as they had hoped at Time 1.

Men also agreed that *the couple* got a satisfactory outcome overall, even though many commented that *their partners* did not necessarily get the career outcomes they wanted. Joseph, for instance, acknowledged that scientist Rebecca's unemployment was not ideal for her. Yet he did not dwell on this fact and felt content with the couple's new chapter in life:

> I don't think much could have happened better. You know, maybe if Rebecca had a job by now, [that] would have been a little bit better because there's not really much to do here at home by herself every day. But in our situation, it wouldn't be necessary. A second income for savings [would be nice]—but it wasn't a huge deal [for her not] to start applying the second we got here.

Joseph thought their outcome was good overall because they were financially stable, even with just his income. Yet rating their outcome based solely on the household's economic well-being minimized Rebecca's professional and emotional well-being as an individual.

Women reported more ambivalence at Time 3 regarding what Pamela Stone and Meg Lovejoy call "privileged domesticity,"[24] upper-class families' ability to financially maintain a nonworking wife at home. On the one hand, many were still coming to terms with the suspended state of their careers. On the other hand, women took pleasure in not working. Scientist Rebecca highlighted both feelings as she reflected on her unemployment:

> It's been weird for me not to be working when I'm perfectly capable of working. And I want to work if I'm not doing anything else 'cause it's boring after a while. Then there's kind of the question of, "how long am I allowed to not be working?" because, you know, I'm able to work. He's supporting me for no reason, really. But breaks come so seldom in your working life so, yeah, I kind of want a break, just because I can.

Rebecca found it "weird" and "boring" and even expressed guilt to not be working. Yet she framed her unemployment positively by calling it a "break," a desirable opportunity given the scarcity of time off for professionals and Joseph's ability to afford her privileged domesticity.

Liz, who stopped searching for a more senior role because her partner Hank was not ready to leave his job, also noted that returning to her data analyst position and not pushing so hard for advancement in her career afforded her more time for leisure:

> I decided to stay with [the data analyst position] for a little while. It wasn't exactly what I wanted to do. The money wasn't exactly what I would have liked. But I think it was the right move. Hank and I made some plans for a month-long trip and [if I were just starting a new role] they obviously wouldn't be happy with me leaving for an entire month.

Despite being dissatisfied with her current role and its pay level (and later questioning whether it was professionally and financially worth it for her to have gone back to school), Liz convinced herself that pausing her career pursuits and returning to her original job was "the right move" because it gave the couple more flexibility to take an extended vacation.

One especially rewarding facet of privileged domesticity for some women was their ability to fully immerse themselves in the pleasures of at-home motherhood. Emily, who left her museum career to move to the West Coast with Brad and stay home with their newborn, bluntly said, "For me, this probably wasn't the best thing. I probably shot my career in the face." At the same time, Emily found deep meaning in full-time motherhood:

> There were a lot of positives, but it's got to be the baby. I mean [the baby is] pretty great. I literally can't imagine not being here with [the baby]. It's not an option that I expected to have. It's an option that I'm glad I have. I honestly didn't feel that [I would] be able to manage that. Thinking about how after three months [of maternity leave] ended, I'd have to go back to work. . . . I mean staying home is challenging and all that stuff, but actually, generally speaking it's a lark. It's fun. It's work, but it's so much fun.

Women could be genuinely happy fulfilling the role of a full-time at-home parent. The problem was the dearth of options for maintaining a career that they could return to on their own terms. Remember that Emily's ideal at Time 1 was to take a parental leave, return to part-time work, and then gradually transition back to full-time work. All-or-nothing professional workplaces are not structured to support such flexibility.[25] Although professional employees may have access to parental leave, they may not be fully paid or be as long as some may want. Further, part-time work is generally unavailable or deeply stigmatized in professions that valorize overwork. Without formal supports to facilitate this work-family pathway, women like Emily had to stop working to enjoy full-time motherhood.

Finally, this individualized response to a societal shortcoming reinforced gender inequality by making women materially dependent on men. Being a stay-at-home mother put women at risk of experiencing several negative consequences in the broader context of a capitalist society. Research suggests that interrupted labor force attachment, more common for women than for men, slows professional growth partly because hiring managers view employment gaps negatively.[26] Women's time away from work could weaken their earnings potential,[27] leading to economic risk for the household if men lose their jobs. If couples break up or get divorced, women without labor force attachment risk being unable to financially support themselves and their children,[28] as women are more likely to get custody when couples separate.[29] Whether or not tending traditional partners knew about these risks, many like Brad insisted at Time 3 that women were not so disempowered by the couple's decision that they would not be able to continue their career pursuits again soon:

> [Emily] could pick up freelancing. I try to help her when I can. I've talked to some people at work about her [research]. Yeah, she seems pretty happy to work from home. The explicit agreement was she would try it—then reassess.

Brad's optimism about freelancing (unfortunately ill-founded) and his assumption that Emily could go back to full-time work if she wanted would dissipate by Time 4,[30] five years after couples entered this neo-traditional work-family ecosystem.

TIME 4: CHALLENGES TO RELAUNCHING WOMEN'S CAREERS AND SHARING WORK RESPONSIBILITIES

At Time 4, tending traditional couples had soured on their gender-imbalanced division of labor. However, feedback between couples' past actions and their subsequent workplace landscapes created many challenges to relaunching women's professional activities and partners' equal sharing of all other responsibilities. Emily built up a small freelancing portfolio but primarily stayed home with her and Brad's two children. Brad changed teams and transferred to another company office in a different city. He earned $210,000 annually in salary, not including yearly bonuses. After a year of unemployment and another year as a temporary contractor, Rebecca secured a permanent research associate position at the same company where Joseph worked. She earned $93,000 a year in salary, the highest salary of any tending traditional woman, but just over half of what her husband Joseph earned in their field. Joseph had moved up from associate scientist to scientist at his biotechnology company and had recently joined a new company as a senior scientist making $165,000 annually. The couple co-parented an eighteen-month-old child. Liz was laid off from her data analyst position and decided to start her own business. Hank continued at his finance firm, making $88,000 plus major bonuses every year. The couple had broken up recently, after going to couples' counseling to try to resolve their problems. The other tending traditional couples' five-year trajectories and Time 4 outcomes appear in table 4.2.

These eventful trajectories, particularly women's shifts from unemployment back into school and work, masked some couples' sentiments of being "stuck" in a power-imbalanced, neotraditional work-family equilibrium. Despite eventually finding work to continue their original careers or pursuing more education to start new ones, these women's professional activities were "tethered" to men's established careers and their children's needs.[31] But men also felt stuck, tied to their jobs to provide their families a certain level of income and access to benefits like health insurance and childcare. For other couples, these trajectories only began to hint at the process of how becoming unstuck from neotraditionalism could involve breaking up.

Women's return to school and work in the five years between Time 3 and Time 4 did not mean that couples stopped leaning traditional in how they thought about gender, careers, and caregiving or in their actual division of labor. Emily and Brad, the most extreme example, largely maintained the husband-earner/wife-caregiver arrangement they had established at Time 3. Although Emily eventually built a freelance portfolio with a handful of clients, her work was not a major source of income for the couple and was limited to the times when their first child was at school and their second child was with a hired nanny. Rather, Emily was primarily responsible for the couple's domestic work and childcare, and Brad was tasked to maintain his career as a data scientist to provide their growing family with income and health insurance.

TABLE 4.2   TENDING TRADITIONAL COUPLES' FIVE-YEAR TRAJECTORIES AND TIME 4 OUTCOMES

Partners & occupations at Time 3	Five-year trajectory	Time 4
Emily, at-home parent Brad, data scientist	She continued as at-home parent He continued as data scientist & transferred offices Remained married & continued living together after moving to new city for his transfer Had 2nd child	She continued as at-home parent (no salary) He continued as a data scientist ($210,000) Remained married & continued living together
Mindy, unemployed Bryan, temporary professor	She started working as teacher, then stopped working to start MS program He became permanent professor at his university Got engaged & then married	She was finishing her MS (no salary) He continued as professor ($90,000) Remained married & continued living together Expecting 1st child
Rebecca, unemployed Joseph, associate scientist	She started contract position, then became permanent research associate at Joseph's firm He moved up to scientist, then advanced to senior scientist at 2nd firm Remained married & continued living together Had their 1st child; she took 6 months' paid and unpaid leave, while he took 8 weeks' paid leave	She continued as research associate ($93,000) He continued as senior scientist ($165,000) Remained married & continued living together Co-parented 1 child

Couple		
Leslie, unemployed Andrew, defense professional	She started working as social worker, then stopped working to start PhD program He continued as defense professional & transferred offices, stopped working to start MPA program, then started as government auditor Remained married & continued living together after moving to new city for his transfer, then moving up to new city for her PhD program	She continued as PhD student ($30,000) He became startup manager ($60,000) Remained married & continued living together
Liz, data analyst Hank, finance professional	She was laid off, then started her own business He continued as finance professional Couple broke up	She continued her small business (salary not given) She began dating new partner He continued as finance professional ($88,000) He remained single
Cheryl, postdoc Gordon, BSN student	She completed her postdoc, then started as professor He completed BSN, then started as medical practitioner The couple divorced after moving to new city for her professor job	She continued as professor ($56,000) She began dating new partner He continued as medical practitioner ($64,000) He remained single
Lauren, unemployed Thomas, law clerk	She started working as teacher, moved to start program director job, then stopped working to move for PhD program She began dating new partner He completed his clerkship, then started as associate lawyer He briefly dated new partner but broke up with her	She continued as a PhD student ($27,000) She continued dating her new partner He continued as associate lawyer ($230,000) He remained single

BSN = bachelor of science in nursing

Neither partner was happy with this arrangement, as it was *too* gender specialized. Brad said, "Neither of us set out to have very traditional gender roles in our home." Emily elaborated:

> He feels crushed by being solely responsible for us financially, and not just for things like our day-to-day, "How are we going to pay the rent? Do we have enough money for groceries in the checking account?" but also things like, "Do we have retirement plans? Do we have savings?" He does feel overwhelmed by it. And I get depressed because we're dependent on him, because I'm dependent on him. I get very depressed about that, especially since the job I have right now, taking care of the kids, is one that Brad could do, but his job is not one I could do. And that makes me feel like there is a power imbalance in our relationship. I wish that we didn't have the financial imbalance, the power imbalance. It bugs me, it bugs Brad, it bugs us for the same reason. It's not what we're used to, it's not what we wanted, and we don't like it.

In contrast to the positive evaluations Emily and Brad had given five years before at Time 3 regarding their gender-traditional career and family arrangement, their opinions about neotraditionalism at Time 4 were decidedly negative. In particular, Emily recognized that their arrangement strained Brad as the sole earner for the family and damaged her own independence and power in the relationship. Neither person expected that the actions they took at Time 2 to establish men's careers and women's caregiving roles would create such a lasting imprint on their relationship.

Yet the partners could not think of anything else they could do and therefore felt stuck with their division of labor. As Brad put it, "We found ourselves in that position and we can't think of better solutions, so we continue to do this." Emily revealed that the couple's high level of economic security discouraged them from disturbing their gender-unequal equilibrium:

> It isn't exactly the relationship either of us envisioned or would want if you asked us, but it works for us right now. It's a very good problem to have, that only one of you is working because you can manage on one income. It's a fortunate problem to have, and just—if that's your big problem, then you're not doing so bad.

Emily accepted the gender inequality in her relationship by framing their gendered power imbalance as a "fortunate problem." Brad's career could afford them privileged domesticity while their youngest child was still nursing (recall these couples' belief that infants *need* their mothers). Consequently, even though it created an unequal power dynamic in their marriage, Emily could not imagine practical alternatives to their neotraditional arrangement.

Brad also felt stuck as the primary earner in their relationship because the couple did not want to give up the excellent health-care benefits his company provided to their family:

> [Our younger child] ended up needing a surgery right after birth, and that was a chronic thing. He still needs another one. [That] has been a real limit for me because I can't move somewhere that doesn't have good health insurance to let us deal with this.

Though many professional workplaces offer high-quality health insurance, Brad considered theirs especially good and would not cede this benefit to disrupt the inequality in his relationship.

Even tending traditional couples who eventually came closer to evening out career imbalances felt stuck with some lingering gender inequalities in their relationship. Couples were hesitant to alter the day-to-day routines that worked for them. Consider how Joseph's career decisions continued creating parameters around Rebecca's career. After leaving her lab to allow Joseph to pursue an out-of-state job, Rebecca remained unemployed for nearly a full year before getting a short-term contract position at Joseph's company. Eventually she landed a full-time, permanent position there. But now she lagged behind Joseph in her career due to her disrupted work history and lack of upward opportunities as a contract employee. (Remember, ironically, that the couple believed at Time 1 that Rebecca had a leg up over Joseph in getting a job due to her degree and work experience.) Still, for a while, both partners carpooled to the same office and after returning from their parental leaves sent their child to the company's on-site day care. These classed privileges gave Rebecca and Joseph access to egalitarianism for some time. However, Joseph had recently changed jobs to take a more senior role at a different company. Initially supportive of Joseph's pursuits, Rebecca later came to grapple with a different kind of "stuck feeling" regarding her ability to advance professionally given Joseph's career moves:

> That was kind of like a slow-realization-shock because I was realizing that if I leave [the biotechnology company to take a better position] then we have to leave the day care immediately. So, it became this stuck feeling. Joseph left his job first, so that puts me in the position of being tied to the day care. So now, all my decisions—about whether I like the job or not, whether I want a new job—have this extra weight to them. Well, do I want it enough to uproot the baby and have to figure out a whole new day-care situation? I wouldn't

have to do it on my own, but it's just tied to that instability [of leaving this
job]. I mean, we weren't really thinking about it at the time, and I think, ret-
roactively, I did get a little upset at him that he didn't foresee that. But that's
just how it worked out and I wouldn't have wanted him to stay, seeing how
he felt [about his lack of growth opportunities]. So, it was just an unfortunate side effect of the situation.

Childcare provided on-site at work was a major benefit allowing both
Rebecca and Joseph to continue their careers. This benefit now tied Rebecca to her job because Joseph had left the company. With workers
increasingly needing to change organizations to move up in their careers,[32] Rebecca's wariness about leaving her job and thus their child's
high-quality, convenient day care became a challenge to her career advancement. Given their two high incomes, the partners were arguably
well positioned to afford a different high-quality day-care facility if
Rebecca wanted to leave the biotech company. But the partners considered it risky to give up this convenient childcare setup given the weak
childcare infrastructure in the United States and the resulting dearth of
attractive options for American parents.[33] In short, tending traditional
couples' class privileges—men's professional jobs that provided couples
high incomes and numerous material benefits and women's "free childcare"—created a gilded cage that prevented some couples from changing their neotraditional equilibrium.

Yet this gilded cage was still a cage. These "stuck" feelings led five of
the seven tending traditional couples to go to couples' counseling to address the unhappiness in their relationships (none of the consistent compromisers or autonomous actors reported going to couples' counseling).
For example, Liz, the data analyst, and Hank, the finance professional,
started going to couples' counseling a year after Liz returned to her
original job. Dissatisfied with the way the partners "would have conversations about the future and what our life together would look like"
after Liz yielded her career goals to Hank's, she sought professional help
for the couple. She hoped an outside moderator could facilitate concrete planning to move the partners toward a more equal prioritization
of their careers. When that issue got worked out, she reasoned, they
could both feel more certain about getting married and raising a child
together.

Although therapy is an immensely valuable (and again, classed) resource for partners grappling with these relationship issues, it is an individualized solution that cannot always overcome the systemic problem
that caused these relationship troubles in the first place. If consistently

supportive workplace contexts, partners' steadfast attitudes about gender egalitarianism, and men's and women's coordinated efforts all need to come together for couples to maintain gender equality in work and family, couples' counseling targeting joint action alone could not disrupt the gendered career imbalance in Liz and Hank's relationship, because gender inequality persisted in their work contexts and in their broader attitudes about careers and family.

After returning to her data analyst job and starting couples' counseling, Liz was laid off from her company. This layoff was directly related to widespread Great Recession–era budget cuts in the public sector, where women are disproportionately concentrated.[34] Hank, working in the private, masculinized finance sector, stayed employed. These gendered economic conditions forced Liz and Hank into even more gender-imbalanced positions in their already deteriorating relationship. In response to Liz's layoff, the partners took mismatched actions reflecting the gendered "Plan B's" described in Kathleen Gerson's research.[35] Liz began building an independent life while Hank, drawing again on existing cultural frameworks for gender, work, and family, leaned even further into neotraditionalism.

Having long aspired to work as a director of an organization, Liz saw her layoff as an opportunity to start her own business. In reflection, she came to realize that building an independent business was related to becoming independent from Hank:

> It was around that time that the business was starting—and in retrospect I don't even think I realized I was doing it—but I started to emotionally check out, just started to feel like, "I'm just going to do whatever I want and I'm not going to worry about you." And I really focused on the business without really sharing. Hank was certainly very supportive of the business, but I didn't include him in conversations about the business. I didn't consult him when I was making plans for the business. I was thinking, "I'm going to stop asking [Hank to make joint career plans with me] because I've been asking for years and I don't feel it's helpful. I'm just going to move forward with my professional development. You let me know when you're ready [to talk about advancing our careers together]." Then over the course of a year or two, that just happened more and more, to the point where I realized that we weren't even in a relationship anymore.

Instead of continuing to put her career plans on hold to allow Hank to advance in his company, Liz opted this time to independently carry out her professional advancement activities without Hank's input. Note, however, that Liz still thought Hank was "very supportive" of her business when she first launched it. This "support" was mostly financial. Hank fully committed himself to a breadwinner role when Liz lost her job. Given that the couple had previously talked about getting married and wanting children in the future, Hank thought Liz's layoff meant that he would be responsible for providing the partners that type of family life on his income alone:

> I was thinking like, "Okay. If I'm still at this [company], maybe they bump [my salary] up to $95,000 in five years. Maybe I'll take the class and try to make a lot more. Then, we can have a kid, buy a bigger house." That was my thought for my job, trying to take on more responsibility. The health care is good, which is important. She was on my health insurance—that was important to me. I was trying to have that stable job and let Liz figure out what she was doing. Then, I was supporting [Liz's business]. I gave them money. I totally was like, "I will support you guys, I will give you some money."

When Liz became unemployed, Hank assumed he needed to step up at work to ensure the couple had continued access to income and health insurance, especially if they wanted a house and a child. Even though he complained throughout his interview that his "high-stress job" in the financial sector constantly had him "staying really late," Hank's career also allowed him to give Liz some money to start up her business. Yet Hank never offered the other type of support Liz wanted: emotional investment in her career plans. Liz wanted Hank to take her professional goals seriously and make interdependent dual-career plans with her. Using different frameworks to understand their situation—Liz wanting to grow professionally alongside Hank after forgoing opportunities for years, and Hank wanting to "take care" of Liz during a time of employment instability—hampered the partners' ability to take coordinated actions to maintain a dual-career relationship. Eventually, Liz ended her decade-long relationship with Hank. More information about what happened to Liz and Hank after breaking up, as well as what happened to other partners who dissolved their relationships, appears in chapter 5.

Of the three tending traditional couples that broke up or divorced after trying to resolve their relationship problems, none had children. Perhaps having children made it harder for partners to separate,[36] even if they were unhappy with their career imbalance. Women certainly valued motherhood, and at least for some couples, fatherhood provided men a chance to enact more equitable sharing. Rather than leaving all childcare to women to maximize their time at work as some research might suggest they would do,[37] these men took on many parenting responsibilities, which women appreciated. Joseph, for example, surprised

Rebecca with his involved parenting even though she assumed his work would come first in relative terms:

> Before we had the baby, I was thinking that maybe taking care of a baby would be more the mother's job. I don't know if I was expecting that men don't do that much, that this is going to be me by myself. And now I see that hasn't been my reality, so I've definitely moved my thinking to, "yes, it should be 50/50 or Joseph can do even more." And that's all right with me and he's doing a great job. He does all the bath times and I think [the baby] kind of favors him in a lot of senses. So, he definitely is very happy to spend a lot of time with her and on the weekends, he'll take her on multiple walks and I can stay at home and get some relaxing time of doing whatever—to the point where sometimes I'm like, "I probably am not doing as much as him."

Rebecca and Joseph's biotech company offered both parents fully paid leave for eight weeks. During this time, the partners reported doing all housework and childcare together. Their story shows that workplaces that make egalitarianism in domestic labor a "reality" via policies like parental leave can shift people's attitudes about caregiving to "yes, it should be 50/50."

Similarly, Brad, who worked for a technology company, enjoyed his children and tried his best to participate in their home life. He made a consistent effort to come home early for family dinners and to relieve Emily from childcare in the evenings and weekends: "I'm very strict about, 'I'm home for dinner four nights a week. I'm at breakfast five days a week. No [work] all weekend.'" Though planning to remain the family's sole earner, Brad spoke at Time 4 about arranging to work from home more frequently to spend more time with his children. These desires may stem from increasingly salient cultural norms promoting involved fatherhood.[38] Such demonstrations of striving for equality, at least with childcare, potentially helped to keep these relationships intact despite the partners' gendered imbalances in their careers. Such patterns indicate that, as we saw in the previous chapter about autonomous actors, people can view gender egalitarianism in careers as separate from gender egalitarianism in the family.[39]

VARIATION ON THE TENDING TRADITIONAL PATHWAY

One exceptional case stood out on the tending traditional pathway. Leslie and Andrew's story reveals that, given sufficient structural support for two careers, a major shift in men's cultural attitudes toward work and relationships could spur joint action to take couples off a tending traditional work-family trajectory.

Long-distance spouses Andrew, a defense industry professional, and Leslie, a social science MA student aspiring to complete a PhD and pursue a research career, shared experiences with the other tending traditional couples from Time 1 to Time 3. At Time 1, they considered it important for Andrew to advance within his organization, which required frequent travel and relocation to move up. They believed Leslie's plans to finish her schooling and launch her career were flexible enough to fit within these parameters. At Time 2, Leslie, like the other tending traditional women, agreed to pause her career pursuits to end the couple's long-distance situation:

> I feel a lot from Andrew that he just, he really needs me. I feel needed in some ways and that's probably part of what's bringing me back to [his city]. I mean he's totally supportive of me, but if he was more supportive of me going and getting a job and working somewhere I would totally do it, but he's not really. He really wants me to come move back to [his city].

Andrew's high-intensity job often left him physically and psychologically drained. Given cultural expectations that tie women to caregiving, Andrew expressed little support for Leslie to seek employment and prepare her PhD applications, and instead pressed that he "needed" her to provide emotional support to him as he finished this challenging work assignment. Without any professional or educational opportunities that suited her career goals in their very small city, Leslie became unemployed at Time 3 while Andrew continued to advance his career.

At Time 4, unlike the other couples on this pathway, Andrew and Leslie had disrupted their power-imbalanced neotraditional division of labor. They were living in a new city where Leslie was pursuing her PhD. For the moment, Leslie had the lead career and Andrew was working in a new occupational sector within those parameters. The threat of divorce between Time 3 and Time 4 had spurred this major shift in this couple's work-family equilibrium.

After two years of unemployment and then underemployment, as well as another cross-country move for Andrew's career and ongoing marital conflict, Leslie began making her own independent plans to apply for her PhD:

> We were actually having some pretty serious marriage problems at the time. Originally my thought was, I'm going to apply to schools where Andrew could potentially be working so that I could do my PhD while he was

working. Then, because I didn't know exactly what was going on with us [in our marriage], I was just going to apply to everything and see what stuck and then see if we could figure it out. I think in the back of my head, because things were so rough for us in the moment, I was like, I need to just go ahead and apply and then see where the cards fall.

Like Liz, the data analyst described previously, Leslie started making plans to pursue her professional goals without accounting for her partner's career. As in the case of Liz and Hank, the combination of Leslie's subpar employment and Andrew and Leslie's relationship troubles led Leslie to make a "Plan B" for independence.

Andrew's response to this situation differed from Hank's response, though. Instead of leaning harder into neotraditionalism to try to "take care" of Leslie during this difficult time in their marriage, Andrew considered it necessary to change his working conditions to preserve his relationship:

> When we started seeing a therapist it was a time to really open up, and that influenced our decision to leave [this company]. It was like, I don't know if she could ultimately trust me when I was constantly traveling. It was just easy to be generally dishonest because of time away from each other. When I knew that I didn't really have a future with her, that was totally important [for the decision to leave my job]. If I would have stayed, I might still be covering up stuff or whatever. I would have been ultra-unhappy. It was a lot easier to just be open and transparent with each other [if I left this job].

Andrew's organization had what Jennifer Berdahl and her coauthors call a masculinity contest culture,[40] in which behaviors like putting work first, aggressive risk-taking, and sexual conquest are valorized. These norms began seeping into the partners' interactions and led Leslie to question "if I wanted to be in my relationship with Andrew at all." The possibility of getting divorced shifted how important Andrew considered his career to be. He prioritized his marriage to Leslie, which contrasted with the logics of the other men on the tending traditional pathway. Whereas others believed that excelling as a breadwinner with a specific type of career would be good for the relationship, regardless of whether women felt similarly, Andrew thought that leaving this line of work would be best for their marriage and would "enable Leslie to do this thing that she wanted to do, go back and get a PhD."

With a new joint plan to give Leslie power to shape the conditions of their lives, the partners moved to a new city close to their extended family where Leslie would start training in the PhD program of her choice.

Andrew did not completely abandon his career pursuits with this move, however. Leslie's university had a graduate program that could translate Andrew's previous professional experience into a career in a new sector. His former employer also had an educational benefit plan that helped Andrew pay for this degree. After finishing his graduate coursework and an internship, Andrew started a job with predictable hours and no travel in a local government office. These professional supports aligned with Andrew's desire "to be stable for her like she was for me" and facilitated his ability to demonstrate his commitment "to really support Leslie while she's studying and doing field research and doing all that stuff."

Andrew's attitudes about the importance of maintaining a family unit and his active support of Leslie's career steered the couple off the tending traditional pathway. However, with Leslie's graduation and job search on the horizon as well as the possibility of becoming parents, this couple's work-family equilibrium could shift again.

CONCLUSION

Although tending traditional couples planned to sequentially establish two careers, they ended up with a neotraditional division of labor or breaking up. Powerful cultural norms about gender, work, and family, exacerbated by men's unemployment and women's pregnancies, led partners to prioritize men's careers and women's caregiving over six years. Gender-complementary actions added up over time to create a greater power imbalance in partners' work-family ecosystems than they expected. Yet because neotraditionalism came with material benefits that were hard to give up, couples pressed on with these relationship arrangements. This trajectory reveals several factors continuing to stall the gender revolution in work and family.

Cultural scripts linking men to paid work and women to relationships and caregiving pose a persistent challenge to gender equality. The cultural norm tying careers to upper-middle-class masculinity posed an especially difficult barrier to equality for these couples. If men and women do not consider, or cannot imagine, other possibilities for themselves in work and family—and if our society at large does not ideologically support gender equality at work and at home—partners are likely to default to reproducing the gendered and unequal status quo.

Yet an expanded "cultural toolkit" with multiple blueprints for possible work-family arrangements also depends on material supports from workplaces and other social institutions.[41] Perhaps "Plan A" for egalitarianism would be more attainable if career opportunities were more available to both men and women. If high levels of economic security were guaranteed to everyone and not perceived by upper-middle-class families to be so tenuous,[42] perhaps men and women would not concede to accepting gender inequality in their relationships in exchange for comfortable incomes and benefits. Further, if it were easier to move in and out of full-time careers and full-time caregiving, and if it were more feasible to work fewer hours so that men and women could do more care work on a regular basis, couples might tend toward egalitarianism rather than gender traditionalism. Without these types of structural support, tending traditional couples perhaps had unrealistic expectations for achieving the dual-professional relationship they thought they could have. They did not foresee that temporarily interrupting women's careers, either for men's career opportunities or for childcare reasons, would be so detrimental to women's professional goals. Gender traditionalism among these highly educated couples may therefore be the result of misjudgments of structural challenges and what it takes to sustain a dual-professional relationship under our current societal conditions.

I elaborate on ideas for moving the gender revolution forward in chapter 6. But first, I provide a more focused comparison of the consistent compromisers, the autonomous actors, and the tending traditional couples in the next chapter. A side-by-side look at the workplace contexts, cultural attitudes, and couple-level interactions of these three trajectories highlights how all three pieces need to come together perfectly to achieve egalitarianism and the work-family outcomes the partners envisioned for themselves at the start.

## CHAPTER 5

Comparing Couples

Having told the stories of the consistent compromisers, the autonomous actors, and the tending traditional couples, I now compare the three pathways to highlight how favorable workplace contexts, unwavering attitudinal support for gender equality in work and family, and partners' coordinated actions needed to align perfectly to produce sustained egalitarianism over time. Then, to show how taking different pathways mattered, I compare the work and family outcomes of the couples in the short term (Time 3, one year after baseline) and in the longer term (Time 4, five to six years after baseline). Finally, I discuss how broader gender inequalities produced key similarities within gender in men's and women's work-family stories regardless of the pathway they traveled.

WHO TAKES WHICH PATHWAY?

Chapters 2, 3, and 4 detailed how different configurations of workplace conditions; cultural attitudes toward gender, work, and family; and partners' interactions came together to produce the three work-family pathways. Even though there could be other factors at play that channeled couples down these three trajectories, several background characteristics were *not* sufficient on their own to reliably distinguish consistent compromisers, autonomous actors, and tending traditional couples. Table 5.1 displays the characteristics of the couples at Time 1 when men and women began their job searches. Partners across the three work-family pathways

TABLE 5.1   TIME 1 BASELINE CHARACTERISTICS

	Consistent compromisers (N = 8)	Autonomous actors (N = 6)	Tending traditional couples (N = 7)
Individual characteristics			
Average age of partners (range 22–35)	28 years	28 years	28 years
Relationship characteristics			
# of married couples	5 (63%)	1 (17%)	4 (57%)
Average relationship length	6 years	4 years	6 years
Average marriage length	3 years	0.5 years	2 years
# of long-distance couples	3 (38%)	3 (50%)	1 (14%)
# of couples that wanted children in the future	6 (75%)	5 (83%)	7 (100%)
Professional characteristics			
# of couples in which partners were in same field	4 (50%)	2 (33%)	2 (29%)

were, on average, twenty-eight years old at the beginning of the study. Recall also that most participants were White, and that most were recruited from elite graduate degree programs. Although age, race, and social class shaped these partners' paths into my study of dual-professional couples, these factors did not differentiate where they traveled over the course of the research.

The demographic factors that did vary across the three trajectories were the couples' specific relationship and professional characteristics. Autonomous actors were much less likely to be married and were in their relationships for a slightly shorter length of time than the couples on the other two trajectories. I detailed in chapter 3 how being unmarried may have made partners more inclined to favor independent decision-making and therefore more likely to travel down the autonomous actor pathway. Still, as described in chapters 2 (consistent compromisers) and 4 (tending traditional couples), being married did not send couples down the same work-family trajectories, because partners attributed different meanings to marriage. Consistent compromisers saw marriage as a promise to always assign equal importance to each person's career in any decision that affected the couple. Tending traditional couples, on the other hand, saw marriage as a guarantee that the couple would even out any short-term inequalities between the partners over time. They were more comfortable prioritizing one partner's career goals at a time because they (perhaps overoptimistically) believed they could focus on the other partner's professional pursuits next.

Tending traditional couples were the least likely to be in long-distance relationships at Time 1 and the most likely to want children in the future (recall that all couples were child free at the start of the study). This stronger aversion to long-distance relationships and stronger desire for children reflected more traditional values surrounding relationships and families that were characteristic of the couples who took the tending traditional pathway.

Finally, partners on the consistent compromiser pathway were the most likely to work in the same field. Still, only half of these couples were made up of partners in the same line of work. I described in chapter 2 that this work-related characteristic was an advantage that likely helped couples maintain two equally important careers and therefore put them on the consistent compromiser trajectory. Nonetheless, there were couples in which both partners worked in the same field on the other two pathways, indicating that this characteristic alone could not explain which trajectory the partners would experience.

What *did* predict which trajectories the couples experienced was the specific combination of workplace conditions, cultural attitudes, and joint actions. Take the stories of consistent compromisers Nora and Rick and tending traditional couple Rebecca and Joseph, for instance. Remember that Nora and Rick were both scientists and had been married for two years when they joined the study. Nora was looking for postdoctoral research positions at universities where Rick was interviewing for faculty jobs. Rebecca and Joseph also both worked in the natural sciences and had been married for about two years at the time of their first interviews. This couple also tried applying to jobs in the same set of target cities with the hope of finding work for both partners. Despite seeming so similar at Time 1, these couples traveled down very different paths based on unique configurations of workplace circumstances, cultural attitudes, and partners' joint actions.

Rick secured multiple job offers at Time 2, several months into the partners' job searches, whereas Joseph continued to be unemployed. With these work-related conditions at play, Rick and Joseph expressed different attitudes about what to do next.

> *Rick:* It boiled down to quality of life and opportunities for Nora, so we
> are going to [a southern university]. . . . My original inclination was [a

mid-Atlantic university] because they gave me a lot more money, but you know, it was not the department for us because they didn't know what to do with the request that I made for a spousal hire [for Nora].

Joseph: We had thought about that [other job search strategies], especially when I applied to a bunch of jobs and hadn't heard anything . . . but . . . I wouldn't want to not work—I couldn't do that. I don't know, there's sort of the breadwinner mentality, like, "males make the money" [whereas] she's completely fine about not having work.

Rick's career decision at Time 2 hinged on what was best for Nora's career. Rick even insisted that he would "be happy to go as the spousal hire" himself if Nora got a good opportunity elsewhere to advance her career: "What's the problem with that? I have very little—and I think that I told her that—that I have very little ties to any lab, and I will move." In contrast, Joseph's professional choices were influenced by a "breadwinner mentality" in which "males make the money." Rick stayed consistent in his attitudes toward a dual-career partnership, but Joseph expressed even stronger traditionalism in his ideas about work and masculinity than he did at Time 1 in response to his employment situation.

Nora and Rebecca stayed on the same page as their husbands in their attitudes, with Nora continuing to endorse egalitarianism and Rebecca downplaying her own feelings about the risks of neotraditionalism. With these shared attitudes in place, the partners in each couple took coordinated action to execute their plans. Nora and Rick picked a job for Rick in a location where Nora had postdoc opportunities as well as an opportunity to interview for a permanent job in the future. This choice helped maintain an equal balance of power across Nora and Rick, as the partners placed equal importance on each person's career. In contrast to Nora and Rick's joint egalitarian actions, Rebecca and Joseph took gender-complementary actions. Rebecca left her job to follow Joseph as he pursued work with an out-of-state employer. This choice created a power imbalance across Rebecca and Joseph, as his career was prioritized over hers.

Although employment conditions contributed to couples' journeys down different paths, workplace contexts alone could not differentiate couples across trajectories without cultural attitudes and partners' joint actions coming into play. Consider the story of consistent compromisers Vanessa and Alex. Like Nora and Rick and Rebecca and Joseph, Vanessa and Alex both wanted careers in the natural sciences. Although not married at the start of the study, Vanessa and Alex were engaged at Time 1. Like Joseph on the tending traditional pathway, Alex also faced continued unemployment at Time 2, months into his job search. However, whereas Joseph responded to his unemployment by asserting the importance to him of pursuing a specific type of job, Alex emphasized the importance of allowing Vanessa to continue working when reassessing his options:

> I didn't get any [academic] offers [near our targeted mid-Atlantic city] at all and so I shifted my attention completely to finding work in the private sector. I looked for nothing outside of [our targeted city]. . . . It has the right kind of jobs, and Vanessa lives there. She already has a job there and we were planning to move in together and so it was just—I am not going to find something somewhere else because I don't want to.

In contrast to Joseph's attitude that his wife Rebecca would be "completely fine about not having work," Alex's attitude was that his fiancée Vanessa "already has a job" that he would not want her to give up. Expressing different attitudes about gender, work, and family, Joseph proceeded to keep pursuing a single type of job, but Alex shifted his job search strategy to look for different kinds of positions in his field. Remember that Rebecca and Vanessa both offered to quit their jobs in response to their partners' continued job searches. These couples ultimately took different paths when Joseph took Rebecca up on her offer, but Alex declined Vanessa's offer. In contrast to Joseph, Alex kept power imbalances in check by viewing Vanessa's career as just as important as his.

Another point of evidence indicating that work-related conditions were not the only factor differentiating the trajectories comes from comparing autonomous actors Julie and Max to consistent compromisers Nora and Rick. Like scientists Nora and Rick, Julie and Max worked in the same field as one another—they both wanted to be medical doctors. Further, both Nora and Julie were behind their partners in their training. Nora was looking to start a postdoc while Rick was finishing his, and Julie was applying to medical residencies while Max was partway through completing his. Both couples also theoretically had access to supportive workplace resources. Nora and Rick could use the spousal hiring policies that many universities offer to accommodate dual-career couples. Julie and Max could use a similar policy, couples matching, that hospitals put in place to hire medical resident couples. Yet the two couples ultimately traveled different paths based on whether men coordinated their job searches with their partners at Time 1:

> *Rick:* I am extremely clear and up front. I sat down [at each department that interviewed me], and the first thing I told the chair is, "I have a

wife that is in science, and if she doesn't have a future as a tenure track faculty [member] then you need to tell me right now because otherwise I wouldn't consider [taking the job]."

Max: I applied to a bunch of places: West Coast, East Coast, some in the Midwest. . . . Out of all the places I interviewed, I liked [the Mountain West institution] the best. Knowingly, it wasn't ideal for our relationship. . . . [I]t would have probably been better to go to places like [the East Coast] where there would be more programs for her to apply to . . . but it was the place I liked the best.

Rick negotiated job opportunities for Nora, directly asking his prospective employers about their spousal hiring policies. Max, on the other hand, as described in greater detail in chapter 3, never considered the possibility of using supportive dual-career policies available to him, like couples matching, and instead took independent action to build his own career without considering Julie's career. On the surface Rick and Max seemed to hold similar attitudes about women's careers. Rick stressed how important it was to him that Nora "go to where the best place is for her." Max similarly stated, "I'm supportive of [Julie] applying everywhere, and if she found a place she really wants to go more than anything, she should go." Yet these men differed in how they acted upon their attitudes in collaboration with their partners. Max's hands-off approach shifted the balance of power in his favor by creating extra coordination work for Julie. Rick's active negotiations to help Nora advance in her career kept the partners' burden of coordination work—and therefore power—balanced. As the stories of Rebecca and Joseph, Vanessa and Alex, Julie and Max, and Nora and Rick show, attitudes and actions came together with workplace conditions to determine couples' trajectories. These stories also show that, in line with quantitative research, *men's* work contexts, attitudes, and actions are particularly influential for what women and couples do.[1]

SHORT- AND LONG-TERM WORK-FAMILY OUTCOMES

Where do these trajectories lead in the short term and over the longer term? Does it matter whether couples take the consistent compromiser, the autonomous actor, or the tending traditional pathway? Table 5.2 shows the couples' work-family outcomes at Time 3, one year after the start of the study, and at Time 4, another five years later. Although the conclusions in this section cannot be extrapolated to represent the experiences of all dual-professional couples, they highlight key patterns that

TABLE 5.2 SHORT- AND LONG-TERM OUTCOMES AT TIME 3 AND TIME 4

	Consistent compromisers (N = 8)		Autonomous actors (N = 6)		Tending traditional couples (N = 7)	
	Time 3	Time 4	Time 3	Time 4	Time 3	Time 4
Relationship characteristics						
# of married couples	5 (63%)	8 (100%)	1 (17%)	4 (67%)	5 (71%)	4 (57%)
# of long-distance couples	0	1 (13%)	2 (40%)	0	0	0
# of couples that divorced/broke up	0	0	1 (17%)	2 (33%)	1 (14%)	3 (43%)
# of women with new partners	—	—	0	1 (50%)	0	3 (100%)
# of men with new partners	—	—	0	2 (100%)	0	0
# of couples with/expecting child	2 (25%)	5 (63%)	1 (17%)	3 (50%)	1 (14%)	3 (43%)
# of women lead parents	0	0	1 (100%)	2 (67%)	1 (100%)	1 (33%)
# of couples child free by choice	0	1 (13%)	1 (17%)	1 (17%)	0	0
Employment characteristics						
# of women employed full-time	8 (100%)	8 (100%)	4 (67%)	5 (83%)	2 (29%)	6 (86%)
# of women precariously employed	0	0	1 (17%)	0	2 (29%)	0
# of women unemployed/out of paid labor force	0	0	1 (17%)	1 (17%)	5 (71%)	1 (14%)
Women's median earnings	—	$120,000	—	$48,000	—	$41,500
Men's median earnings	—	$116,500	—	$64,500	—	$90,000

NOTE: Time 3 outcomes were measured 1 year from baseline. Time 4 outcomes were measured 5–6 years from baseline. Couples that broke up before Time 3 or before Time 4 were excluded from reports of the proportions of long-distance couples at each time point. Those in school or out of the labor force were included in median earnings calculations as earning $0.

should be tested in larger quantitative studies in the future. Importantly, these data cannot disentangle selection effects or determine causal direction. It is possible, and consistent with some recent research,[2] that taking the consistent compromiser pathway results in better financial outcomes because couples are more egalitarian. However, egalitarianism may be related to economic status in the opposite direction. For instance, consistent compromisers' higher earning potential might make these partners more committed to men's and women's equal participation in paid work. This section uses the qualitative patterns from this study to generate hypotheses that serve as a starting point for future quantitative research that can help us better understand selection and causal directionality.

Relationship Outcomes

Autonomous actors continued being the least likely to be married and were the only couples to be in long-distance relationships at Time 3. By Time 4, all eight consistent compromiser couples were married, but only four of six autonomous actor couples (67%) and four of seven tending traditional couples (57%) were married. Although getting married was not a priority for everyone, no one reported wanting to end their relationship at any point in the study. Yet two autonomous actor couples (33%) and three tending traditional couples (43%) broke up or got divorced by Time 4. Interestingly, among the five couples that ended their relationships, four of the women began new ones (80%), but only two of the men did the same (40%). The number of breakups is small and may not reflect the rate of relationship dissolution in the population. However, men's and women's experiences of this life event are informative for understanding the mechanisms linking work-family pathways to relationship outcomes, so I expand on this pattern later. For now, we see that relationship stability was highest on the consistent compromiser pathway (100% stayed together) and lower on the other two pathways.

Getting Their Desired Family Life

Table 5.1 shows that 75 percent of consistent compromisers, 83 percent of autonomous actors, and 100 percent of tending traditional couples wanted to have children at Time 1. Table 5.2 shows that by Time 3, two consistent compromisers had or were expecting a child (25%), compared to one autonomous actor couple (17%) and one tending traditional couple (14%). By Time 4, 63 percent of consistent compromisers had children or were expecting a child, but only 50 percent of autonomous actors and 43 percent of tending traditional couples reported the same. Note that whereas all consistent compromisers co-parented, women were lead parents in two of three (67%) autonomous actor couples by Time 4, though none of these women had imagined this arrangement at Time 1. One of the three (33%) tending traditional couples with or expecting a child had a woman lead parent. The expectant couple described going on parental leave at the same time, suggesting a desire to co-parent, and the remaining tending traditional couple co-parented and were pleasantly surprised by how much they liked this arrangement. Only one consistent compromiser couple and one autonomous actor couple opted to remain child free over the course of the study. Altogether, then, those on the consistent compromiser pathway were the most likely to get the family life they wanted over time.

Work-Related Outcomes

Turning to employment outcomes, consistent compromiser women had the highest rates of working full-time in both the short and long terms. All eight of these women maintained full employment at Times 3 and 4. Tending traditional women, in contrast, had the lowest rate of full-time employment (29%) and the highest rate of unemployment (71%) at Time 3. By Time 4, over 80 percent of women on both the autonomous actor and tending traditional pathways reported full-time employment (including going to school full-time), though one woman on each of these pathways was fully out of the labor force. Men across all pathways maintained full-time employment at both Time 3 and Time 4 (not shown). These gendered patterns of employment—men's consistent participation in full-time work across time and women's heterogeneous employment trajectories—mirror those found in larger quantitative studies.[3]

Finally, consistent compromiser men and women had the highest earnings at Time 4. Consistent compromiser women's average salary was $120,000, compared to $48,000 for autonomous actor women and $41,500 for tending traditional women. This stark difference was related to higher proportions of women in school or completely out of the labor force on these two latter pathways at Time 4. Consistent compromiser men's average salary at Time 4 was $116,500, compared to $64,500 for autonomous actor men and $90,000 for tending traditional men. Taking the salaries of men and women together, consistent compromiser households had the highest earnings out of all the couples because they were the most likely to be made up of two full-time working professionals. Further, the difference in men's and women's average salary, which serves as a measure of power imbalance, was much smaller for consistent compromisers ($3,500 in women's favor) than for autonomous actors ($16,500 in men's favor) or for tending traditional couples ($48,500 in men's favor).

This descriptive exploration suggests that the consistent compromisers had the most favorable outcomes in work and family life at Times 3 and 4. Although these data do not permit statistical testing, these patterns provide a starting point for hypothesis generation and tests of causality in future studies using quantitative, population-level data.

DIFFERENT PATHS LEAD TO THE SAME OUTCOME

Even though examining work-family outcomes can be instructive, considering outcomes on their own could mask crucial variation in the processes that led to them. For example, couples could end up with a neotraditional division of labor by taking the autonomous actor pathway or the tending traditional pathway. Take the story of autonomous actors Janelle and Stephen. When PhD student Stephen said at Time 2 that "we're just going to have to wait and see" about MA student Janelle continuing into a PhD program at a foreign university, Janelle responded to Stephen's noncommittal stance by abandoning her career plans. She assumed the couple would not be able to juggle his career, her career, and their new baby:

> I kind of let this slip to the back burner because we had so much going on the last couple of months, and you know, the trip [back to my university abroad] kind of fell through. I brought it up to Stephen and he was like, "Well, why haven't you gotten on this?" And I was like, "Well, I guess I just figured that we didn't have a whole lot of money and there were all these different reasons and it just wasn't going to be easy and affordable for us right now [with the baby coming]."

Without active support for her career from Stephen, Janelle "independently chose" to give up her PhD pursuits by Time 3 to support Stephen's career and their growing family. The partners maintained this neotraditional division of labor through Time 4 because Stephen continued to passively "allow" Janelle to "choose" stay-at-home motherhood rather than actively encouraging her to return to her career.

Tending traditional couple Emily and Brad took a more direct path to reach neotraditionalism. When Brad asserted at Time 2 "If I had the choice, I'd go to work," the couple proceeded to act on his explicit wishes. They established a husband-earner/wife-caregiver equilibrium by Time 3. Brad and Emily remained "stuck" in this neotraditional ecosystem through Time 4 despite disliking the power imbalance in their relationship. They were hesitant to disrupt an economic arrangement that worked well enough for them and to give up the convenience of "free childcare" Emily could provide the couple.

Likewise, couples could arrive at an egalitarian division of labor by taking the consistent compromiser or autonomous actor pathway. Reaching egalitarianism was more direct for consistent compromisers, as couples like Vanessa and Alex, the environmental scientists, continually worked together to secure and maintain two careers in the same location. Achieving two careers while keeping a relationship together on the autonomous actor pathway, in contrast, hinged on *women* doing the work to make it happen. Aspiring doctors Julie and Max were able to end their long-distance relationship and complete medical residencies at the same hospital because *Julie* put in an enormous amount of effort to match to Max's hospital. Considering Julie and Max's outcome alone overlooks the gender-unequal burden on women to build and maintain a dual-career partnership, which overlooks a gendered power imbalance stemming from inequality in who labors on behalf of the couple. Further, as Max grew more interdependent with Julie in building an equal dual earner-caregiver partnership in the five years between Time 3 and Time 4, it made a difference to examine their long-term pathway and not just consider a recent snapshot of their work and family equilibrium.

SAME ACTIONS, GENDERED RESULTS

Whereas the previous section demonstrates that different paths could lead to the same outcome, a comparison of the couples' stories also shows that men and women could take the same actions but experience different results. Consider what happened when men compromised on their ideal career plans compared to when women did. Consistent compromiser Alex changed his job application strategy from targeting academic positions to targeting private sector ones when it became clear he could not have his ideal career in the city where his fiancée Vanessa had already started hers. But because the couple targeted their applications to a city with many job opportunities for scientists in their field, Alex was able to maintain a career in environmental science research while enabling Vanessa to continue hers. Alex's compromise did not harm his career trajectory, as he insisted: "[Our targeted city] is a large enough area, and there's enough stuff in environmental and energy science that I should be able to find a job here. . . . If I expand even a little bit beyond academia, [our targeted city] is one of the best places I could be."

In contrast, when tending traditional partner Emily compromised on her ideal career plans to work in a museum, she ended up leaving her career altogether. Because her husband Brad pivoted from pursuing academic work in Europe to looking for technology sector work on the West Coast, in response to his lack of job offers, the couple was no longer going to a location that could support Emily's career. Given these circumstances, Emily worked on changing her feelings instead:

> I thought I'd be looking for work [in Europe], which would have been great. I'm still sorry we're not going there. . . . It made me feel really uncomfortable at first to feel like I was putting my husband's career first. [But] I try to encourage him as much as possible because it'll be good for him. . . . [H]e's got to go where the work is.

Even when women did not completely give up their careers, women who compromised on their ideal career plans had to work harder to stay employed in their fields. Autonomous actor Julie, for example, did extra work to arrange an away rotation at her partner Max's hospital to ensure a favorable outcome for her residency application at his institution. As Max's hospital was the only one with a residency program for Julie in the entire state, she could not simply apply to multiple programs nearby:

> The frustrating part is that places like [this Mountain West city] only have one program in the entire state—it didn't give me a lot of options for applying to different programs. The East Coast [would have been] a little easier just 'cause it's a little denser with programs. So, would [Max's hospital] be number one if Max wasn't there? I don't know.

These stories show that when men compromise on their ideal careers, they can still leverage external circumstances to work out in their favor because workplaces systematically advantage men. When women compromise on their ideal careers, however, because the landscape of work is systematically stacked against women, they have to either change their own feelings about pursuing a career, as the tending traditional women did, or work much harder to continue their careers, as we saw with autonomous actor women. These patterns support the argument raised in chapter 2 that gendered workplace barriers make it difficult for partners to maintain an equal balance of power in their relationship.

Now consider what it looked like for men and women to "support" their partners' careers. Across all pathways, women actively adjusted their career plans to facilitate their partners' career goals and keep the couple together. Consistent compromiser Vanessa, for example, refrained from applying to jobs across the country and targeted one mid-Atlantic city that worked for both her and Alex at Time 1. At Time 2, when Alex continued being unemployed, she offered to try to transfer to another office within her company or start a whole new job search in the southwestern city where Alex had a promising lead. Similarly, autonomous actor Julie prioritized Max's hospital in a Mountain West city for her residency while forgoing good training options in her specialty on the East Coast. She even arranged to work at Max's hospital to boost her application. Finally, tending traditional partner Rebecca only applied to jobs once Joseph got interviews at Time 1 and then quit her job to support his search when he remained unemployed at Time 2.

The only men who supported women's careers in a similarly active fashion were consistent compromiser men. For instance, Alex changed job search strategies at Time 2 to target private sector work in the couple's targeted mid-Atlantic city even though he could have pursued an academic opportunity in the Southwest. He reasoned that it would be unfair to ask Vanessa to move to a smaller city with limited career opportunities when he could easily find a job in his field if he simply expanded the types of jobs he would be willing to take.

Autonomous actor men and tending traditional men, on the other hand, supported their partners' careers in words but not actions, creating a power imbalance due to unequal investment in effort to support the couple. Remember that autonomous actor Max was "supportive of [Julie] applying everywhere" for residency at Time 1 but made no changes to his own career plans to make it easier for Julie to continue her career in the same place as him. Similarly, tending traditional partner Joseph said at Time 3 that he would be happier "if Rebecca had a job by now." But even after she gave up her job to support his out-of-state job search, Joseph did little to help Rebecca find a new one when they moved. He ultimately thought "it wouldn't be necessary" for her to work because he could "support" her financially on just his income.

In sum, gender shaped action in systematic ways. The same actions taken by women produced different results when they were taken by men. Additionally, "supporting" a partner's career looked different when men did the supporting compared to when women did it. The following section reveals the extent to which gender inequalities built into the workplace shaped men's and women's career experiences over the five years between Times 3 and 4.

GENDERED WORKPLACES

Across all pathways, women faced challenges at work that slowed their professional growth over the longer term. For example, remember that consistent compromiser Vanessa contended with an abusive boss, was passed over for important work assignments, and as a result changed jobs three times in five years. Chapter 2 showed that poor mentorship, overt harassment and subtle discrimination, and job churning were major factors that slowed other women's career growth compared to the men on the consistent compromiser pathway.

These barriers were not unique to consistent compromiser women. Autonomous actor and tending traditional women also reported these challenges. Consider how Cassandra, the aspiring professor on the autonomous actor pathway, received poor mentorship that ultimately drove her away from advancing her academic career. She reported at Time 4 that her relationship with her postdoc supervisor became strained when he "had basically given me negative feedback" for producing work targeting wider, nonacademic audiences on top of her scholarly research. Initially, she felt "guilty" about working on projects she was passionate about rather than spending all her energy on academic re-search. Eventually she became "disheartened" and "disenchanted" with the insular culture surrounding traditional academic careers. Therefore, she concluded that academia was not right for her and transitioned into a different kind of research role within higher education.

As Cassandra continued her story, she highlighted an additional factor that hindered women's careers across all pathways: economic disinvestment in the public and nonprofit sectors, where women are likely to be concentrated.[4] After working as a research analyst for a public college for several years, Cassandra's career stalled when her employer could not afford to promote her:

> I enjoyed my work at [the midwestern college], but it was a rocky time because funding higher education has been really thorny. Those years I had at [the midwestern college], they were really unstable. I was never threatened to be laid off or anything like that, but it really precluded me getting

promoted. There wasn't money to promote people like me, people who were performing at a higher level than their job description. I kind of hit this point where I was just very aware of the fact that I was being exploited because they were pretending I was working as an analyst but I was really a director, but there was no money to actually pay for a director. Money was short because our legislature has hacked away our tax revenue stream for several years.

Working in a state that had continually cut budgets for public education, Cassandra did the work of a director with neither the formal title nor the pay. This exploitative situation prompted Cassandra to leave the college even though she liked her work and "would have probably stayed" if she had had more of a career ladder to climb. Instead, she changed institutions (though she remained in public education) and started trying to work her way up in a new setting. Cassandra's initiative and hard work could only take her so far, however, as she could do little on her own to change the larger issue of state disinvestment in public education.

Adverse economic conditions hampered other women's public sector and nonprofit careers, too. Recall that tending traditional partner Liz, the data analyst who went back to school for an MPP, was laid off from her company following government budget cuts in the aftermath of the Great Recession. Losing her job when federal funds for nonprofit work dried up meant losing opportunities to advance in an organization with strong internal career ladders. Liz saw this moment as an opportunity to start her own business, but entrepreneurship is inherently risky, and Liz could lose even more. In sum, broader economic forces in the United States negatively affected women's, but not men's, careers by dispro-portionately impacting the jobs that women were more likely to hold. Though this study cannot explain why public sector and nonprofit work faced financial disinvestment, previous scholarship has suggested that work done by women is devalued simply because it is done by women.[5]

Finally, women with children across all the pathways highlighted how their parental status affected their careers in ways that did not seem to affect men. Remember, for example, that consistent compro-miser Cristina worried that the timing of her maternity leave would dis-rupt her integration into a new work team. Tending traditional partner Rebecca voiced a similar concern that her maternity leave had hurt her career progression:

> [My career growth] seems slower than some people around me. Like, having to go through the route of the contractor and then having the work delay because of maternity leave and things like that. So, people [around me] are

being promoted slowly and I'm relatively older, so it's like now I'm starting to lag behind them in terms of the progress being made.

In contrast, Rebecca's husband Joseph did not see his parental leave as a professional hindrance even though he worked for the same company and received the same parental leave as Rebecca. In fact, he was hired into a more senior role at a new company shortly after returning to work from his parental leave.

Recall also that consistent compromiser Nora constantly questioned whether keeping strict work hours at her research lab to accommodate day-care pickup stigmatized her as less than an ideal worker. Autonomous actor Janelle likewise worried that being a mother would cause her professional colleagues and supervisors to look down on her:

> I have not told anyone [that I'm pregnant] and I don't know exactly whether that's the very politic thing to do because I don't know what I'm worth more as, you know, someone who has a kid or someone who doesn't. I don't know if [my adviser] would be as serious about me if I was—I don't know. I guess that's my own self-consciousness going—I'm coming from the standpoint of you know, once you have a kid, you're less valuable in the workplace.

Although MA student Janelle perceived that in academia "once you have a kid, you're less valuable in the workplace," her husband Stephen, also a graduate student, never mentioned this concern for his own career. These stories reflect women's (accurate) assessment that professional work cultures specifically stigmatize motherhood but not fatherhood.[6]

Whereas women contended with unfriendly and even hostile workplaces that impeded their careers, men across the three pathways described positive work experiences that bolstered their confidence as professionals. For example, in contrast to his wife Vanessa, consistent compromiser Alex characterized his career progression as "super successful":

> At the [first] small firm I had good quality of life, got to do cool stuff, [and] they gave me elevating levels of responsibility. Then this new job transition, I have moved up a level. . . . Plus, I still have my quality of life. And my boss likes me. So I feel super successful.

Alex's trajectory of increasing work responsibilities along with a good quality of life resulted in a sense of confidence in his continued career growth:

> I feel more comfortable that I can transition between lots of spaces and be successful in different career fields. Like, academia over here, tech over here,

government consulting. There's a bunch of different things I feel like I could be successful in. So, I guess mostly I have more confidence.

Alex's feeling that he had been, and would continue to be, successful in his professional life was expressed by men on the other two pathways, too. Take these examples from autonomous actor Max and tending traditional partner Joseph from Time 4:

> *Max:* Once you're done with the residency you can always get a job. . . . I think [my career has] gone exceptionally well. I mean, I basically got through the fellowships I wanted to, got through the training I wanted to. I got the journey I wanted. . . . Now it looks like they would hire me at [a nearby hospital]. I mean, there's demand for physicians.

> *Joseph:* From fresh PhD [with] no industry experience to where I am now, I think [my career progression has] been great. I think the company's growing [my] role. I think there's lots of opportunities for growth and fun work. Yeah, I think [I'm] pretty optimistic. I'm generally pretty happy, but if I'm not, I know that leaving [one position for a better one] was not that hard, and I don't expect the job market to be that hard. I'm just open to change if it needs to be. Yeah, I'm like, "Leaving's great. It's the best thing ever. Why not leave again? Just keep going."

Max thought his career progression had "gone exceptionally well," and Joseph likewise thought his professional growth had "been great." These experiences led both men to expect the same looking forward. These patterns also indicate that, whereas men's workplace contexts, attitudes, and actions mattered a lot for women's career outcomes, women's situations mattered less for men's professional outcomes.

In chapter 3 I suggested that men's professional security prompted autonomous actor men to make more career compromises to account for their partners and families. This pattern was evident among consistent compromisers and tending traditional couples, too, indicating that men may be more willing to be egalitarian in their relationships when they have confidence in their own employment circumstances. We saw in chapter 2 that consistent compromiser Rick leveraged his security as a professor at Time 4 to advocate for his wife Nora's career:

> We had been trying for [my university] to hire her, or at least interview her, as it was in my contract, for about two years. And they kept bumping the ball down. I kind of got fed up with that. But when [my grant] money started coming, I started realizing I had leverage. . . . When I told [the department chair] that I had interviews, that I was considering the possibility of leaving [and taking my grant money with me], and that I had been approached by [another institution], they actually started the process of hiring Nora.

Rick's workplace confidence also enabled him to take on more than 50 percent of the couple's childcare responsibilities:

> I spend a lot of time with [our child.] . . . On Thursdays I pick her up at 1 p.m. and take her to a library, so I spend a whole afternoon there. On Saturdays and Sundays, I don't even open my computer, I spend it completely with her. I can do it because I don't have to write papers at this point. I am going to get tenure. Usually, one grant almost guarantees tenure. I got three.

Rick's career success allowed him to feel confident considering jobs at other universities that would more willingly invest in Nora's career. Rick also felt confident in receiving tenure, so he chose to do more childcare rather than more research.

Even tending traditional men like Brad showed this pattern. At Time 4 he plainly stated, "My professional career has been beyond what I can imagine." Feeling confident that his skills were in demand and that he would continue growing in his career, he wanted to help his wife Emily return to her own career (within the parameters that he would remain the primary earner): "I'd rather her be writing. She loves writing. She cares deeply about it." As such, he put firm boundaries around his work to relieve Emily from childcare and enable her to build up her freelance portfolio:

> I'll watch them in the evenings or on the weekend afternoons so she can write. Like this weekend, Saturday and Sunday, I'll watch the kids for like hours so that she'd be able to write. She's ready to get back to writing [so] we have sitters come in and we pay for it.

Having consistently passed his company's performance reviews, Brad was confident that he could maintain his career while taking on more childcare in the evenings and on weekends. Further, he thought it was reasonable to pay for childcare so Emily could spend more time expanding her professional portfolio. Although he could advance more quickly in his company if he put in longer hours, he preferred to be an active parent and to get Emily back into her career.

These stories emphasize how workplaces systematically advantage men and disadvantage women in multiple ways that compound over time. The men and women in my study all started in the same place (finishing graduate degrees and trying to launch careers) but did not have similar journeys or equal outcomes. Unequal workplaces thus played a major, though not exclusive, role in perpetuating gendered power imbalances in couples and gender inequality more broadly over the course of this six-year study.

SEARCHING FOR EQUAL PARTNERS

Earlier in this chapter I noted that two autonomous actor couples and three tending traditional couples broke up or divorced over time. Table 5.2 shows that four of the five women who left their original relationships started new ones. The way these women described their breakups and their new partners underscored their desires for egalitarian relationships. Take these examples from autonomous actor Cassandra and tending traditional partner Liz. Recall that Cassandra worked to foster a sense of "we-ness" in her ongoing long-distance relationship with David at Time 3 (without equal effort from him). And remember that Liz initiated couples' therapy after Time 3 to try establishing a more egalitarian balance of career importance following the continued prioritization of Hank's career. Both stories highlight that women wanted power-balanced relationships in which partners built a shared life with two equally prioritized careers and equally shared relationship and family responsibilities.

Women on the autonomous actor pathway dissolved their relationships when men did not meet the women's expectations for collaboratively constructing a shared life. Specifically, Cassandra broke up with David in part because she did not see him working to sustain the relationship and felt them drifting apart: "We don't talk enough. It's too much checking out." Women on the tending traditional pathway broke up with men because, although men were working to build a shared life, they were constructing one in which the man's career was more important than the woman's. Specifically, Liz ended her relationship with Hank by Time 4 when she tired of asking him to make joint career plans with her: "I started to emotionally check out. . . . I'm going to stop asking [Hank to make joint career plans with me.] . . . I'm just going to move forward with my professional development."

In contrast to their previous partners, Cassandra and Liz described their new partners as more deliberate in intertwining their lives, including coordinating their two careers and maintaining a shared family life:

Cassandra: It's framed a little differently. It's more like, "Okay, we're family. We're attached now." We are each other, so to speak. . . . [I]t's more like, "Let's do what's best for everyone, together."

Liz: [My new partner] and I have had conversations about, would it make more sense for him to try to move back here? To maintain a lifestyle in two places? Or does it make sense for me to try to move to [his state] where there are a lot more opportunities [for my business]? We're not committed just yet, but we're having them in a more concrete way where it's, "Let's explore what those options are." And I think his emotional availability and desire to be very communicative, it's like, "I'm looking for somebody I can share a life with." And I like that in a person.

Cassandra characterized her partner as wanting to "do what's best for everyone, together." Liz felt that her partner was "looking for somebody [he] can share a life with." Both women liked that their new partners were more equal contributors to maintaining a dual-career relationship. These examples suggest that professional women who leave gender-unequal relationships may start new ones with partners who work more cooperatively toward shared goals.

Further evidence that some professional women may not settle for nonegalitarian partners comes from the repartnering patterns among men. Both of the autonomous actor men who experienced a breakup started new relationships over the course of the study, but none of the three tending traditional men who exited their original relationships did. Remember that autonomous actor men like David shifted from autonomy to interdependence with their new partners by Time 4. Instead of making individual plans for his own university teaching career, David supported his new partner's career as a tenure track professor by taking lecturer or instructor positions wherever his spouse was working. This shift toward joint career planning and active compromising may have contributed to these men's repartnering trajectories.

The men on the tending traditional pathway, on the other hand, remained single after their original relationships ended. At least one man cited his work schedule as a barrier to dating. Another said his casual relationships usually ended when he was unwilling to increase his commitment to his dating partners. Perhaps tending traditional men's reluctance to compromise on their careers and integrate their lives with their partners led to their continued singlehood.

One area in which many men were enthusiastic about equal sharing was in parenting. Consistent compromisers like Rick often did more than 50 percent of the childcare. Some tending traditional men like Joseph surprised their wives by being involved fathers even though they placed high importance on their careers. Finally, even though some autonomous actor men passively "allowed" women to be the lead parent, others like Max wanted to be active parents:

I always knew I wanted to have kids, but when you finally get there, it's pretty satisfying. So, I've been really happy in that. I guess I always knew that I would want to make sure that my career allowed me to spend a good amount of time with family and kids. Now actually looking at jobs, I guess it's more clear what that looks like. For example, if I got the opportunity to do an academic job where I had ideal research opportunities but would be working all the time and have limited vacation, limited days off, versus a career that had less ideal academic opportunities and more time with family, more days off, or more vacation, I would take the second one.

Max thought parenting was "pretty satisfying" and outlined exactly what it meant for him to "spend a good amount of time with family and kids": take a job that was less ideal for him professionally if it gave him more time to invest in his family. Notably, men like Joseph and Max readily adjusted their work for their children, though they had not done the same in the past for their partners (unlike consistent compromiser men). Perhaps autonomous actor and tending traditional men believed women could adjust their working conditions to them, but that their children could not. Perhaps fatherhood changed men's outlook on life to focus more on caring for the next generation rather than on themselves.[7] These cases suggest that parenthood can shift a couple's work-family equilibrium not only by changing the material conditions of their life, but also by changing the attitudes they hold about how to live a good life.

Altogether, these patterns indicate that men and women had more control over egalitarianism in their relationships and families compared to the workplace. Yet when work delineates what might be possible for partners and families, and workplaces remain gender unequal, we will most likely see continued gender inequality at home. Even though scholarly and popular narratives often suggest that gender inequality at home leads to gender inequality at work, this study suggests that the reverse is also true.[8]

CONCLUSION

The comparisons in this chapter underscore how workplace structures; cultural attitudes about gender, work, and family; and partners' joint and coordinated actions all need to come together for couples to experience egalitarian work-family trajectories. Work-related supports for dual-professional couples—such as strong labor markets for two careers in the same city or formal processes to help spouses of employees with job placement—must exist for partners to maintain two equally important careers. As we have seen, though, these conditions are difficult to find because the existing landscape of work is gendered and unequal. Without more favorable labor market conditions, partners may see no other option than to enter and sustain a power-imbalanced, gender-unequal equilibrium of work and family.

Still, workplace or other external supports on their own are not enough to produce egalitarianism if couples do not hold consistently egalitarian attitudes and do not jointly take action to leverage those resources. If partners prioritize autonomy and independently pursue career opportunities instead of making shared plans for equally and consistently compromising, they can miss opportunities to take coordinated actions to achieve gender-equal work-family outcomes. Note, however, that "taking coordinated actions" cannot simply mean that men and women act the same as each other; men and women can take the same actions but experience different results, partly because what it means to "support" a partner or "compromise" one's career is gendered. Even if men and women end nonegalitarian relationships to pursue more equal ones, and even if men and women do their best to co-parent under otherwise gender-unequal conditions, we cannot individualize the societal issue of gender inequality.

A comparison of relationship, family life, and employment outcomes suggests that couples taking the consistent compromiser pathway—the most egalitarian of the three pathways—were the most likely to get what they wanted over time. This association needs to be tested in larger, quantitative datasets, but it does suggest that egalitarianism may be related to relationship stability, realizing family goals, and achieving greater household income.

These outcomes should be possible to achieve for all men and women who want them. Conditions in the United States are not currently set up to produce the perfect alignment of structure, culture, and joint action needed for gender egalitarianism—but they could be. The final chapter discusses what we can do as individuals, as couples, as organizations, and as a society to address the challenges we face to advancing the gender revolution.

## CHAPTER 6

Pathways Forward

Julie and Max experienced many professional and personal life events after they joined this study. They sustained a long-distance relationship while each person finished medical school. They started living together for the first time when Julie matched to the residency program at the hospital where Max was completing his. They bought a house and got married while Julie finished her residency and Max completed a fellowship program. At the time of their final interviews, Julie was wrapping up a fellowship at the same hospital, Max was coming to the end of a second fellowship he had taken on to stay in the same place as Julie, the couple had a six-month-old baby, and the partners were searching for permanent jobs together. Reflecting on everything they had gone through over the past six years, Julie said:

> I feel like we've grown together instead of individually or separately. . . . [I]t feels more like it's a partnership and we're evenly sharing dinner and cleaning and baby care and walking the dog and all that kind of stuff. . . . I think that although the scales are tipped pretty heavily towards work, I think that the balance, right now, it's pretty good.

Experiencing this equilibrium for the last several years and seeing how the two of them collaboratively sustained it made Julie feel hopeful that they could continue their rhythm even as they prepared for another life change:

With figuring out where we're going to be for [more permanent] jobs, I think that a difficult compromise decision is coming up. Finding good jobs where we can both achieve the goals that we want to and be doing the kind of work that we want to do, I think would be ideal, no matter where that is. . . . I guess I look forward to just seeing where we end up and what opportunities there are.

If both partners could find fulfilling jobs in the same location to advance their careers, Julie believed they could continue "what we're doing already, as far as the family and relationship stuff" and could enjoy "seeing our daughter grow up. The changes that she's gone through already are pretty incredible, and so I'm looking forward to that." We cannot know whether the partners landed two jobs that were ideal for each person's career without more data. Further, as I completed the final interviews before the COVID-19 pandemic hit the United States, we cannot know how the major changes to work and family during this time of global crisis affected Max and Julie's lives. But we could pose hypotheses about what happened using the work-family ecosystems framework. In the epilogue, I demonstrate the usefulness of this framework beyond this particular study. I analyze the configuration of partners' workplace resources; their attitudes toward gender, work, and family; and their approaches to taking joint action to describe possible responses to the pandemic. Before I complete this exercise, I discuss the broader implications of this research for scholars, policy makers, workplaces, and individuals.

I have shown how couples like Julie and Max replicated and resisted patterns of gender inequality in the early years of their shared work and family trajectory. Based on these men's and women's stories, I can offer answers to the three questions that motivated this book: What work-family trajectories do contemporary young adults in different-gender relationships follow as they launch and build careers, maintain relationships, and start families? How do conditions at work and cultural norms shape these pathways? What do these trajectories tell us about the state of the gender revolution and its likely future?

I found that aspiring dual-professional couples experienced three work-family trajectories. Partners traveled the consistent compromiser pathway, the autonomous actor pathway, or the tending traditional pathway. Different combinations of workplace supports or challenges; partners' attitudes toward gender, work, and family; and men's and women's joint actions came together to send couples down these distinct paths. Supportive workplaces, unwavering egalitarian attitudes, and partners' well-coordinated actions put men and women on the consistent compromiser pathway and created gender equality in couples' careers, relationships, and families (chapter 2). Attitudinal support for individuals to make independent decisions while refraining from restricting a partner's autonomy, regardless of partners' workplace resources, led to gender-unequal patterns of career compromise on the autonomous actor pathway, despite some couples' achievement of two careers and a relationship (chapter 3). Finally, acceptance of cultural norms for man-breadwinner/woman-caregiver relationships, intensified by men's unemployment, resulted in gender-complementary joint action that sent men and women down the gender-unequal tending traditional pathway (chapter 4).

Feedback between partners' work landscapes, cultural attitudes, and joint actions created path dependence in these couples' work-family trajectories. For example, tending traditional couples' early decision to prioritize men's careers and women's family responsibilities made it difficult for couples to change their division of labor later because couples did not want to give up their economic security and convenient childcare arrangements. Likewise, consistent compromisers' initial access to workplace support for dual-career couples made it easier for both partners to sustain careers and become equal caregivers across their transition to parenthood. Still, changes in any of these factors could result in a new equilibrium of work and family for these couples. For instance, gender inequality in who adjusted their professional pursuits to support the couple among autonomous actors dissipated when men established security in their careers.

The many contours along these three pathways suggest that movement of the gender revolution among young, mostly White, American professionals in different-gender couples is complex, advancing in some ways and remaining stalled in others. The consistent compromiser pathway offers the most optimistic picture for the future of the gender revolution. Scholars have argued that the gender revolution has stalled partly because men have not changed their paid work and domestic labor attitudes and activities as much as women have.[1] Consistent compromiser men counter this narrative. They firmly believed in the importance of both partners having careers and both partners being responsible for maintaining a relationship and family. Situated in a broader societal landscape that systematically advantages men and disadvantages women in work and family, consistent compromiser men resisted reproducing gendered power imbalances in their partnerships by taking action to support women's professional pursuits. They adapted their own work activities to women's careers and took on 50 percent or more of the work at home. Yet these attitudes and actions may not have been possible without couples' access to workplace and other external supports. In line with what other researchers have shown, the consistent compromisers' stories underscore that finishing the gender revolution requires institutional support and not just individual action.[2]

The tending traditional pathway, on the other hand, suggests that the gender revolution may continue to stall into the future. Beliefs in the centrality of continuous, full-time paid work for men (but not women) and expectations that mothers (but not fathers) will take time away from their careers to care for young children prove to be persistent cultural blocks to advancing the gender revolution. If such attitudes are prevalent across the general American population—as some survey research suggests is the case[3]—and no changes occur in workplace and public policies to support men's caregiving and women's professional advancement, we can expect to see continued gender complementarity and gender inequality in work and family.

We may be especially likely to see a continued stall in the gender revolution if other couples follow in the tending traditional couples' footsteps and choose a gender-unequal division of labor over ending their relationships when egalitarianism is out of reach. This work-family trajectory provides additional insight into questions raised by previous research. Kathleen Gerson found that young men and women had gendered "Plan B's" for what to do if external conditions at work made "Plan A" for equal sharing difficult to achieve.[4] Men preferred neotraditionalism, but women favored forgoing partners to work while independently raising children. Because Gerson asked her study participants to speculate about the future but did not collect data on what they actually did, we have not had clear answers about what happens when a man and a woman in a couple cannot have "Plan A" and have to come up with a "Plan B" together. The tending traditional couples' stories indicate that partners may turn to men's "Plan B's" first. Women only enacted their "Plan B" for independence when they became unhappy with neotraditionalism and had no barriers to leaving the relationship.

The autonomous actor pathway perhaps most clearly demonstrates that the future of the gender revolution will not be a straightforward story of advancement or stagnation. These partners held gender-neutral attitudes favoring a "separately, together" version of women's "Plan B" for independence in work and family. Yet these attitudes translated into gender-unequal behaviors (and not necessarily breakups, at least not right away) that continued to stall the gender revolution. Men chose whatever was best for their own careers without considering women's careers or their relationships and families. Women, on the other hand, "made a personal choice" to adjust their professional activities to men's careers and their relationships and families. The autonomous actors' experiences thus provide evidence supporting what other scholars have argued: using gender-neutral language and logics can, but does not necessarily, produce gender equality.[5] When partners assume that they have the same understanding of autonomy, they can overlook or even justify gendered actions because couples can agree that they both supported independence and individual freedom of choice. It can seem coincidental that men enacted autonomy in one way but women did so in another. Couples may also dismiss gender inequality in their actions if partners achieve nominally equal outcomes in work and family. Along with the finding that tending traditional couples go with men's "Plan B's" first, the finding that autonomous actors go with a modified version of women's "Plan B" for independence but leave the work that comes with that decision to women reveals men's greater power in their relationships more broadly. This persistent gendered power imbalance within relationships is a key hurdle in the advancement of the gender revolution.

In addition to answering questions about the state of the gender revolution, this research extends other theoretical debates about gender, work, and family and raises new questions that should be explored in future research. The consistent compromisers' experiences raise the question of whether egalitarianism is always desirable. These partners' commitment to equal participation in paid work and domestic responsibilities required constant, concerted effort and used up time and energy that they would have otherwise spent on personal hobbies and maintaining friendships. Egalitarianism may therefore not be desirable if achieving it requires unrelenting resistance to existing structural and cultural circumstances and ongoing interpersonal negotiation. Still, it is not clear that men and women would have had better access to leisure time in nonegalitarian arrangements, as autonomous actors and tending traditional partners also lamented a lack of free time. Further, prior research suggests that men and women lose out on leisure time for different reasons when work and family responsibilities are unequally divided across partners based on gender.[6] Finally, partners with more egalitarian arrangements seemed the happiest and most satisfied in their relationships, suggesting that the effort to maintain equality was worth it to them. Scholars should continue studying the conditions that make egalitarianism in work and family more, and less, desirable.

The autonomous actors' stories alert us to the ambiguous meaning of "egalitarian" and encourage us to ask whether that descriptor can accurately characterize individuals or couples. Other scholars have revealed a "gender equality paradox,"[7] in which people express support for gender equality but behave in inegalitarian ways. They caution us to distinguish between attitudes and actions. The autonomous actor pathway pushes our thinking in this area forward by revealing that "attitudes supporting gender equality" may not mean just one thing. Whereas consistent compromisers considered egalitarianism to mean men and women cooperatively and evenly participating in paid work and unpaid domestic responsibilities, autonomous actors understood egalitarianism to mean men's and women's "equal right" to freely make individual choices and men's and women's "equal responsibility" to preserve each partner's autonomy.

The autonomous actors' case also indicates that the relationship between attitudes and behaviors may be even more complicated than the gender equality paradox suggests. Not only can attitudinal support for gender equality be paired with unequal, gender-complementary behaviors, but nominally egalitarian attitudes can be paired with gendered and mismatched behaviors in which men act in their own interests (and encourage women to do the same) while women act on behalf of the couple (and do not expect the same from men).

The autonomous actor trajectory additionally directs us to consider both processes and outcomes to fully understand egalitarianism. *How* men and women come to different work and family outcomes is just as relevant for examining gender equality as *what* those outcomes are. Moreover, gender equality in attitudes and actions, and in process as well as outcomes, can change over time. Researchers should be careful about classifying people as "egalitarian" or "gender unequal" based on a single, point-in-time snapshot of their lives.

The tending traditional pathway challenges our theories about gender equality in the public versus the private sphere. Recent scholarship suggests that people readily embrace egalitarianism in school and work but are slower to endorse and enact equality at home and in the family.[8] Although the autonomous actors' experiences contribute additional evidence to support this claim, as some men passively "allowed" women to take the lead in parenting even as they came to more actively support women's careers, tending traditional couples' stories indicate the opposite pattern. Tending traditional men were loath to give up their primary earner status, but many were enthusiastic to co-parent with their wives. These heterogeneous patterns about when couples want and enact egalitarianism warrant continued research. One hypothesis that may explain this contradiction is that couples consider themselves to be equal partners overall as long as they are equal in at least one domain of life—either in their careers or at home. This type of thinking will likely slow the progress of the gender revolution, as couples stop short of full equality across all domains of a shared life.

The experiences of all the couples in the study lead us to ask: What will it take to achieve equality in work and family? Because weaknesses in workplace supports, inegalitarian attitudes, and uncoordinated actions can channel couples away from an equal division of labor and put women at a disadvantage in their careers and at home, I turn now to outline what organizations, governments, men, and women can do to shore up those weaknesses. Ultimately, unstalling the gender revolution for professionals who aspire to be equal partners in work and family requires simultaneous change at all three levels—structural, cultural, and interactional—and buy-in from all actors.

WORKPLACE AND OTHER STRUCTURAL SUPPORTS

Dual-professional couples could benefit from workplace policies like spousal hiring and partner job placement services to ensure that no one becomes detached from their careers when one partner receives a good job opportunity that requires relocation. Consistent compromisers Rick and Nora were able to take advantage of such a policy, as Rick's academic job offer explicitly included a promise from his employer to interview Nora for a position as well. If employers put such mechanisms in place, they can be careful to ensure that they are made available to all prospective and current employees, that partner hire candidates meet all job qualifications, and that workers hired through these policies are not stigmatized as "people who are here just because of their partner." Mindful implementation of these practices can buffer against class and race inequalities stemming from hiring through networks rather than on merit and can guard against gender inequality stemming from the possibility that women may be especially likely to be penalized as workers hired through this process.[9]

Better remote work options could also stem career interruptions and overcome challenges in nonthriving local job markets for dual-professional couples who want to move to pursue a job for one of the partners. Several couples described considering this option to facilitate two careers, pointing to people's openness to using telework policies if they were more widely available. Autonomous actor Janelle, for instance, may not have given up pursuing her graduate education if her university abroad or her husband Stephen's American university had offered formal options for both partners' remote degree completion. Employers can feel confident about offering telework to employees, too, as research indicates that work-from-anywhere does not harm productivity and includes benefits to workers.[10] If these possibilities were more widely available, men could work remotely so women could pursue their career opportunities, or vice versa. It is important that not only women take this option, though, because gender inequality can emerge through the consistent pairing of men and women with different activities that can then become differently valued and resourced.[11]

Parental leave that is fully paid, adequate in length, and flexible in timing is crucial for allowing dual-professional partners to maintain equality in work and family across the transition to parenthood. For example, and consistent with patterns found in other studies,[12] tending traditional couple Rebecca and Joseph actually established a more egalitarian division of labor after their first child was born because their company gave both of them generous parental leave. Rebecca reported: "I spent a lot of time breastfeeding at the beginning, so Joseph had time to do those other things. He was just trying to do as many as he could and is continuing still. Even some of the chores that I didn't do when I was pregnant, he just continued doing. So I'm trying not to mess with that [laughs]." Establishing domestic routines together without worrying about income or job security provided a foundation for Rebecca and Joseph to continue equally sharing domestic labor even when they returned to work. Governments can follow the example of New York, California, New Jersey, Rhode Island, Washington, and Washington, D.C., of requiring employers to provide paid parental leave to employees. In particular, incentivizing fathers to take paternity leave can boost gender equality at work and at home.[13]

Beyond the early months of caring for an infant, men and women professionals can more easily maintain gender equality given access to affordable, quality childcare. After Rebecca and Joseph's parental leave, both partners were able to return to work full-time because they enrolled their child at the daycare located on-site at their employer's campus. The convenient location facilitated their ability to do drop-offs and pickups together. The day care's hours also lined up with the partners' work hours, shielding them from having to make hard choices about who would cut back on paid work to better accommodate childcare. Better infrastructure making childcare centers (and schools) more available and closer to business centers would ease the logistics of working and parenting. State and federal governments could fund day-care centers, but businesses also have incentives to invest in childcare infrastructure, as experienced workers like Rebecca would be more inclined to stay with their companies: "The job decisions become tied to that. It's a very nice day care. We feel like she's safe there. We feel like she's having fun. They get to play outside and they do all different types of learning initiative things, so it's nice."

Men and women professionals could also benefit from other real options for supporting personal, household, and family care responsibilities that may change over time. Offering part-time and flexible working arrangements, as well as concrete off-ramps and on-ramps for exiting and reentering careers, could help couples maintain gender equality. Such resources might have protected Emily's career on the tending traditional pathway. If there had been specific mechanisms in place to facilitate her desire to take parental leave, work part-time for a few years, and then return to full-time work, Emily may have been able to enjoy immersive motherhood for a little while without taking such a hit to her career.

If companies give employees options to work part-time, to work flexibly, and off- and on-ramps, they need to also make sure that promotion criteria do not penalize workers for using these policies. Clearly defined career ladders across a profession that account for part-time and flexible work as well as workplace leaves could keep workers on track to grow professionally even if they work on a different rhythm or take time off. These workplace supports may have helped Emily's husband Brad imagine more possibilities for himself other than full-time work in a single career: "I don't know a lot of part time [academic researchers]. I know a lot of people who quit being [academics] to work in research firms but I don't know many people who have been able to transfer [back in]. I have not seen examples. Professionally, that's really weird." If there had been real options for him to move in and out of an academic career or to work as a part-time academic, he might not have been so focused on pursuing a specific type of career, to the detriment of Emily's career. Again, it is important for men to use these options as well so that such activities do not become gendered and unequally regarded and rewarded.

Adequate mentorship is necessary for helping channel employees along this upward trajectory. People like consistent compromiser women who repeatedly came up against workplace barriers to career progression may gain the most from these formal supports. For example, consistent compromiser Cristina was able to continue moving up in her organization even as she went on maternity leave because she had a boss who supported her integration into a new work team. Appropriate mentorship to support women's careers also needs to account for how women of color can face unique challenges to advancement.[14]

Finally, companies and governments have to prevent and address workplace harassment to narrow the gap between men's and women's professional progression. Women like consistent compromiser Vanessa might not feel compelled to jump from job to job if their working conditions were better. Her career as an environmental scientist could have been smoother and shown more upward movement like her husband Alex's, who did the same type of work she did, if she had not had to face overt harassment and subtle gender discrimination from her superiors.

Although the workplace supports and protections outlined here may specifically facilitate gender equality among professional men and women, many of them are likely to support other workers' well-being and ability to maintain egalitarianism as well. People who work at childcare centers, who clean dual-career couples' homes and care for their yards, and who keep professional offices stocked and secure deserve access to paid parental leave, affordable childcare, and protections against workplace harassment, too. In fact, we know that more robust parental leave policies and expanded childcare options would especially benefit women of color, women without college degrees, and women in same-gender relationships, as well as their families.[15] Gender equality in work and family for people in White, upper-middle-class, different-gender couples should not, and does not have to, come at the price of exacerbating inequalities across race, class, and sexual orientation.

CULTURAL CHANGE

Changing cultural attitudes and beliefs about gender, work, and family requires, at a minimum, imagination. Brainstorming different ideas can expand the set of blueprints professional men and women may reach for when imagining their work and family lives and can aid in building organizations and communities that support that vision.

Cultural norms linking full-time, uninterrupted engagement in paid work—and nothing else—to masculinity have to be disrupted. Having such a narrow set of activities deemed appropriate for men sets up dual-career couples to fail. For example, the only pathways that included breakups and divorces were the autonomous actor and tending traditional pathways. These men were more likely to have a single-minded focus on their careers than consistent compromiser men, who were more flexible about their own professional activities and more attentive to women's careers and their families' needs. By following dominant, White, upper-middle-class cultural models for work and manhood, autonomous actor and tending traditional men's exclusive attention on their careers resulted in several negative consequences for themselves, their partners, and their relationships. Our beliefs about "what men do" have to include meeting the responsibilities of doing care work and relationship work beyond providing financial resources to the couple. More expansive models of masculinity emphasizing equitable relationships and care for family and community already exist among men of color and working-class men;[16] they provide examples of what is possible for other men. Further, men's secure attachment to employment cannot be a prerequisite for them to endorse egalitarianism (see chapters 3 and 5). Workplaces can contribute to this culture change by creating a results-only work environment while resisting ideal worker norms and expectations for long hours and overwork.[17]

At the same time, cultural beliefs assigning women ultimate responsibility for maintaining relationships and families have to shift. We cannot understand the work of attending to the well-being of partners and children as only women's work. Instead, let us think like the consistent compromisers: working for pay, completing housework, caring for children and family members, and nurturing the relationship—as well as strategizing how to manage them all—are responsibilities that belong to everyone. And "everyone" includes workplaces and governments. Let us reimagine personal well-being as society's collective responsibility as much as individual men's and women's responsibility. This vision, already put into practice by Black mothers and queer couples,[18] can guide us in building social institutions that promote people's ability to connect with and care for one another.

In addition to changing the way we think about how gender aligns with work and family, we can change the way we value care work. As discussed in chapter 4, part of the problem of linking femininity to relationships and family in the context of a different-gender relationship is that the work of nurturing social ties is unpaid and lower in status than paid market work.[19] In a capitalist society, the consistent pairing of women with economically devalued labor results in continued gender inequality.[20] We can start recognizing that care work is just as valuable as the work done in the paid labor market if we remunerate domestic labor that is currently unpaid. Family care stipends and universal basic income may be good first steps to address this inequality.

On top of changing our ideas about what women do and what men do, we can rethink the models we have for *how* dual-career partners can do everything together. The autonomous actors' stories alert us to the downsides of privileging each person's individual choice and preserving each partner's independence. One partner, usually a woman like Julie, could end up making more compromises and doing more work to get the outcome a couple wants. Remember that for Julie's partner Max, privileging Julie's freedom to choose the medical residencies she wanted and maintaining her independence meant not getting involved at all in making career plans for the two of them as a dual-physician couple. This thought process effectively left Julie with sole responsibility for "making the independent choice" to maintain the partners' two careers and their relationship. The autonomous actors therefore show us that a "separate but parallel" strategy is a risky one for couples hoping to maintain equality while remaining together. Still, this ideological orientation does not reflect individuals' or couples' shortcomings. As shown in chapter 3, people adopt this cultural framework for understanding work and family in response to job insecurity and employer assumptions that workers are individuals with neither outside responsibilities nor attachments to other workers. People's attitudes toward autonomy can change if these workplace conditions and logics change.

The tending traditional couples' experiences underscore how uncritically accepting the ideas that men "happened" to have stronger career preferences while women "happened" to feel more comfortable scaling back paid work to care for children could lead couples to enter a more gender-differentiated and gender-unequal work-family equilibrium than they expected for themselves. Tending traditional couples also fell into a trap of prioritizing the person with "the harder job to find" or "the higher paying job." Because gender influences individuals' career orientations and the material conditions of the workplace, the person that couples prioritize will likely be the man. We can more carefully consider how using supposedly gender-neutral logics to make decisions can still result in gender-unequal outcomes. Men and women can recognize that when we degender our thinking we risk overlooking gender inequality. The tending traditional couples show us that "prioritizing him for now" or "going with whatever is practical or economically rational" is unlikely to help couples achieve equality.

Instead, we can take inspiration from the consistent compromisers. Their approach of simultaneously considering each person as an equally important member of, and an equally responsible member to, a collective, was key to sustaining gender egalitarianism in work and family. Under this model, partners act in tandem, not separately. And men and women take similar or gender-progressive actions, not traditionally gender-complementary ones, to maintain equality in careers and family. In fact, their stories highlight how using a logic of equity, not just equality, is necessary when the professional and domestic playing fields are stacked against women. Recall, for example, that scientist Rick thought it was fair for him to do a greater share of housework and childcare than his wife and fellow scientist Nora. He recognized that she needed this extra support to advance in their male-dominated field and reach the high level of professional success that he had. To get equal outcomes, the partners had to put in equitable, not just equal, levels of effort.

JOINT ACTION

Although broad-scale structural and cultural changes are the surest way to produce widespread and enduring conditions for gender egalitarianism, these societal-level shifts may take a long time to achieve. Partners can take joint action now to build egalitarianism into their relationships and to push for structural and cultural change in their communities.

Within a relationship, partners can actively look for professional opportunities for each other. Because men, especially those who are privileged along race and class lines, may have more advantages and face less discrimination at work than women, it is especially important for them to leverage their resources to support women's careers and their families. Men can look to consistent compromiser Anthony as an example. He restricted his applications to locations that had good job opportunities for his wife Cristina. When the couple opted for the best offer for him, he invested active effort in helping Cristina land a position in the same city that would advance her career. He looked through job ads with her, read her cover letters, and practiced interview questions with her. After they both started their new positions, he made sure the partners made time for their relationship and for setting up their new home. When they became parents and Cristina felt overwhelmed by the demands of work and motherhood, Anthony encouraged her not to give up her career and stepped up his provision of childcare. He used the flexibility of his job to do day-care drop-offs and pickups and to be the designated parent for emergencies. Taking these kinds of actions does not hurt men's careers in the same way these actions hurt women's careers, either, as I show in chapter 5. Highly educated men with professional careers are unlikely to lose out at work and can afford to act intentionally on behalf of their partners and families.

Men can take care to be mindful, too, of whether they are acting too autonomously. Chapter 3 reveals that "independent" decisions and actions inevitably ripple out and affect others when people are embedded in partnerships and families. Taking individual action can inadvertently leave other people (in this society, usually women) to contend with the consequences of those actions. Women cannot be the only ones accounting for their relationships and families when making career decisions. Men can better reciprocate in concrete ways.

In reciprocating, men and women can be cautious in using a "trading off" strategy for being career leaders in a dual-professional relationship, especially if partners start in gender-traditional positions. Couples who want a dual-career relationship can get stuck in a husband-earner/wife-caregiver arrangement and not actually reshuffle the division of labor. When tending traditional couple Liz and Hank, for example, kept prioritizing Hank's finance career, data analyst Liz realized she would never get "her turn" to go next. She ultimately ended the relationship to build the career she wanted with a new partner who was more invested in realizing her vision alongside her. Simultaneously and mutually building both partners' careers can be a lot of work, but that work may be worth it for stable and egalitarian relationships. Investing equally in both men's and women's careers could be especially beneficial for relationship stability in the face of unexpected challenges like illness or unemployment, which may be particularly prominent among working-class families.[21]

To ensure that taking jointly coordinated actions in a relationship does not lead to the concentration of resources among race- and class-privileged couples, dual-professional partners can take collective action with people outside their households to build communities that foster and support egalitarian relationships. Men and women can organize with their coworkers who may not have access to the same advantages that professional workers do to advocate for the employee-centered policies listed here. Outside the workplace, men and women can take collective action to hold government officials and policy makers accountable for making gender equality a reality for all families. Men and women can demand, support, and vote for policies that make it easier for dual-earner partners to also be dual-caregiver families. They can get involved with community organizations already working on these work-family issues. Perhaps there are efforts to organize cooperative caregiving for children and older adults in the neighborhood. Perhaps there are professional training and networking events in the community for people to provide and receive mentorship and information about job opportunities. Imagine what gender equality in work and family could be if these efforts included and supported *everyone* across race, class, and sexual orientation.

Structure, culture, and joint action need to come together, and dual-career men and women have to work for change to finish the gender revolution. Structural support is necessary but not sufficient if cultural models for action do not lead them to think of using such resources. And these favorable workplace landscapes and progressive cultural attitudes do not matter if partners cannot collaboratively work together—and with other actors in their social worlds—to make the most of the situation. Men and women *can* be equal partners and *can* have egalitarianism in work, relationships, and families if we all get to work making this life possible for everyone, together.

Epilogue

Less than a year after I finished conducting the final round of interviews for this book in 2019, the COVID-19 pandemic hit. I was deep into the analysis and writing stage of this project but knew that I could potentially follow up again with the couples to see how they responded to the global crisis. Who kept their job, and who lost theirs? Who shifted to working from home, and who continued going into the office? If both people started working from home, who got a dedicated desk or office space, and who was relegated to the kitchen table? What did parents do about childcare for very young children, and what did they do for older children's virtual school? Although these questions were all intriguing to me, I ultimately decided against another round of data collection.

First, I felt uncomfortable asking these men and women to give me more of their time at a moment when everyone was trying to figure out how to continue working and what to do with their children now that schools and day cares were closed. Second, I was personally stretched too thin and could not imagine myself conducting more interviews. I lacked time needed for systematically collecting high-quality data as I scrambled to revise my college classes for online delivery. I also had greatly reduced energy for more data collection due to the mental and emotional effort I needed to expend to simply function without my usual sources of rejuvenation; dinners and social events with friends, group exercise and leisure activities, and traveling to see family were all, for good reason, off the table. I can imagine that a number of the study participants would have appreciated an opportunity to tell their stories, but I was unsure I had the emotional capacity to hold and process those stories this time. I am in awe of the other scholars who were able to collect this important information and am grateful for their work on gender, work, and family during the pandemic. We have since learned that women bore the brunt of the pandemic fallout[1]—higher levels of unemployment, greater reduction in work hours, and greater responsibility for homeschooling children—despite men's increased time spent in housework and childcare.[2] We might expect a similar pattern among the couples in this study. We could also make a few other predictions based on the work-family ecosystems framework and empirical patterns from these couples' past experiences.

Consistent compromisers experienced a combination of structural support for two careers, egalitarian attitudes, and well-coordinated joint action that created a gender-equal work-family equilibrium in their lives. Gendered workplace challenges constantly threatened this balance, but partners took gender-equitable action together to maintain equality in men's and women's careers. We can think of the pandemic as posing yet another gendered workplace challenge to equality in consistent compromisers' lives. We might predict that consistent compromiser men again stepped up their domestic contributions and made arrangements in their paid work to shield women from experiencing greater losses in their careers and a disproportionate burden of housework and childcare during the COVID-19 lockdowns.

Autonomous actors had access to structural support to facilitate a dual-career relationship but did not leverage these resources for each other because they held attitudes in favor of men's and women's equal right to make independent choices and men's and women's equal responsibility for preserving their partner's autonomy. This gender-neutral logic led to a gendered pattern of actions in which men made their own plans and stated passive support for whatever women wanted to do, but women actively compromised their careers for the couple. These couples experienced a more gender-equal equilibrium in work and family when men became more secure in their careers over time. If the pandemic shook autonomous actor men's confidence in their professional security, we might predict a return to more independent action: men may have made arrangements to maintain their own careers and may have left it up to women to figure out what to do about their own jobs and the couple's family responsibilities. A more optimistic take would be that feedback between structure, culture, and joint action from just before the pandemic made egalitarianism more possible for autonomous actors during the pandemic, with both partners having relatively high professional security, a different attitude endorsing interdependence, and more experience in taking collaborative action on behalf of each other and their children.

Tending traditional couples were more accepting of conventional cultural norms surrounding gender, work, and family, which were made explicit by structural challenges to men's professional identities. This combination of gender attitudes and workplace circumstances prompted couples to take gender-complementary action to prioritize men's careers and women's caregiving roles. This gender-unequal equilibrium persisted over time due to feedback between structure, culture, and gendered joint action. The pandemic may have exacerbated gender inequality in work and family among these couples who already emphasized men's attachment to paid work and women's responsibility for maintaining the relationship and the family.

I am eager to see future scholarship that tests these hypotheses using new sources of empirical data and other research methods.

Acknowledgments

This book exists thanks to many people. First, I thank the men and women who participated in the study. I am grateful to each of you for spending hours with me to share your experiences. It is a big ask to complete so many follow-up interviews, so thank you for agreeing to talk to me each time.

My thanks also to go to Andrew Penner, Linda Waite, Kristen Schilt, and Jenny Trinitapoli. I have the research skills that are necessary to complete a study like this one because of your training. I would not have gone to graduate school at all without Andrew's mentorship. Thank you for presenting that option to me and pointing me toward how to become a sociologist. I would not have completed my dissertation, which formed the foundation for this book, without guidance from Linda, Kristen, and Jenny. Thank you, Linda, for helping me keep the big picture in mind when I got lost trying to tell a coherent story. Thank you, Kristen, for pushing me to think carefully about theory. Thank you, Jenny, for encouraging me to be deliberate when making methodological choices. I hope my work reflects well on all of you. Thank you to my community at the University of Chicago Center for the Study of Gender and Sexuality, NORC, and the Department of Sociology for supporting me through the challenging early stages of data collection, analysis, and writing. I am grateful to have learned from and with you through writing group meetings, workshops, and spontaneous conversations.

Thank you to Abigail Ocobock for inviting me to join a book writing group along with Ellen Lamont, Monica Liu, and Jessi Strieb. I had not even started collecting follow-up interviews when we started meeting, and now I have a whole book! Your feedback all along the way has been invaluable. Thanks to everyone for reviewing drafts of my study protocol, my interview guide, my book proposal, and my book chapters. Your comments were the perfect combination of encouraging and critical. Thank you for showing me what "writing a book" looks like as well. I am so much more confident in my capacity to complete a large project like this thanks to you.

Others provided feedback when they read, or saw presentations of, parts of this book while it was in progress and deserve thanks, too. Thank you to Carla Pfeffer, Jennifer Augustine, Caroline Hartnett, Andrea Henderson, and Léa Pessin for reading very early drafts of several of my chapters. Thank you to those who engaged with my presentations of this work at the 2020 meetings of the American Sociological Association and the Work and Family Researchers Network, including Richard Petts and Gayle Kauffman. Thank you to Kathleen Gerson, Sarah Damaske, and Amanda Miller for providing excellent reviews that helped me strengthen the analysis for the final version of this book.

Thank you to Naomi Schneider and Summer Farah for ushering the manuscript through the publication process. Thank you to Megan Routh for your stellar research assistance. What a pleasure it was to work with all of you.

Finally, my deepest gratitude goes to my family for your support and love. Thank you to Victor and Sylvia Wong for enabling me to pursue these endeavors, including letting me live in your basement during the first fall of the COVID-19 pandemic when I was negotiating the book contract. Thank you to Jessica Wong and Alex Weissman for doing fun things with me, like going wine tasting to celebrate completing a full draft of the book manuscript. Thank you to Daphne Haas-Kogan, Suzanne Ezrre, Shira Kogan, Maetal Haas-Kogan, Scott Kogan, Elijah Selby, Erin Selby, Scott Yu, and Lee Bashant for your ongoing interest in my work. Our conversations remind me that my research is relevant and worth doing. And thank you to Yonatan Kogan for, quite literally, everything. You are the first person I turn to when I want to brainstorm ideas and work through my thoughts out loud. Thank you for generously listening to me, responding with your honest reactions, and helping me articulate my arguments. Writing this book was so much easier and a lot more fun to do with your companionship and support.

Portions of this book were previously published in J. S. Wong, "Competing Desires: How Young Adult Couples Negotiate Moving for Career Opportunities," *Gender & Society* 31, no. 2 (2017): 171–196. Copyright © SAGE Publications. doi: 10.1177/0891243217695520; and J. S. Wong, "Aspiring Dual-Professional Couples' Career Launch Plans and Childbearing Timing," *Journal of Family Issues* 42, no. 5 (2021): 1092–1115. Copyright © SAGE Publications. doi: 10.1177/0192513X20983380.

Methodological Appendix

This project started with an observation. When I graduated from college, I noticed that a few of the women I was friends with who had graduated alongside me decided to follow their boyfriends to wherever the men had gotten jobs. The women did not have jobs lined up for themselves or social networks where they were going. They hoped to figure things out when they arrived in their new cities, but it was uncertain whether things would turn out okay for them. Another friend I had, this one a man, made a different decision. He broke up with his girlfriend because her post-college career plans were incompatible with his own professional next steps. At least that is what he said. I eventually learned that he had his heart set on launching his career in one specific city and did not consider whether he had opportunities in the location where his ex-girlfriend would be pursuing her profession. As a young scholar in the sociology of gender, work, and family, I had a hunch that broader social forces were playing a role in my friends' different professional and relationship trajectories. I wondered whether these cases might reflect processes occurring more widely among highly educated men and women and decided to systematically explore this idea.

STUDY DESIGN

Although my life inspired this project, my research is firmly grounded in a broader scholarly conversation about gender, work, and family. As detailed in chapter 1, the literature led me to ask: What work-family trajectories do contemporary young adults in different-gender relationships follow as they launch and build careers, maintain relationships, and start families? How do conditions at work and cultural norms shape these pathways? Further, what do these trajectories tell us about the state of the gender revolution and its likely future? To answer these questions, I designed a longitudinal interview study of young, dual-career couples. I decided to talk to child-free couples in which at least one partner was actively graduating from a graduate or professional degree program and applying for jobs nationally and internationally. I strategically chose this empirical case and purposefully chose a longitudinal design to document evolving gender dynamics as young adults launched careers and formed families together.

Aspiring dual-professional couples present an ideal case for examining gender inequality in work and family because highly educated men and women with strong career orientations and high earnings potential are particularly likely to want and achieve egalitarianism in work and family. Highly educated individuals are more likely than people with lower levels of education to express attitudinal support for gender equality.[1] Further, men and women pursuing two high-paying professional careers made it likely that couples would have financial resources to facilitate an egalitarian work-family arrangement.[2] Yet maintaining two demanding careers may create conflicts that couples are forced to resolve. Talking to educated, dual-career couples therefore would allow me to assess what conditions could facilitate gender equality in work and family and what challenges remain for those otherwise well positioned to equally share all responsibilities.

Studying child-free young adults who were actively transitioning from school to work was especially useful for documenting the evolution of people's work and family pathways. Men and women at this life stage were likely to be making major decisions about careers, relationships, and families during the timeframe of my study. I used the case of couples who were considering moving for job opportunities after graduation as an ideal starting point for my investigation of gendered processes of work and family in early adulthood. The possibility of geographic relocation made decisions about relationships and families especially salient. Taking a job in one's current city might not impact a relationship very much, but considering a job in a different region of the country or a different part of the world might prompt couples to talk explicitly about whether to continue their relationship; whether to start, stop, or continue living together; whether and when they might get married; and whether and when they might have children. Relocating for a career opportunity therefore represented one of the first of many life events with implications for gender inequality in work and family that young dual-professional couples on a normative life course might face together.

I conducted four interviews with each partner of a couple over the course of six years to capture how career and family pathways unfolded organically over time. Other studies that interview people at one point in time are limited in their ability to examine the development of work-family trajectories. Studies relying on a single retrospective account are prone to people's misremembering or reinterpreting how things happened. Studies relying on a single hypothetical account in which people imagine their future cannot verify whether any of the projected events actually take place. By following up with the same people at multiple points over time, I could accurately record people's work-family trajectories, directly compare their ideals or expectations to their subsequent behaviors and outcomes, and more precisely document change over time.

I conducted Time 1 baseline interviews between January and April 2013, when men and women were preparing for graduation and starting to search for jobs. I collected Time 2 follow-up interviews between April and August 2013, when job seekers received (or did not receive) offers and couples had to decide what to do. Then I conducted Time 3 follow-up interviews between August 2013 and August 2014, when men and women had started settling into their new jobs and adjusting to new living conditions if they had moved. Finally, I conducted Time 4 follow-up interviews five years after Time 3, between November 2018 and June 2019, to capture whether and how men and women had advanced, changed, or left their careers; gotten married or ended their relationships; and transitioned to parenthood.

It was important to me to interview both partners in each couple. Many studies on gender inequality in work and family include women only,[3] and just a handful of researchers have spoken to men about these issues.[4] Yet decisions about work, relationships, and family life are often made jointly by partners, not independently by individuals. Further, combining findings from separate studies with independent samples of women and men may not accurately reflect couple-level processes. Therefore, talking to two people in each partnership could provide additional insights into men's and women's career and family trajectories.[5] This methodological choice allowed me to confirm key events in a couple's unfolding story. Additionally, discrepancies or disagreements across partners' accounts served as valuable data points on differences in men's and women's experiences of events that happened to a couple. Although inviting both partners to participate in separate interviews may have resulted in a sample of couples with relatively high relationship quality, the prospective study design made it possible to observe conflicts develop and relationships dissolve over time.

RECRUITMENT AND FINAL INTERVIEW SAMPLE

With this study design in place, I sent out my call for research participants using university email lists. I started by recruiting participants from the universities within driving distance of a major midwestern city. I also relied on referrals from my networks and from the interviewees. I used theoretical and quota sampling to achieve even representation of couples across a number of relevant characteristics. Because different professions have different structures and norms surrounding career launch, I aimed to interview men and women pursuing careers across three broad fields: the social sciences and humanities; science, technology, engineering, and mathematics (STEM); and professions like public policy, medicine, business, and law. Because marriage is a social institution with legal implications and cultural expectations for how partners relate to each other regarding gender, work, and family,[6] I decided to split my sample into half married and half unmarried couples in any living arrangement (living together or apart). Finally, because I expected gender to shape partners' career and family pathways, I specifically recruited couples in which the man was graduating and actively applying for jobs, the woman was actively graduating and applying for jobs, and both partners were completing degrees and actively looking for work.

My final sample included forty people from twenty-one couples. I spoke with twenty-one graduate and professional school students who were in the final year of their degree programs and nineteen of the students' spouses or romantic partners. Two of the twenty-one partners declined to join the study after I had already confirmed a Time 1 interview with the student who had contacted me to participate in the research. One partner declined to be interviewed because they were living abroad and had logistical barriers to participation due to time differences and the inability to receive a call from outside their country of residence. Another partner declined to be interviewed because of privacy concerns. Although I invited these partners to join the study at each subsequent point of data collection, they continued to decline my requests. Forty individuals from twenty-one couples may seem like a small sample, but larger samples are not always necessary based on the case study logic of qualitative research.[7] I stopped recruiting couples into the study when I reached a minimum number of interviews necessary for strategic comparisons based on my theoretical sampling guidelines,[8] and when I began hearing the same sorts of stories while gaining less new information from each additional interview.

The men and women in the final sample were twenty-two to thirty-five years old and twenty-eight years old on average at the beginning of the study. Ten of the couples were married and eleven unmarried, including two engaged couples. The median relationship duration was five years among all couples, and the median marriage duration among married couples was two years. All couples were composed of different-gender partners, and 80 percent of the forty participants were White. Although I did not initially screen out transgender, nonbinary, and gender expansive individuals, nor did I exclude lesbian, gay, and other queer couples from my research, none volunteered to participate. Thus, I decided to focus my research on cisgender men and women in different-gender partnerships to understand how gender differences within couples—rather than between couples—shaped men's and women's career and family pathways. Relying on volunteers to participate in my study also affected the racial composition of my final interview sample, so the work-family pathways I identified may largely reflect White men's and women's experiences of gender, careers, and family.

These highly educated, mostly White, different-gender couples are not demographically representative of dual-earner couples in America. Still, they provide a useful case for examining gender egalitarianism and inequality. This group arguably had the best shot at successfully launching two careers while maintaining equality in their relationship and at home due to their multiple advantages. A close examination of highly educated couples who have economic resources to overcome structural challenges to gender equality helps me illuminate variation in how partners navigate work and family during a time of contested cultural gender ideologies. Studying socially advantaged actors offers me a way to document processes of joint agency,[9] as professional men and women have high levels of resources to leverage for themselves, their partners, and their relationships as they build their lives.

I hypothesize that work-family pathways among less-advantaged groups would be further shaped by marginalization due to capitalism, cisnormativity, heteronormativity, and racism. On the one hand, occupying disadvantaged social positions might make equal sharing very difficult for people to achieve because workplace resources to accommodate outside responsibilities and the financial means to outsource housework and childcare are more limited.[10] On the other hand, people facing social disadvantages may create other models for equally sharing work and family responsibilities, potentially by relying on extended kin and fictive kin networks to get everything done for their families.[11] Future research should seek to better understand how working-class and poor couples, gender expansive individuals and queer couples, and couples of color and interracial couples navigate the stalled gender revolution in building careers and families.

Although the background characteristics of my sample do not reflect those of all families in the larger American population, the broader theories I develop about gender, work, and family processes may be generalizable beyond my empirical case.[12] For instance, my argument that supportive workplaces, steadfast attitudes toward gender egalitarianism, and partners' well-coordinated actions must come together if we are to see equal work-family arrangements may also apply to groups other than White, upper-middle-class professionals in different-gender couples. Likewise, the idea that feedback between structure, culture, and joint action sustains an equilibrium in couples' work-family life, and the idea that changes in any facet of this ecosystem can ripple out to shift the balance, might also accurately reflect other couples' experiences.

STUDY PROCEDURES

Once I had recruited couples for the study, I met each person individually at a university office, a coffee shop, or the interviewee's workplace or home to complete the Time 1 and Time 2 interviews. I conducted a handful of phone interviews at Time 1 and Time 2 with participants who lived outside of driving distance from me. By Time 3, most people had moved away to take a job, so I relied on phone interviews for this point of data collection. At Time 4, I exclusively used online video calls to conduct interviews. The interviews at Time 1 and Time 2 generally took a little over an hour to complete, while the Time 3 interviews lasted thirty-five minutes on average. The Time 4 interviews usually took two to three hours to cover people's five-year work and family histories.

I collected more than two hundred hours of conversations from 156 interviews by the end of the six-year data collection period. Although four interviews from forty individuals should have resulted in 160 interviews in total, one participant missed their Time 2 interview due to a work-related travel conflict (but completed their Time 3 and Time 4 interviews), one participant declined to participate in their Time 3 and Time 4 interviews, and one participant declined to participate in their Time 4 interview. In each of these instances, I gathered as much basic information about the work and relationship status of each individual as possible over email and on publicly visible professional websites like LinkedIn and company webpages, as well as social media websites like Facebook and Twitter. I also relied on their partners' interviews for additional details.

I used an interview guide at each wave of data collection to cover topics including each partner's work or school status; their short-, medium-, and long-term career plans; how they saw their careers fitting in with their personal, relationship, or family goals; and whether and how men and women worked together with their partners to coordinate their work and family activities. These interview guides are available in this appendix. I made sure to probe into topics that were contentious for the couples to better understand sources of work-life conflict and how partners resolved those tensions. I recorded all interviews so I could transcribe and analyze them later. Otherwise, I focused on keeping our conversations as natural as possible. Most people were forthcoming in sharing their life details and their thoughts and feelings about them with me because the topic of work and relationships was at the top of many men's and women's minds. Conducting repeated interviews with the same people over six years bolstered my ability to gather intimate details about people's professional and personal experiences because I became knowledgeable about their histories but always maintained a nonjudgmental and empathetic enthusiasm for hearing their stories.

I was a graduate student when I started collecting data for this study, and I positioned myself as someone who wanted to learn about my older peers' experiences with navigating professional jobs, relationships, and family. Over the course of the study, I also transitioned from graduate school to working full-time as a professor. My similar social status as an early-career professional could have prompted interviewees to assume that I shared their knowledge and worldviews, but I was able to probe for more details by reminding them I was much less experienced and working in a different professional field than they were. I did not disclose my relationship status or my opinions about other family-related topics, so I was able to keep interviewees focused on describing their own experiences with, and ideas about, their relationships and families.

I transcribed interviews from Times 1, 2, and 3 myself but used professional transcription services for the interviews from Time 4. I analyzed the data in multiple steps largely following Deterding and Waters's flexible coding approach.[13] First, I wrote memos after each interview to catalog each person's background information and note any striking details about their story. Second, I read transcripts and listed major themes by hand for each time point and then for all time points as a trajectory. I carried out these two stages of analysis first for individuals and then for couples. Finally, I systematically coded transcripts in NVivo based on emerging themes from my memos and initial readings of the interviews. This multistage analysis process helped me identify key similarities and differences between couples that distinguished the consistent compromisers, the autonomous actors, and the tending traditional couples. Because two of the twenty-one partners never opted into the study, I only had complete couple-level information for nineteen couples. To ensure that these cases did not bias my analyses, I started by analyzing the complete couple interviews first before turning to analyze the individual student interviews. The individual interviews that were missing their partner interviews were similar in detail to, and echoed themes from, the complete couple interviews, so I included them as additional data to support my emerging findings.

INTERVIEW GUIDES

Interview Guide for Time 1

Background
First could you tell me a little about yourself?
What is your current program of study/job?
What were you doing before you started this program/job?
How did you meet your current partner?
(If married) When did you get married?
Is your partner in school, or does he/she currently work?

Job Search Plans
Now I'd like to ask you about your immediate plans for after graduation.
Are you planning to continue your education or are you looking for work right now? Or do you have some other plans for after you graduate?
(If applying to higher education) Can you describe how you chose these programs?
(If looking for work) Can you describe how you search for and apply for jobs?
(If applying to school/work) Do you have criteria for where to apply? How did you decide to target these locations?
(If already has a job lined up) Can you tell me how you found this job? Did you have any other job offers before you chose this one? Why did you choose this job over the others?
Do you discuss these plans with your partner? Could you describe how those conversations usually go?
What role does your partner play in the search process?
(If partner is also applying to school/work) What role do you play in his/her search process?
Did your plans ever come into conflict with your partner's plans? Give me an example.
How did you resolve that?
What are some things you and your partner both agree on about your postgraduation plans?
How often do you talk about your future together?
How do your visions of the future line up or diverge?
(If applying to higher education program decisions or jobs) Can you describe the best outcome for you? Why is that ideal?
(If already has a job lined up) Would you say this position is ideal for you? Why or why not?

Work and Family in the Future
Let's talk about your long-term goals.
What is your ideal job?
What would you need to do to get that type of job?
Do you think you will have to change companies or relocate often for your career?
Do you think your career path is compatible with your partner's?
Explain why or why not.
Do you ever think about (if unmarried: getting married and) starting your own family?
Have you discussed these ideas about (if unmarried: getting married and) having kids with your partner? Tell me more about that.
Do you think that your current career plans are compatible with having a family? Why or why not?
(If considering marriage and/or family) When is an ideal time for you to get married? When is an ideal time for you to have children?

Reflections and Wrap-Up
Let's reflect on your experience up to this point.
How do you think your experiences and decisions would be different if you were single?
(If unmarried) What if you and your partner were married?
(If married) What if you and you partner were in a relationship but not legally married?
(If married) Do you ever think you got married too early?
What advice would you give to someone, like a younger sibling, in a similar situation, given the experiences you've had?

Interview Guide for Time 2

Updates
Last time we met, you had plans to [fill in for specific respondent].
Tell me about your plans now. Have any of your career plans changed since we last spoke?
(If applying to higher education) Which programs did you get into?
Have you accepted any offers? How did you choose this program?
(If looking for work) What other jobs did you apply to between our first interview and today's interview?
Have you gotten any offers? Which position did you take? Why did you choose this position?
(If already has a job lined up) Are you still planning to work at [fill in for specific respondent]?
What other options did you consider, if any, since the last time we spoke?
Tell me about how you made the final decision.
What were the most important factors in the decision?
Did you discuss these decisions with your partner? What role did your partner play in choosing among the options?

How did those discussions go? What did you agree and disagree about?
Can you describe any other important decisions you made between our first
interview and today's interview?

> How did you make that decision? Did you discuss these decisions with
> your partner? How did that conversation go? What did you agree or
> disagree about?

Have any of your partner's plans changed since we last spoke?
What were the most important factors in the decision?
Did you discuss these decisions together? What role did you play in
choosing among the options?

Reflections and Wrap-Up

*Let's reflect on your experience up to this point. How do you feel about your
current situation as you move forward?*

Do you feel like you are taking the necessary steps to move forward in your
professional life?
Do you feel like you are taking the necessary steps to move forward in your
personal life?

> Have you changed your mind about marriage and family since we last
> spoke? Why? Have you discussed your thoughts with your partner?

Do you think you would be making different choices if you were single?

> (If unmarried) What if you and your partner were married?
> (If married) What if you and you partner were in a relationship but not
> legally married?

What have you learned from your experience so far?

> Was there anything in particular that stood out to you during this
> process?
> What was the most disappointing part of your experience?
> What was the best?
> What advice would you give to someone, like a younger sibling, in a
> similar situation, given the experiences you've had?

Interview Guide for Time 3

Updates

Last time we met, you had plans to [fill in for specific respondent].
What are you doing now? Working, going to school, or something else?
(If school/job offer required relocation) Where did you move?
(If school/job offer required relocation) Did your partner move? What is
your partner doing now? Working, going to school, or something else?

Reflection and Wrap-Up

*Have you noticed any changes in your work or daily habits since you started
school/started work/moved?*

Have you noticed any changes in your relationship since you started
school/started work/moved?

How happy are you with the way things turned out?

Was this a good move for you professionally and personally? Why or why not?
Was this a good move for your partner professionally and personally? Why or why not?

Do you have any more plans for (if unmarried: marriage or) kids and family?
Any other long term plans?

Would your experience and the outcome be very different if you were single?
(If unmarried) What if you were a married couple?
(If married) What if you were in a relationship but not legally married?

What have you learned from this experience of making career and relocation decisions?
Was there anything in particular that stood out to you during this process?
If you had to do it again, do you think you would have done anything differently? What? Why?

Interview Guide for Time 4

Updates
The last time we talked was five years ago and you were [insert relationship/career details].
Are you working now? What are you doing?

Career History
Will you take me through a timeline of events in your career starting in 2013 leading up to now?
How did you decide to take that job? Was your partner involved in that decision? How did that affect your relationship?
Was that a good job for your professional trajectory? Why or why not?
Why did you leave that job? Was your partner involved in that decision?

Relationship and Partner's Career History
I'd like to fill in some gaps in your relationship history. In 2013 you were married to/in a relationship with [partner's name].
(If same partner) Will you walk me through any major events in his/her career and your relationship starting in 2013 leading up to now?
(If no longer in relationship with 2013 partner) Can you tell me about the major events in that relationship from 2013 up until it ended?
Can you walk me through your relationship history after that relationship ended to now?
How was that relationship different from your previous relationship(s) with [partner(s) name(s)]?
Why did that relationship end?
(If currently has new partner) What does your current partner do?
What is this relationship like compared to the one you had with [2013 partner]?

[Confirm details of job relationship history.] Now that I know more about what you've been doing for the last five years, I need just a few more details about your work.

How much money do you currently make a year from this job? And how about your partner?

Reflections
Thinking about the last five years, how do you feel things have gone in your career or professional life up to this point?
Do you think your ideas about what you want from work have changed over time?
Are there any specific events or people that shaped how your ideas changed?
How are you currently feeling about your career?
Thinking about the last five years, how do you feel things have gone in your relationship(s) up to now?
Do you think you have grown or changed as a couple?
Have your ideas about what you want from a relationship changed over time?
Are there any specific events or people that shaped how your ideas changed?
How are you currently feeling about your relationship?
Thinking about the last five years, how do you feel things have gone regarding having kids or your own family up to this point?
Have your ideas about what you want from family life changed over time?
Are there any specific events or people that shaped how your ideas changed?
How are you currently feeling about having kids?
Thinking about the last five years, how do you feel things have gone in terms of balancing work, relationships, family, and your personal life up to this point?
What were some of the most difficult decisions you had to make to balance work/relationships/family/personal life up to this point?
Do you feel like you ever had to compromise on your work/relationships/family/personal life to balance everything?
How about your partner(s)?
How are you currently feeling about the balance of work and life that you have now?
What would you consider to be an ideal balance?
If you could go back, would you do anything differently in your professional or personal life?

Future Plans and Wrap-Up
Now I'd like you to think ahead. Do you have any major goals or plans for your career, relationship, family, or personal life in the next year or two?
Do you anticipate any barriers or challenges to these goals or plans?
What are you most excited about for the next year or two? How about in the longer term?

Notes

CHAPTER 1. GENDER, WORK, AND FAMILY
IN THE TWENTY-FIRST CENTURY

1. Goldin, "Grand Gender Convergence"; Bellani, Anderson, and Pessin, "When Equity Matters"; and Lamont, *Mating Game*.

2. Cherlin, "Happy Ending?"

3. England, "Gender Revolution"; England, "Reassessing Uneven Gender Revolution"; and England, Levine, and Mishel, "Progress toward Gender Equality."

4. US Bureau of Labor Statistics, "Labor Force Statistics"; and US Bureau of Labor Statistics, "Employment Status."

5. US Census Bureau, "Graphic: Earnings Differences."

6. Institute for Women's Policy Research, "Gender Wage Gap."

7. Cohen, "Persistence of Workplace Segregation"; and McKinsey & Company and Leanin.org, "Women in the Workplace."

8. Goldin, "Grand Gender Convergence."

9. Killewald and García-Manglano, "Tethered Lives"; and Killewald and Zhuo, "U.S. Mothers' Employment Patterns."

10. Landivar and deWolf, "Mothers' Employment."

11. Pedulla, "Penalized or Protected?"

12. Emerson, "Power-Dependence Relations."

13. Pupo and Duffy, "Unpaid Work."

14. Craig, "Does Father Care?"; and Bianchi et al., "Is Anyone Doing Housework?"

15. Carlson, Petts, and Pepin, "Changes in Domestic Labor."

16. Wight, Bianchi, and Hunt, "Explaining Racial/Ethnic Variation"; Usdansky, "Gender-Equality Paradox"; Bianchi et al., "Housework"; and Sayer, "Gender, Time and Inequality."

17. Sullivan, "Analyzing Housework Separately"; and Craig, "Does Father Care?"

18. Pepin, Sayer, and Casper, "Mothers' Time Use"; and Cha, "Reinforcing Separate Spheres."

19. Pupo and Duffy, "Unpaid Work."

20. Blair-Loy, *Competing Devotions.*

21. Berdahl et al., "Work as Masculinity Contest."

22. Collins, *Making Motherhood Work.*

23. Usdansky, "Gender-Equality Paradox."

24. Dow, *Mothering While Black*; Barnes, *Raising the Race*; and Damaske, *For the Family?*

25. Acker, "Hierarchies, Jobs, Bodies"; and Collins, "Who to Blame."

26. Acker, "Hierarchies, Jobs, Bodies."

27. Weeden, Cha, and Bucca, "Long Work Hours"; Coser, *Greedy Institutions*; and Sullivan, "Greedy Institutions."

28. Damaske, *For the Family?*; and Landivar, *Mothers at Work.*

29. Collins, *Making Motherhood Work*; and Hertz, *More Equal Than Others.*

30. Collins, *Making Motherhood Work*; and Collins, "Who to Blame."

31. Although a man-breadwinner/woman-homemaker arrangement is not actually a traditional family form, it is culturally viewed as such; see Coontz, *Way We Never Were*; Gerson, *Unfinished Revolution*; Pedulla and Thébaud, "Can We Finish?"; and Stone, *Opting Out?*

32. Blair-Loy, *Competing Devotions*; and Stone, *Opting Out?*

33. Acker, "Hierarchies, Jobs, Bodies."

34. Hays, *Cultural Contradictions of Motherhood.*

35. Stone and Lovejoy, *Opting Back In.*

36. General Social Survey, "Key Trends."

37. Scarborough, Sin, and Risman, "Attitudes and Gender Revolution."

38. Institute for Women's Policy Research, "Work Supports for Health."

39. Madgavkar et al., "Future of Work."

40. Kan, Sullivan, and Gershuny, "Gender Convergence"; and Pepin and Cotter, "Separating Spheres?"

41. Lamont, *Mating Game.*

42. Miller and Carlson, "Great Expectations?"; and Miller, Carlson, and Sassler, "His Career, Her Job."

43. Gerson, *Unfinished Revolution*; and Pedulla and Thébaud, "Can We Finish?"

44. Gerson, *Unfinished Revolution*; and Pedulla and Thébaud, "Can We Finish?"

45. Usdansky, "Gender-Equality Paradox."

46. Usdansky, "Gender-Equality Paradox."

47. Damaske, *For the Family?*

48. US Census Bureau, "2018 Median Household Income."

49. Barnes, *Raising the Race*; and Li, "Hitting the Ceiling."

50. Dow, *Mothering While Black*.
51. Crouch and McKenzie, "Logic of Small Samples."
52. For example, Blair-Loy, *Competing Devotions*.
53. For example, Gerson, *No Man's Land*.
54. Hertz, "Separate but Simultaneous Interviewing."
55. Sewell, "Theory of Structure."
56. Elder, "Time, Human Agency." Han and Moen, "Work and Family."
57. Han and Moen, "Work and Family."
58. Emerson, "Power-Dependence Relations."
59. Pupo and Duffy, "Unpaid Work."
60. Association of American Medical Colleges, "Active Physicians by Sex."
61. Hoff and Lee, "Gender Pay Gap."
62. Schippers, "Recovering the Feminine Other."
63. Hoff and Lee, "Gender Pay Gap."
64. Vespa, "Gender Ideology Construction"; Gerson, *Unfinished Revolution*; and Damaske, *For the Family?*
65. Zhou, "Motherhood, Employment, Gender Attitudes."

CHAPTER 2. CONSISTENT COMPROMISERS

1. Coser, *Greedy Institutions*; and Sullivan, "Greedy Institutions."
2. Geist and Ruppanner, "Mission Impossible?"; Stack, *All Our Kin*; and Stafford, "Measuring Relationship Maintenance Behaviors."
3. Berdahl et al., "Work as Masculinity Contest"; and Minnotte and Legerski, "Sexual Harassment."
4. National Academies of Sciences, *Sexual Harassment of Women*.
5. Alon and Tienda, "Job Mobility"; Kalleberg and Mouw, "Occupations, Organizations, Career Mobility."
6. Patterson, Damaske, and Sheroff, "Gender and the MBA."
7. King et al., "Benevolent Sexism at Work"; and Stone, *Opting Out?*
8. Acker, "Hierarchies, Jobs, Bodies"; Blair-Loy, *Competing Devotions*; and Correll, Benard, and Paik, "Getting a Job."
9. Hays, *Cultural Contradictions of Motherhood*; Blair-Loy, *Competing Devotions*; and Acker, "Hierarchies, Jobs, Bodies."
10. Stone, *Opting Out?*
11. Miller, "Women Did Everything Right"; Cha, "Reinforcing Separate Spheres"; and Stone, *Opting Out?*
12. Misra et al., "Ivory Ceiling."

CHAPTER 3. AUTONOMOUS ACTORS

1. Acker, "Hierarchies, Jobs, Bodies"; and Acker, "Inequality Regimes."
2. Pugh, *Tumbleweed Society*.
3. Blair-Loy, *Competing Devotions*; and Valian, *Why So Slow?*
4. Hamilton, "Revised MRS"; and Stone and Lovejoy, "Fast-Track Women."
5. Cherlin, "Happy Ending?"; Farrell, VandeVusse, and Ocobock, "Family Change"; and Sassler and Lichter, "Cohabitation and Marriage."

6. Benson, "Rethinking Two-Body Problem"; and Stone and Lovejoy, "Fast-Track Women."

7. Daminger, "De-Gendered Processes."

8. Dalessandro, James-Hawkins, and Sennott, "Strategic Silence."

9. Geist and Ruppanner, "Mission Impossible?"; Stack, *All Our Kin*; and Stafford, "Measuring Relationship Maintenance Behaviors."

10. Blair-Loy, *Competing Devotions*.

11. Dernberger and Pepin, "Gender Flexibility."

CHAPTER 4. TENDING TRADITIONAL COUPLES

1. Schippers, "Recovering the Feminine Other."

2. Benson, "Rethinking Two-Body Problem."

3. Institute for Women's Policy Research, "Gender Wage Gap."

4. Daminger, "De-Gendered Processes."

5. Berdahl et al., "Work as Masculinity Contest."

6. These individual-level explanations overlook how "personal preference" is also shaped by cultural scripts for gender; see Friedman, "Still a 'Stalled Revolution'?"

7. Providing childcare is not free when taking opportunity costs into account, however; see Joshi, "Opportunity Costs of Childbearing."

8. Bass, "Preparing for Parenthood?"; and Miller, Carlson, and Sassler, "His Career, Her Job."

9. Dengate, "How Does Family Policy."

10. Blair-Loy, *Competing Devotions*.

11. Hess, Ahmed, and Hayes, "Providing Unpaid Work"; and Pupo and Duffy, "Unpaid Work."

12. Collins, *Making Motherhood Work*.

13. Williams, "Life Support."

14. Geist and Ruppanner, "Mission Impossible?"

15. England and Kilbourne, "Markets, Marriages."

16. Gerson, *Unfinished Revolution*.

17. See also Rao, *Crunch Time*.

18. Larson, Ghaffarzadegan, and Xue, "Too Many PhD Graduates."

19. Blair-Loy, *Competing Devotions*.

20. See also Rao, "Stand By Your Man."

21. Schippers, "Recovering the Feminine Other."

22. Stone and Lovejoy, *Opting Back In*.

23. Cha and Weeden, "Overwork."

24. Stone and Lovejoy, *Opting Back In*.

25. Stone and Hernandez, "All-or-Nothing Workplace."

26. Rosenfeld, "Women's Work Histories"; and Cha, "Reinforcing Separate Spheres"; Patterson, Damaske, and Sheroff, "Gender and the MBA"; Kalleberg and Mouw, "Occupations, Organizations"; Pedulla, "Penalized or Protected?"; and Lovejoy and Stone, "Opting Back In."

27. Stone and Lovejoy, "Fast-Track Women."

28. Sayer et al., "She Left, He Left"; and England and Kilbourne, "Markets, Marriages."

29. Cancian et al., "Who Gets Custody Now?"

30. Mai, "Unclear Signals, Uncertain Prospects."

31. Killewald and García-Manglano, "Tethered Lives."

32. Kalleberg and Mouw, "Occupations, Organizations, Career Mobility."

33. OECD, "Family Benefits Public Spending."

34. Christensen, "He-Cession? She-Cession?"

35. Gerson, *Unfinished Revolution*.

36. Tach and Edin, "Sources of Union Dissolution."

37. Barnes, "Gender Differentiation."

38. Marsiglio and Roy, *Nurturing Dads*; Petts, Shafer, and Essig, "Masculine Norms Shape Behavior?"

39. Dernberger and Pepin, "Gender Flexibility."

40. Berdahl et al., "Work as Masculinity Contest."

41. Swidler, "Culture in Action."

42. Cooper, *Cut Adrift*.

CHAPTER 5. COMPARING COUPLES

1. Stertz, Grether, and Wiese, "Gender-Role Attitudes."

2. Gonalons-Pons, Schwartz, and Musick, "Changes in Couples' Earnings."

3. Killewald and García-Manglano, "Tethered Lives"; and Killewald and Zhuo, "U.S. Mothers' Employment Patterns."

4. US Department of Labor, "Women in Labor Force"; and Mandel, "Process of Occupational Feminization."

5. Mandel, "Process of Occupational Feminization"; and Levanon, England, and Allison, "Occupational Feminization and Pay."

6. Weeden, Cha, and Bucca, "Long Work Hours."

7. Roy, "Fathering."

8. Miller, "Young Men Embrace Equality"; Miller, "Gender Pay Gap"; Padavic, Ely, and Reid, "Explaining Gender Inequality"; and Dernberger and Pepin, "Gender Flexibility."

CHAPTER 6. PATHWAYS FORWARD

1. England, "Gender Revolution"; and England, Levine, and Mishel, "Progress toward Gender Equality."

2. Pedulla and Thébaud, "Can We Finish?"

3. Dernberger and Pepin, "Gender Flexibility."

4. Gerson, *Unfinished Revolution*.

5. Roth, *Selling Women Short*; and Daminger, "De-Gendered Processes."

6. Women's housework and childcare responsibilities, and men's long hours in paid employment, restrict their leisure time; see Pepin, Sayer, and Casper, "Mothers' Time Use"; Sayer, "Gender, Time and Inequality"; and Sullivan, "Greedy Institutions."

7. Usdansky, "Gender-Equality Paradox."

8. Pepin and Cotter, "Separating Spheres?"

9. New research indicates that assortative mating does not exacerbate class inequalities, however; see Schwartz, Wang, and Mare, "Opportunity and Change."

10. Choudhury, Foroughi, and Larson, "Work-from-Anywhere."

11. Ridgeway, "Social Construction of Status."

12. Almqvist and Duvander, "Changes in Gender Equality?"

13. Andersen, "Paternity Leave"; and Rehel, "When Dad Stays Home."

14. Barnes, *Raising the Race*; and Li, "Hitting the Ceiling."

15. Barcus, Tigges, and Kim, "Time to Care"; and Maume, "Can Men Make Time."

16. Rogers, Sperry, and Levant, "Masculinities"; Walters and Valenzuela, "More Than Muscles"; Lu and Wong, "Stressful Experiences of Masculinity"; and Williams, Blair-Loy, and Berdahl, "Cultural Schemas."

17. Kelly et al., "Gendered Challenge, Gendered Response"; and Kelly and Moen, *Overload*.

18. Dow, *Mothering While Black*; and Goldberg, Smith, and Perry-Jenkins, "Division of Labor."

19. Though care work is associated with greater power in lesbian couples; see Moore, "Gendered Power Relations."

20. Ridgeway, *Framed by Gender*.

21. Damaske, *For the Family?*

EPILOGUE

1. Collins et al., "COVID-19 Gender Gap"; Collins et al., "Gendered Consequences"; and Petersen, "Other Countries."

2. Carlson, Petts, and Pepin, "Changes in Domestic Labor."

METHODOLOGICAL APPENDIX

1. Usdansky, "Gender-Equality Paradox."

2. Damaske, *For the Family?*

3. For example, Blair-Loy, *Competing Devotions*.

4. For example, Gerson, *No Man's Land*.

5. Hertz, "Separate But Simultaneous Interviewing."

6. Cherlin, *Marriage-Go-Round*.

7. Small, "How Many Cases."

8. Gerson and Damaske, *Science and Art of Interviewing*.

9. Sewell, "Theory of Structure."

10. Cherlin, "Happy Ending"; Legerski and Cornwall, "Working-Class Job Loss"; and Barnes, *Raising the Race*.

11. Dow, *Mothering While Black*; and Gerstel and Clawson, "Class Advantage."

12. Crouch and McKenzie, "Logic of Small Samples."

13. Deterding and Waters, "Flexible Coding."

Bibliography

Acker, Joan. "Hierarchies, Jobs, Bodies: A Theory of Gendered Organizations." *Gender & Society* 4, no. 2 (1990): 139–58. https://doi.org/10.1177/0891243 90004002002.

———. "Inequality Regimes: Gender, Class, and Race in Organizations." *Gender & Society* 20, no. 4 (August 2006): 441–64.

Almqvist, Anna-Lena, and Ann-Zofie Duvander. "Changes in Gender Equality? Swedish Fathers' Parental Leave, Division of Childcare and Housework." *Journal of Family Studies* 20, no. 1 (April 1, 2014): 19–27. https://doi.org/10 .5172/jfs.2014.20.1.19.

Alon, Sigal, and Marta Tienda. "Job Mobility and Early Career Wage Growth of White, African-American, and Hispanic Women." *Social Science Quarterly* 86, no. s1 (December 1, 2005): 1196–1217. https://doi.org/10.1111/j.0038 -4941.2005.00342.x.

Andersen, Signe Hald. "Paternity Leave and the Motherhood Penalty: New Causal Evidence." *Journal of Marriage and Family* 80, no. 5 (2018): 1125–43.

Association of American Medical Colleges. "Active Physicians by Sex and Specialty, 2017." 2017. www.aamc.org/data-reports/workforce/interactive-data /active-physicians-sex-and-specialty-2017.

Barcus, Miriam, Leann Tigges, and Jungmyung Kim. "Time to Care: Socioeconomic, Family, and Workplace Factors in Men and Women's Parental Leave Use." *Community, Work & Family* 22, no. 4 (August 8, 2019): 443–64. https://doi.org/10.1080/13668803.2019.1629876.

Barnes, Medora W. "Gender Differentiation in Paid and Unpaid Work during the Transition to Parenthood." *Sociology Compass* 9, no. 5 (2015): 348–64.

Barnes, Riché J. Daniel. *Raising the Race: Black Career Women Redefine Marriage, Motherhood, and Community*. New Brunswick, NJ: Rutgers University Press, 2015.

Bass, Brooke Conroy. "Preparing for Parenthood? Gender, Aspirations, and the Reproduction of Labor Market Inequality." *Gender & Society* 29, no. 3 (2015): 362–85. https://doi.org/10.1177/0891243214546936.

Bellani, Daniela, Gosta Esping Anderson, and Lea Pessin. "When Equity Matters for Marital Stability: Comparing German and U.S. Couples." *Journal of Social and Personal Relationships* 35, no. 9 (2018): 1273–98. https://doi.org/10.1177/0265407517709537.

Benson, Alan. "Rethinking the Two-Body Problem: The Segregation of Women into Geographically Dispersed Occupations." *Demography* 51, no. 5 (2014): 1619–39.

Berdahl, Jennifer L., Marianne Cooper, Peter Glick, Robert W. Livingston, and Joan C. Williams. "Work as a Masculinity Contest." *Journal of Social Issues* 74, no. 3 (2018): 422–48.

Bianchi, Suzanne M., Melissa A. Milkie, Liana C. Sayer, and John P. Robinson. "Is Anyone Doing the Housework? Trends in the Gender Division of Household Labor." *Social Forces* 79, no. 1 (September 2000): 191–234.

Bianchi, Suzanne M., Liana C. Sayer, Melissa A. Milkie, and John P. Robinson. "Housework: Who Did, Does or Will Do It, and How Much Does It Matter?" *Social Forces* 91, no. 1 (2012): 55–63.

Blair-Loy, Mary. *Competing Devotions: Career and Family among Women Executives*. Cambridge, MA: Harvard University Press, 2003.

Cancian, Maria, Daniel R. Meyer, Patricia R. Brown, and Steven T. Cook. "Who Gets Custody Now? Dramatic Changes in Children's Living Arrangements after Divorce." *Demography* 51, no. 4 (August 1, 2014): 1381–96. https://doi.org/10.1007/s13524-014-0307-8.

Carlson, Daniel L., Richard J. Petts, and Joanna R. Pepin. "Changes in US Parents' Domestic Labor during the Early Days of the COVID-19 Pandemic." *Sociological Inquiry*, September 26, 2021. https://doi.org/10.1111/soin.12459.

Cha, Youngjoo. "Reinforcing Separate Spheres: The Effect of Spousal Overwork on Men's and Women's Employment in Dual-Earner Households." *American Sociological Review* 75, no. 2 (April 1, 2010): 303–29. https://doi.org/10.1177/0003122410365307.

Cha, Youngjoo, and Kim A. Weeden. "Overwork and the Slow Convergence in the Gender Gap in Wages." *American Sociological Review* 79, no. 3 (April 8, 2014): 457–84. https://doi.org/10.1177/0003122414528936.

Cherlin, Andrew J. "A Happy Ending to a Half-Century of Family Change?" *Population and Development Review* 42, no. 1 (2016): 121–29.

———. *The Marriage-Go-Round: The State of Marriage and the Family in America Today*. New York: Vintage Press, 2010.

Choudhury, Prithwiraj (Raj), Cirrus Foroughi, and Barbara Larson. "Work-from-Anywhere: The Productivity Effects of Geographic Flexibility." *Strategic Management Journal* 42, no. 4 (April 1, 2021): 655–83. https://doi.org/10.1002/smj.3251.

Christensen, Kimberly. "He-Cession? She-Cession? The Gendered Impact of the Great Recession in the United States." *Review of Radical Political Economics* 47, no. 3 (September 3, 2014): 368–88. https://doi.org/10.1177/0486613414542771.

Cohen, Philip N. "The Persistence of Workplace Gender Segregation in the US." *Sociology Compass* 7, no. 11 (November 1, 2013): 889–99. https://doi.org/10.1111/soc4.12083.

Collins, Caitlyn. *Making Motherhood Work: How Women Manage Careers and Caregiving*. Princeton, NJ: Princeton University Press, 2019.

———. "Who to Blame and How to Solve It: Mothers' Perceptions of Work–Family Conflict across Western Policy Regimes." *Journal of Marriage and Family* 82, no. 3 (June 1, 2020): 849–74. https://doi.org/10.1111/jomf.12643.

Collins, Caitlyn, Liana Christin Landivar, Leah Ruppanner, and William J. Scarborough. "COVID-19 and the Gender Gap in Work Hours." *Gender, Work & Organization* 28, no. S1 (January 1, 2021): 101–12. https://doi.org/10.1111/gwao.12506.

Collins, Caitlyn, Leah Ruppanner, Liana Christin Landivar, and William J. Scarborough. "The Gendered Consequences of a Weak Infrastructure of Care: School Reopening Plans and Parents' Employment during the COVID-19 Pandemic." *Gender & Society* 35, no. 2 (April 1, 2021): 180–93. https://doi.org/10.1177/08912432211001300.

Coontz, Stephanie. *The Way We Never Were: American Families and the Nostalgia Trap*. New York: Basic Books, 2016.

Cooper, Marianne. *Cut Adrift: Families in Insecure Times*. Oakland: University of California Press, 2014.

Correll, Shelley J., Stephen Benard, and In Paik. "Getting a Job: Is There a Motherhood Penalty?" *American Journal of Sociology* 112, no. 5 (2007): 1297–1338.

Coser, Lewis A. *Greedy Institutions; Patterns of Undivided Commitment*. New York: Free Press, 1974.

Craig, Lyn. "Does Father Care Mean Fathers Share? A Comparison of How Mothers and Fathers in Intact Families Spend Time with Children." *Gender & Society* 20, no. 2 (2006): 259–81.

Crouch, Mira, and Heather McKenzie. "The Logic of Small Samples in Interview-Based Qualitative Research." *Social Science Information* 45, no. 4 (December 1, 2006): 483–99. https://doi.org/10.1177/0539018406069584.

Dalessandro, Cristen, Laurie James-Hawkins, and Christie Sennott. "Strategic Silence: College Men and Hegemonic Masculinity in Contraceptive Decision Making." *Gender & Society* 33, no. 5 (May 29, 2019): 772–94. https://doi.org/10.1177/0891243219850061.

Damaske, Sarah. *For the Family? How Class and Gender Shape Women's Work*. New York: Oxford University Press, 2011.

Daminger, Allison. "De-Gendered Processes, Gendered Outcomes: How Egalitarian Couples Make Sense of Non-Egalitarian Household Practices." *American Sociological Review* 85, no. 5 (2020): 806–29.

Dengate, Jennifer L. "How Does Family Policy 'Work'? Job Context, Flexibility, and Maternity Leave Policy." *Sociology Compass* 10, no. 5 (May 1, 2016): 376–90. https://doi.org/10.1111/soc4.12368.

Dernberger, Brittany N., and Joanna R. Pepin. "Gender Flexibility, but Not Equality: Young Adults' Division of Labor Preferences." *Sociological Science* 7 (2020): 36–56.

Deterding, Nicole M., and Mary C. Waters. "Flexible Coding of In-Depth Interviews: A Twenty-First-Century Approach." *Sociological Methods & Research*, October 1, 2018. https://doi.org/10.1177/0049124118799377.

Dow, Dawn Marie. *Mothering While Black: Boundaries and Burdens of Middle-Class Parenthood*. Oakland: University of California Press, 2019.

Elder, Glen H. "Time, Human Agency, and Social Change: Perspectives on the Life Course." *Social Psychology Quarterly* 57, no. 1 (1994): 4–15. https://doi.org/10.2307/2786971.

Emerson, Richard M. "Power-Dependence Relations." *American Sociological Review* 27, no. 1 (February 1962): 31–41.

England, Paula. "The Gender Revolution: Uneven and Stalled." *Gender & Society* 24, no. 2 (2010): 149–66.

———. "Reassessing the Uneven Gender Revolution and Its Slowdowns." *Gender & Society* 25, no. 1 (2011): 113–23.

England, Paula, and Barbara Stanek Kilbourne. "Markets, Marriages, and Other Mates: The Problem of Power." In *Beyond the Marketplace: Rethinking Economy and Society*, edited by Roger Friedland and A. F. Robertson, 163–89. New York: Aldine de Gruyter, 1990.

England, Paula, Andrew Levine, and Emma Mishel. "Progress toward Gender Equality in the United States Has Slowed or Stalled." *Proceedings of the National Academy of Sciences*, March 26, 2020, 201918891. https://doi.org/10.1073/pnas.1918891117.

Farrell, Betty, Alicia VandeVusse, and Abigail Ocobock. "Family Change and the State of Family Sociology." *Current Sociology* 60, no. 3 (May 1, 2012): 283–301. https://doi.org/10.1177/0011392111425599.

Friedman, Sarah. "Still a 'Stalled Revolution'? Work/Family Experiences, Hegemonic Masculinity, and Moving toward Gender Equality." *Sociology Compass* 9, no. 2 (February 1, 2015): 140–55. https://doi.org/10.1111/soc4.12238.

Geist, Claudia, and Leah Ruppanner. "Mission Impossible? New Housework Theories for Changing Families." *Journal of Family Theory & Review* 10, no. 1 (February 26, 2018): 242–62. https://doi.org/10.1111/jftr.12245.

General Social Survey. "Key Trends: Better for Man to Work and Woman to Stay Home." GSS Data Explorer, n.d. https://gssdataexplorer.norc.org/trends/.

Gerson, Kathleen. *No Man's Land: Men's Changing Commitments to Family and Work*. New York: Basic Books, 1993.

———. *The Unfinished Revolution: Coming of Age in a New Era of Gender, Work, and Family*. New York: Oxford University Press, 2010.

Gerson, Kathleen, and Sarah Damaske. *The Science and Art of Interviewing*. New York: Oxford University Press, 2020.

Gerstel, Naomi, and Dan Clawson. "Class Advantage and the Gender Divide: Flexibility on the Job and at Home." *American Journal of Sociology* 120, no. 2 (September 2014): 395–431.

Goldberg, Abbie E., JuliAnna Z. Smith, and Maureen Perry-Jenkins. "The Division of Labor in Lesbian, Gay, and Heterosexual New Adoptive Parents." *Journal of Marriage and Family* 74, no. 4 (August 1, 2012): 812–28. https://doi.org/10.1111/j.1741-3737.2012.00992.x.

Goldin, Claudia. "A Grand Gender Convergence: Its Last Chapter." *American Economic Review* 104, no. 4 (2014): 1091–1119.

Gonalons-Pons, Pilar, Christine R. Schwartz, and Kelly Musick. "Changes in Couples' Earnings Following Parenthood and Trends in Family Earnings Inequality." *Demography* 58, no. 3 (June 1, 2021): 1093–1117. https://doi.org/10.1215/00703370-9160055.

Hamilton, Laura T. "The Revised MRS: Gender Complementarity at College." *Gender & Society* 28, no. 2 (2014): 236–64.

Han, Shin-Kap, and Phyllis Moen. "Work and Family over Time: A Life Course Approach." *Annals of the American Academy of Political and Social Science* 562, no. 1 (1999): 98–110.

Hays, Sharon. *The Cultural Contradictions of Motherhood*. New Haven, CT: Yale University Press, 1996.

Hertz, Rosanna. *More Equal Than Others: Women and Men in Dual-Career Marriages*. Berkeley: University of California Press, 1986.

———. "Separate but Simultaneous Interviewing of Husbands and Wives: Making Sense of Their Stories." *Qualitative Inquiry* 1, no. 4 (December 1, 1995): 429–51. https://doi.org/10.1177/107780049500100404.

Hess, Cynthia, Tanima Ahmed, and Jeff Hayes. "Providing Unpaid Household and Care Work in the United States: Uncovering Inequality." Briefing Paper. Washington, DC: Institute for Women's Policy Research, 2020. www.iwpr.org/wp-content/uploads/2020/01/IWPR-Providing-Unpaid-Household-and-Care-Work-in-the-United-States-Uncovering-Inequality.pdf.

Hoff, Timothy, and Do Rim Lee. "The Gender Pay Gap in Medicine: A Systematic Review." *Health Care Management Review* 46, no. 3 (2021). https://journals.lww.com/hcmrjournal/Fulltext/2021/07000/The_gender_pay_gap_in_medicine__A_systematic.11.aspx.

Institute for Women's Policy Research. "The Gender Wage Gap by Occupation 2019; and by Race and Ethnicity." 2020. https://iwpr.org/wp-content/uploads/2020/07/2020-Occupational-wage-gap-FINAL.pdf.

———. "Work Supports for Health: The Role of Paid Family and Medical Leave." 2019. https://iwpr.org/wp-content/uploads/2019/06/Work-Supports-for-Adult-Health.pdf.

Joshi, Heather. "The Opportunity Costs of Childbearing: More Than Mothers' Business." *Journal of Population Economics* 11, no. 2 (1998): 161–83.

Kalleberg, Arne L., and Ted Mouw. "Occupations, Organizations, and Intragenerational Career Mobility." *Annual Review of Sociology* 44, no. 1 (July 30, 2018): 283–303. https://doi.org/10.1146/annurev-soc-073117-041249.

Kan, Man Yee, Oriel Sullivan, and Jonathan Gershuny. "Gender Convergence in Domestic Work: Discerning the Effects of Interactional and Institutional

Barriers from Large-Scale Data." *Sociology* 45, no. 2 (April 1, 2011): 234–51. https://doi.org/10.1177/0038038510394014.

Kelly, Erin L., Samantha K. Ammons, Kelly Chermack, and Phyllis Moen. "Gendered Challenge, Gendered Response: Confronting the Ideal Worker Norm in a White-Collar Organization." *Gender & Society* 24, no. 3 (2010): 281–303.

Kelly, Erin L., and Phyllis Moen. *Overload: How Good Jobs Went Bad and What We Can Do about It.* Princeton, NJ: Princeton University Press, 2020.

Killewald, Alexandra, and Javier García-Manglano. "Tethered Lives: A Couple-Based Perspective on the Consequences of Parenthood for Time Use, Occupation, and Wages." *Social Science Research* 60 (2016): 266–82. https://doi.org/10.1016/j.ssresearch.2016.03.007.

Killewald, Alexandra, and Xiaolin Zhuo. "U.S. Mothers' Long-Term Employment Patterns." *Demography* 56, no. 1 (February 1, 2019): 285–320. https://doi.org/10.1007/s13524-018-0745-9.

King, Eden B., Whitney Botsford, Michelle R. Hebl, Stephanie Kazama, Jeremy F. Dawson, and Andrew Perkins. "Benevolent Sexism at Work: Gender Differences in the Distribution of Challenging Developmental Experiences." *Journal of Management* 38, no. 6 (April 1, 2010): 1835–66. https://doi.org/10.1177/0149206310365902.

Lamont, Ellen. *The Mating Game: How Gender Still Shapes How We Date.* Oakland: University of California Press, 2020.

Landivar, Liana Christin. *Mothers at Work: Who Opts Out?* Boulder, CO: Lynne Rienner, 2017.

Landivar, Liana Christin, and Mark deWolf. "Mothers' Employment Two Years Later: An Assessment of Employment Loss and Recovery during the COVID-19 Pandemic." Washington, DC: Women's Bureau, US Department of Labor, May 2022. www.dol.gov/sites/dolgov/files/WB/media/Mothers-employment-2%20-years-later-may2022.pdf.

Larson, Richard C., Navid Ghaffarzadegan, and Yi Xue. "Too Many PhD Graduates or Too Few Academic Job Openings: The Basic Reproductive Number R0 in Academia." *Systems Research & Behavioral Science* 31, no. 6 (December 11, 2014): 745–50.

Legerski, Elizabeth Miklya, and Marie Cornwall. "Working-Class Job Loss, Gender, and the Negotiation of Household Labor." *Gender & Society* 24, no. 4 (2010): 447–74.

Levanon, Asaf, Paula England, and Paul Allison. "Occupational Feminization and Pay: Assessing Causal Dynamics Using 1950–2000 U.S. Census Data." *Social Forces* 88, no. 2 (December 1, 2009): 865–91. https://doi.org/10.1353/sof.0.0264.

Li, Peggy. "Hitting the Ceiling: An Examination of Barriers to Success for Asian American Women." *Berkeley Journal of Gender Law & Justice* 29 (2014): 140.

Lovejoy, Meg, and Pamela Stone. "Opting Back In: The Influence of Time at Home on Professional Women's Career Redirection after Opting Out." *Gender, Work & Organization* 19, no. 6 (November 2012): 631–53.

Lu, Alexander, and Y. Joel Wong. "Stressful Experiences of Masculinity among US-Born and Immigrant Asian American Men." *Gender & Society* 27, no. 3 (2013): 345–71.

Madgavkar, Anu, James Manyika, Sven Smit, Kweilin Ellingrud, Mary Meaney, and Olivia Robinson. "The Future of Work after COVID-19." McKinsey Global Institute, 2021. www.mckinsey.com/featured-insights/future-of-work /the-future-of-work-after-covid-19.

Mai, Quan D. "Unclear Signals, Uncertain Prospects: The Labor Market Consequences of Freelancing in the New Economy." *Social Forces* 99, no. 3 (March 1, 2021): 895–920. https://doi.org/10.1093/sf/soaa043.

Mandel, Hadas. "A Second Look at the Process of Occupational Feminization and Pay Reduction in Occupations." *Demography* 55, no. 2 (April 1, 2018): 669–90. https://doi.org/10.1007/s13524-018-0657-8.

Marsiglio, William, and Kevin Roy. *Nurturing Dads: Social Initiatives for Contemporary Fatherhood*. New York: Russell Sage Foundation, 2012.

Maume, David J. "Can Men Make Time for Family? Paid Work, Care Work, Work-Family Reconciliation Policies, and Gender Equality." *Social Currents* 3, no. 1 (March 1, 2016): 43–63. https://doi.org/10.1177/2329496515620647.

McKinsey & Company and Leanin.org. "Women in the Workplace." 2019. https://wiw-report.s3.amazonaws.com/Women_in_the_Workplace_2019.pdf.

Miller, Amanda J., and Daniel L. Carlson. "Great Expectations? Working-and Middle-Class Cohabitors' Expected and Actual Divisions of Housework." *Journal of Marriage and Family* 78, no. 2 (2016): 346–63. https://doi.org/10 .1111/jomf.12276.

Miller, Amanda J., Daniel L. Carlson, and Sharon Sassler. "His Career, Her Job, Their Future: Cohabitors' Orientations toward Paid Work." *Journal of Family Issues* 40, no. 11 (April 15, 2019): 1509–33. https://doi.org/10.1177/01 92513X19841090.

Miller, Claire Cain. "The Gender Pay Gap Is Largely Because of Motherhood." *New York Times*, May 13, 2017. www.nytimes.com/2017/05/13/upshot/the -gender-pay-gap-is-largely-because-of-motherhood.html.

———. "Women Did Everything Right: Then Work Got 'Greedy.'" *New York Times*, April 26, 2019. www.nytimes.com/2019/04/26/upshot/women-long -hours-greedy-professions.html.

———. "Young Men Embrace Gender Equality, but They Still Don't Vacuum." *New York Times*, February 11, 2020. www.nytimes.com/2020/02/11/upshot /gender-roles-housework.html.

Minnotte, Krista Lynn, and Elizabeth M. Legerski. "Sexual Harassment in Contemporary Workplaces: Contextualizing Structural Vulnerabilities." *Sociology Compass* 13, no. 12 (December 1, 2019): e12755. https://doi.org/10 .1111/soc4.12755.

Misra, Joya, Jennifer Hickes Lundquist, Elissa Holmes, and Stephanie Agiomavritis. "The Ivory Ceiling of Service Work." *Academe* 97, no. 1 (2011): 22–26.

Moore, Mignon R. "Gendered Power Relations among Women: A Study of Household Decision Making in Black, Lesbian Stepfamilies." *American Sociological Review* 73 (January 1, 2008): 335–56.

National Academies of Sciences, Engineering, and Medicine. *Sexual Harassment of Women: Climate, Culture, and Consequences in Academic Sciences, Engineering, and Medicine*. Washington, DC: National Academies Press, 2018. https://doi.org/10.17226/24994.

Organisation for Economic Co-operation and Development (OECD). "Family Benefits Public Spending." 2021. doi:10.1787/8e8b3273-en.

Padavic, Irene, Robin J. Ely, and Erin M. Reid. "Explaining the Persistence of Gender Inequality: The Work–Family Narrative as a Social Defense against the 24/7 Work Culture." *Administrative Science Quarterly* 65, no. 1 (February 14, 2019): 61–111. https://doi.org/10.1177/0001839219832310.

Patterson, Sarah E., Sarah Damaske, and Christen Sheroff. "Gender and the MBA: Differences in Career Trajectories, Institutional Support, and Outcomes." *Gender & Society* 31, no. 3 (April 10, 2017): 310–32. https://doi.org/10.1177/0891243217703630.

Pedulla, David S. "Penalized or Protected? Gender and the Consequences of Nonstandard and Mismatched Employment Histories." *American Sociological Review* 81, no. 2 (March 2, 2016): 262–89. https://doi.org/10.1177/0003122416630982.

Pedulla, David S., and Sarah Thébaud. "Can We Finish the Revolution? Gender, Work-Family Ideals, and Institutional Constraint." *American Sociological Review* 80, no. 1 (2015): 116–39. https://doi.org/10.1177/0003122414564008.

Pepin, Joanna, and David Cotter. "Separating Spheres? Diverging Trends in Youth's Gender Attitudes about Work and Family." *Journal of Marriage and Family* 80, no. 1 (February 2018): 7–24.

Pepin, Joanna R., Liana C. Sayer, and Lynne M. Casper. "Marital Status and Mothers' Time Use: Childcare, Housework, Leisure, and Sleep." *Demography* 55, no. 1 (February 1, 2018): 107–33. https://doi.org/10.1007/s13524-018-0647-x.

Petersen, Anne Helen. "Other Countries Have Social Safety Nets: The U.S. Has Women." *Culture Study*, November 11, 2020. https://annehelen.substack.com/p/other-countries-have-social-safety.

Petts, Richard J., Kevin M. Shafer, and Lee Essig. "Does Adherence to Masculine Norms Shape Fathering Behavior?" *Journal of Marriage and Family* 80, no. 3 (June 1, 2018): 704–20. https://doi.org/10.1111/jomf.12476.

Pugh, Allison J. *The Tumbleweed Society: Working and Caring in an Age of Insecurity*. New York: Oxford University Press, 2015.

Pupo, Norene, and Ann Duffy. "Unpaid Work, Capital and Coercion." *Work Organisation, Labour and Globalisation* 6, no. 1 (2012): 27–47. https://doi.org/10.13169/workorgalaboglob.6.1.0027.

Rao, Aliya Hamid. *Crunch Time: How Married Couples Confront Unemployment*. Oakland: University of California Press, 2020.

———. "Stand By Your Man: Wives' Emotion Work during Men's Unemployment." *Journal of Marriage and Family* 79, no. 3 (2017): 636–56. https://doi.org/10.1111/jomf.12385.

Rehel, Erin M. "When Dad Stays Home Too: Paternity Leave, Gender, and Parenting." *Gender & Society* 28, no. 1 (2014): 110–32.

Ridgeway, Cecilia. "The Social Construction of Status Value: Gender and Other Nominal Characteristics." *Social Forces* 70, no. 2 (December 1991): 367–86.

Ridgeway, Cecilia L. *Framed by Gender: How Gender Inequality Persists in the Modern World.* New York: Oxford University Press, 2011.

Rogers, Baron K., Heather A. Sperry, and Ronald F. Levant. "Masculinities among African American Men: An Intersectional Perspective." *Psychology of Men & Masculinity* 16, no. 4 (2015): 416–25. https://doi.org/10.1037/a0039082.

Rosenfeld, Rachel A. "Women's Work Histories." *Population and Development Review* 22 (1996): 199–222. https://doi.org/10.2307/2808012.

Roth, Louise Marie. *Selling Women Short.* Princeton, NJ: Princeton University Press, 2006.

Roy, Kevin. "Fathering from the Long View: Framing Personal and Social Change through Life Course Theory." *Journal of Family Theory & Review* 6, no. 4 (2014): 319–35.

Sassler, Sharon, and Daniel T. Lichter. "Cohabitation and Marriage: Complexity and Diversity in Union-Formation Patterns." *Journal of Marriage and Family* 82, no. 1 (February 1, 2020): 35–61. https://doi.org/10.1111/jomf.12617.

Sayer, Liana C. "Gender, Time and Inequality: Trends in Women's and Men's Paid Work, Unpaid Work and Free Time." *Social Forces* 84, no. 1 (September 2005): 285–303.

Sayer, Liana C., Paul D. Allison, Paula England, and Nicole Kangas. "She Left, He Left: How Employment and Satisfaction Affect Women's and Men's Decisions to Leave Marriages." *American Journal of Sociology* 116, no. 6 (May 2011): 1982–2018.

Scarborough, William J., Ray Sin, and Barbara Risman. "Attitudes and the Stalled Gender Revolution: Egalitarianism, Traditionalism, and Ambivalence from 1977 through 2016." *Gender & Society* 33, no. 2 (November 8, 2018): 173–200. https://doi.org/10.1177/0891243218809604.

Schippers, Mimi. "Recovering the Feminine Other: Masculinity, Femininity, and Gender Hegemony." *Theory and Society* 36, no. 1 (2007): 85–102.

Schwartz, Christine R., Yu Wang, and Robert D. Mare. "Opportunity and Change in Occupational Assortative Mating." *Social Science Research* 99 (September 1, 2021): 102600. https://doi.org/10.1016/j.ssresearch.2021.102600.

Sewell, William H. "A Theory of Structure: Duality, Agency, and Transformation." *American Journal of Sociology* 98, no. 1 (1992): 1–29. https://doi.org/10.1086/229967.

Small, Mario Luis. "'How Many Cases Do I Need?' On Science and the Logic of Case Selection in Field-Based Research." *Ethnography* 10, no. 1 (2009): 5–38.

Stack, Carol B. *All Our Kin: Strategies for Survival in a Black Community.* New York: Basic Books, 1975.

Stafford, Laura. "Measuring Relationship Maintenance Behaviors: Critique and Development of the Revised Relationship Maintenance Behavior Scale." *Journal of Social and Personal Relationships* 28, no. 2 (September 14, 2010): 278–303. https://doi.org/10.1177/0265407510378125.

Stertz, Anna M., Thorana Grether, and Bettina S. Wiese. "Gender-Role Attitudes and Parental Work Decisions after Childbirth: A Longitudinal Dyadic
Perspective with Dual-Earner Couples." *Journal of Vocational Behavior* 101
(2017): 104–18.

Stone, Pamela. *Opting Out? Why Women Really Quit Careers and Head Home.*
Berkeley: University of California Press, 2008.

Stone, Pamela, and Lisa Ackerly Hernandez. "The All-or-Nothing Workplace:
Flexibility Stigma and 'Opting Out' among Professional-Managerial Women."
Journal of Social Issues 69, no. 2 (2013): 235–56.

Stone, Pamela, and Meg Lovejoy. "Fast-Track Women and the 'Choice' to Stay
Home." *Annals of the American Academy of Political and Social Science* 596
(2004): 62–83.

———. *Opting Back In: What Really Happens When Mothers Go Back to
Work.* Oakland: University of California Press, 2019.

Sullivan, Oriel. "What Do We Learn about Gender by Analyzing Housework
Separately from Child Care? Some Considerations from Time-Use Evidence."
Journal of Family Theory & Review 5, no. 2 (June 1, 2013): 72–84. https://
doi.org/10.1111/jftr.12007.

Sullivan, Teresa A. "Greedy Institutions, Overwork, and Work-Life Balance."
Sociological Inquiry 84, no. 1 (February 1, 2014): 1–15. https://doi.org/10
.1111/soin.12029.

Swidler, Ann. "Culture in Action: Symbols and Strategies." *American Sociological Review* 51, no. 2 (April 1986): 273–86.

Tach, Laura, and Kathryn Edin. "The Compositional and Institutional Sources
of Union Dissolution for Married and Unmarried Parents in the United
States." *Demography* 50, no. 5 (October 1, 2013): 1789–1818. https://doi
.org/10.1007/s13524-013-0203-7.

US Bureau of Labor Statistics. "Employment Status of the Civilian Population
by Sex and Age." November 1, 2019. www.bls.gov/news.release/empsit.t01
.htm.

———. "Labor Force Statistics from the Current Population Survey." January
2019. www.bls.gov/cps/cpsaat03.htm.

US Census Bureau. "2018 Median Household Income in the United States."
September 26, 2019. www.census.gov/library/visualizations/interactive/2018
-median-household-income.html.

———. "Social Media Graphic: Earnings Differences." September 10, 2019. www
.census.gov/library/visualizations/2019/comm/social-earnings-differences
.html.

US Department of Labor. "Women in the Labor Force: A Databook." US Bureau
of Labor Statistics, 2019. www.bls.gov/opub/reports/womens-databook/2019
/home.htm.

Usdansky, Margaret L. "The Gender-Equality Paradox: Class and Incongruity
between Work-Family Attitudes and Behaviors." *Journal of Family Theory
& Review* 3, no. 3 (September 1, 2011): 163–78. https://doi.org/10.1111/j
.1756-2589.2011.00094.x.

Valian, Virginia. *Why So Slow? The Advancement of Women.* Cambridge, MA:
MIT Press, 1999.

Vespa, Jonathan. "Gender Ideology Construction: A Life Course and Intersectional Approach." *Gender & Society* 23, no. 3 (May 22, 2009): 363–87. https://doi.org/10.1177/0891243209337507.

Walters, Andrew S., and Ivan Valenzuela. "More Than Muscles, Money, or Machismo: Latino Men and the Stewardship of Masculinity." *Sexuality & Culture* 24, no. 3 (2020): 967–1003.

Weeden, Kim A., Youngjoo Cha, and Mauricio Bucca. "Long Work Hours, Part-Time Work, and Trends in the Gender Gap in Pay, the Motherhood Wage Penalty, and the Fatherhood Wage Premium." *RSF: The Russell Sage Foundation Journal of the Social Sciences* 2, no. 4 (2016): 71–102.

Wight, Vanessa R., Suzanne M. Bianchi, and Bijou R. Hunt. "Explaining Racial/Ethnic Variation in Partnered Women's and Men's Housework: Does One Size Fit All?" *Journal of Family Issues* 34, no. 3 (March 1, 2013): 394–427. https://doi.org/10.1177/0192513X12437705.

Williams, Christine L. "Life Support: The Problems of Working for a Living." *American Sociological Review* 86, no. 2 (March 22, 2021): 191–200. https://doi.org/10.1177/0003122421997063.

Williams, Joan C., Mary Blair-Loy, and Jennifer L. Berdahl. "Cultural Schemas, Social Class, and the Flexibility Stigma." *Journal of Social Issues* 69, no. 2 (June 1, 2013): 209–34. https://doi.org/10.1111/josi.12012.

Zhou, Muzhi. "Motherhood, Employment, and the Dynamics of Women's Gender Attitudes." *Gender & Society* 31, no. 6 (December 1, 2017): 751–76. https://doi.org/10.1177/0891243217732320.

Index

Founded in 1893,
UNIVERSITY OF CALIFORNIA PRESS
publishes bold, progressive books and journals
on topics in the arts, humanities, social sciences,
and natural sciences—with a focus on social
justice issues—that inspire thought and action
among readers worldwide.

The UC PRESS FOUNDATION
raises funds to uphold the press's vital role
as an independent, nonprofit publisher, and
receives philanthropic support from a wide
range of individuals and institutions—and from
committed readers like you. To learn more, visit
ucpress.edu/supportus.